DATE DUE

RHYTHM
AND
RESISTANCE

Media and Society Series

J. Fred MacDonald, General Editor

RHYTHM AND RESISTANCE

Explorations in the Political Uses of Popular Music

Ray Pratt

PRAEGER

New York
Westport, Connecticut
London

Copyright Acknowledgments

Material in Chapters 4 and 8 is based on substantially revised versions of material originally published as "The Politics of Authenticity in Popular Music: The Case of the Blues," *Popular Music and Society* 10:3 (1986), pp. 55–78 and "Is A Dream A Lie If It Don't Come True or Is It Something Worse? A Commentary on Political Implications of the Springsteen Phenomenon," *Popular Music and Society* 11:1 (1987). Adapted with permission.

Library of Congress Cataloging-in-Publication Data

Pratt, Ray.
    Rhythm and resistance : explorations in the political uses of
popular music / Ray Pratt.
        p.   cm.—(Media and society series)
    Includes bibliographical references.
    ISBN 0-275-92624-9 (alk. paper)
    1. Popular music—Political aspects.   2. Music and society.
I. Title. II. Series.
ML3470.P7   1990
306.4'84—dc20   89-16197

Library of Congress Catalog Card Number: 89-16197
ISBN: 0-275-92624-9

First published in 1990

Praeger Publishers, One Madison Avenue, New York, NY 10010
An imprint of Greenwood Publishing Group, Inc.

Printed in the United States of America

The paper used in this book complies with the
Permanent Paper Standard issued by the National
Information Standards Organization (Z39.48-1984).

10 9 8 7 6 5 4 3 2 1

Contents

Preface

Rhythm and Resistance is an interpretive exploration of "political" uses of popular music from the era of slavery through the present. Many recent theorists of popular culture have stressed the way "marginality" has, in Stuart Hall's words, become "at last a productive space." This phenomenon is by no means "new," but extends back two centuries to the cultural creations of slaves—the black church, spirituals, work songs, field hollers—and then to the blues and gospel. All these forms are reflected in later jazz, blues, rhythm and blues, rock 'n' roll, rock, and rap. These earlier forms were taken up by whites and invested with new energies such that they appeared as virtually new, or "reinvented," forms but were really extensions of earlier forms.

This book conceives of popular or "people's" music as part of a continuing effort to create forms of community in response to social transformations—the trauma of modernization—that empty out all the "little worlds" (Marshall Berman's term) in which people live. Human existence is conceived as a quest for community or, more specifically, for "free spaces" and "utopias" to which popular culture is a manufactured response.

The human reality is conceived as a "contested" reality in which people struggle in what M. M. Bakhtin would call a "dialogic" process to create a satisfying existence out of the raw materials provided by "culture industries." In this sense *Rhythm and Resistance* constitutes a fundamental critique of the approach (probably started by T. W. Adorno's 1944 essay "The Culture Industry") that sees popular culture as imposed on an inert public.

The Springsteen phenomenon of the 1980s, for example, is examined at length because of that artist's effort to remind us of what we have lost and to reassert values of community in the context of a searching critique of U.S. society in terms of its own values. Thus his anthemic "Born to Run" becomes for many a part of a collective search for new values and new forms of community in spite of the essentially lethal outcomes of the "normal" life choices chronicled in his songs.

In many ways *Rhythm and Resistance* works both backward and forward from the 1960s efforts to establish a political popular music, seeking to understand the nostalgic fetishization of "the Sixties" music as an expression of more fundamental social longings that should not be dismissed as mere nostalgia.

An important limitation on 1960s and post–1960s music is that it has functioned largely as an expression of male efforts to establish individual "authenticity" (Berman). As a consequence, as I argue in Chapter 7 (a long exploration of women's voices and silences in popular music), the impact of that music has been much less than some of its proponents might wish, though still of immense significance.

Other forms of popular culture, particularly popular films, as these became a mass cultural phenomenon, and the pervasive influences of the collective electronic community established by television, are frequently considered as supplementary data on trends discussed.

Certain forms of popular music, notably country, are not covered in detail, though the nostagic appeal of country music as reflective of a deeper longing for eroded forms of community is an important concern of Chapter 5, which considers folk music and its uses. These exclusions are due partly to problems of space, partly to a recognition of certain works as having said much of what I wanted to say already. Among these are Bill C. Malone's *Country Music— U.S.A.* and Peter Guralnick's *Sweet Soul Music: Rhythm and Blues and the Southern Dream of Freedom*, and several works on jazz.

Throughout the book I have written in the first person whenever I have tried to relate a particularly powerful personal experience of a kind of music that left an enduring impression that I have, over the years, tried to understand. The adoption of this mode also grows out of my conviction that work and life are too often separated by conventions of "scholarship" that deny the important and intimate connections between life and what one writes about.

A Bruce Springsteen concert in 1985 was the single most significant catalyst in the writing of this book. Following the incredible wave of advertising for Springsteen in the mid–1970s I refused for five years to listen seriously to an artist hyped by his recording company as the future of rock. Only after two close friends urged it did I listen to an album, see his performance in the 1979 *No Nukes* concert film, and come to appreciate the energy he brings to concerts (the effort expended in his filmed performance was staggering but seemed to have no "political" content nor link at all to the theme of the Musicians United for Safe Energy [MUSE] concerts). Repeated listening to songs such as "Born to Run," "Thunder Road," and "Jungleland" (especially Clarence Clemons' sax solo on the latter) "hooked" me. By the time I heard his live show at the Pontiac

Silverdome in 1985 (I was repeatedly told, ''You've *got* to hear him live''), I was, as they said I would be, ''blown away.'' A song-by-song examination of every one of the Springsteen albums, as many of his singles as could be found, and reading and collecting articles and reviews on the ''phenomenon,'' ultimately proved so moving and intellectually engrossing that *Rhythm and Resistance* was the result.

Acknowledgments

This book is dedicated to my parents, the late Mildred E. Riddle, who passed away May 2, 1988, and my father, Raymond W. Pratt. Both contributed to my appreciation of the expressive uses of music from the first days of my existence.

Carl Boggs and George Lipsitz contributed searching comments on each chapter at crucial stages and helped me keep on keeping on when I sometimes doubted it was worth the struggle. Both men are models of the best in critical consciousness and remain brothers in struggle who remind me of the best in myself. Carl and I were "blues brothers" a decade before the other guys.

Sara Goulden was an extraordinarily supportive companion throughout the three years of writing on this project. Without her I might have finished, but she made it a lot easier.

My daughter Leah has carried forward my love for all sorts of music and is a source of inspiration as her talent develops.

Many friends, too numerous to list and thank individually, contributed in a variety of ways that I could write about, and will, one day, but not here.

Two teachers, especially, helped me discover the ways people fight when and where they can using whatever means they have. Sociologist James B. McKee's course "Social Movements and Ideologies" and several others at Michigan State University, more years ago than I care to recall, introduced me to the sociological imagination. Daniel Goldrich's courses on Latin America over many years at Michigan State and Oregon helped me to appreciate the power of the human spirit and the politics of liberation from Zapata and Sandino to contemporary struggles to create new forms of community.

Work that has found its way into this book was supported in its earliest stages by a National Endowment for the Humanities Fellowship in Residence for College

Teachers at the University of California, Santa Barbara, in the department of anthropology during 1978–79. Paul Bohannan, as my advisor, encouraged my explorations of the functions of music as an expression of ethnic identity. Montana State University provided a much-needed sabbatical leave during 1987–88, which permitted full-time writing.

Since January 1979 I have produced and hosted a weekly radio program on the black music tradition: first, during 1979 on KCSB-FM, Santa Barbara, and, since fall of 1979, "The Blues Tradition" on KGLT-FM, Bozeman, Montana. The staff of these stations and the listeners over a decade have provided me with an immense source of satisfaction. But it is to the scores of musicians I have met and interviewed and to the thousands whose music I have heard and whose recordings have become a part of my life that I want to give the greatest credit. To have helped to make their music heard a bit better than it was before is more than adequate compensation.

But perhaps the greatest reward comes from those who have told me, "You have changed the way I listen to music."

1

Popular Music and Politics

Three seemingly isolated incidents of cultural practice illuminate the political problems raised by popular music in the late 1980s. In the acclaimed film *Platoon*, between the gut-wrenching agonies of the "search and destroy" missions, some of the men are shown in a bunker drinking and smoking pot, and they begin dancing, arms around each other's shoulders, to Smokey Robinson and the Miracles' "The Tracks of My Tears." The scene illustrates an important dimension of the political functions of popular music: The political meaning of any music depends on its use. In the horrific madness of Vietnam combat, dancing together to a popular song becomes for the men an affirmation of their humanity in the face of their task as killers who themselves confront the imminence of death. This assertion of their humanity comes as they are resting between episodes of a war that permanently scarred America's consciousness, leaving well over a million Vietnamese dead during the U.S. involvement in addition to the generally recognized 55,000 Americans. Over 20 years after the events portrayed, given the power of the "substitute imagery"[1] of the film to move the audience and the ability of music to evoke the mood of the era, one emerges from the film shaken and emotionally drained. It could not have been done otherwise if the audience is to recall the pain (not just of our losses, but the losses of millions of Vietnamese), begin to heal the deep emotional wounds, and then move on to whatever future we as a national community have before us.

In September 1985 Bruce Springsteen and the E Street Band were completing the last weeks of the "Born in the USA" tour, appearing at the Pontiac, Michigan, Silverdome with a crowd of over 70,000 (Michigan Bell Telephone reported 650,000 calls to the ticket agency). I was part of that crowd. The spectacle of thousands of people shouting in unison the lines of song after song made evident the many ways music is used and the variety of its meanings. As Springsteen introduced his version of Woody Guthrie's "This Land Is Your Land," he said, "This is the greatest song ever written about America" but added, "I'm not sure this song is true anymore. I hope it is, but I'm not sure. It's about a promise that's eroding every day for a lot of people. Just remember, with nations, as with people, it's easy to let the best of yourself slip away." Then, in a voice of raw pain that Immamu Amiri Baraka compared to that of the great black blues and soul shouters,[2] he began a solo vocal, harmonica, and guitar version slower than any other previously recorded. It had a somber, solemn quality and yet grew in intensity to a determined, almost march-like processional anthem for the dispossessed that engulfed the stadium. As it ended Springsteen said resolutely, "Remember, nobody wins unless *everybody* wins!" What did this mean? What was he trying to say? What could it possibly mean to the audience?

In September 1988 Springsteen, Sting, Peter Gabriel, Tracy Chapman, and Senegalese star Youssou N'dour launched the Amnesty International "Human Rights Now!" world tour with an entourage of some 160 people and projected costs of $23 million, the deficit to be covered through a sponsorship by the Reebok sports shoe company. At a London news conference Springsteen said, "I like to believe that music can change people's minds and feelings about their own humanity, and in doing so may change the way they look at the next guy."[3] Was he correct?

The soundtrack of *Platoon,* the "Born in the USA" tour, and the Amnesty International "Human Rights Now!" world tour strike this observer as powerful evidence of the political potential of popular music in the late 1980s. Certainly Springsteen's performance of Guthrie's "This Land Is Your Land" is one of the more eloquent versions of any song of protest. But what does the audience do with it? To paraphrase the Buffalo Springfield's 1967 "For What It's Worth," something *is* happening here, but what it is "ain't exactly clear." The Springsteen phenomenon of the 1980s and the many recent efforts to fuse rock and other forms of popular music to political causes provide significant and deeply moving examples of mass popular culture consumed and experienced by millions of people that may, some suggest, function simultaneously as a national and perhaps even international language. Yet precisely what are its functions and effects? Does it carry messages? If so, are the particular messages really heard? If heard, how are they heard and interpreted? If understood, how is the audience affected?

From the time of Plato (428–348 B.C.) observers of political life have seen the significance of music to political attitudes and behavior. Socrates is reported by Plato in *The Republic* as saying:

When the poet says that men care most for "the newest air that hovers on the singer's lips," they [the Guardians] will be afraid lest he be taken not merely to mean new songs, but to be commending a new style of music. Such innovation is not to be commended, nor should the poet be so understood. The introduction of novel fashions in music is a thing to beware of as endangering the whole fabric of society, whose most important conventions are unsettled by any revolution in that quarter.[4]

In the 1980s the alliance between politics and popular music has become closer than before. From the use of the music video format in political commercials to John Cougar Mellencamp's eloquent evocation of the plight of farmers to the simultaneous effort to appropriate Bruce Springsteen's "Born in the USA" by both Ronald Reagan and Walter Mondale in the 1984 presidential election, connections between popular music and politics pervade the era. To appreciate the complex political impulses in popular music one must go beyond traditional liberal Anglo-American institutionally based conceptions of participation in politics such as voting, influencing the behavior of officials, proposing legislation, and running for office. Contemporary conceptions of what politics is all about have in recent years become much more open and expansive. As Sheldon Wolin pointed out, the political dimension originally meant "public" things—of, or pertaining to, the whole community.[6] However, as Carole Pateman has more recently argued, this conception has built into it a distinction between public and private that ignores some of the profound biases in the concrete reality of "private" existence.[7] Important dimensions of conflict may exist within the private realm. Politics—understood in terms of the "authoritative allocation of values"[8]—exists within the home and family and in any organizational setting.

The emergence of feminist theory with its critique of repressive aspects of both conventional family structures and the power exerted by men in virtually every dimension of social existence has made significant contributions to the infusion of new concerns and broader visions of what constitutes "the political" in public discourse.[9]

THE PERSONAL AND THE POLITICAL

Especially within the last half century, "private" existence has increasingly been seen as the seat of profound discontents, alienation, and oppressions that have provided significant source material for popular music. While the women's movement has in recent decades brought heretofore "personal" issues into consideration as being publicly (hence politically) relevant, even before the advent of this wave of feminism, the sociologist C. Wright Mills provided an important link between the personal and political in *The Sociological Imagination*.[10] Drawing a distinction between personal "troubles" and social "issues" in such a way that apparently uniquely individual troubles become (at least theoretically) transformed into (essentially political) social issues, Mills demonstrated how, through the mechanism of public communication with others, a common recognition of shared concern is made. As a result public (and public policy) relevance is brought to consciousness. Such "basic human needs"[11] as those for food, housing, shelter, love and belonging, and sexual satisfaction and such "higher order" needs and desires as those for self-esteem, dignity, and self-actualization, as well as the rich dreams and fantasies of all people,[12] can in this way achieve significant political relevance and a position on society's public "agenda"[13] through increasing recognition of their collectively shared nature.

In chapters that follow, ways are explored through which the popular music consumed by Americans functions, especially through its use of what Alan Gowans has termed "substitute imagery,"[14] as an important way in which individuals and wider publics identify, name, and may begin to work to satisfy such needs and desires. Psychological categories are frequently employed because they have become essentially political categories. In the present era traditional borderlines between individual psychology on one side and political and social philosophy on the other have become obsolete. As Herbert Marcuse put it, "Formerly autonomous and identifiable psychical processes are being absorbed by the function of the individual in the state—by . . . public existence." In this way psychological problems become political problems, "private disorder reflects more directly than before the disorder of the whole, and the cure of personal disorder depends more directly than before on the cure of the general disorder."[15]

Music functions in important ways as political *behavior*. In the silent film *Napoleon* by Abel Gance, there is a scene in which "La Marseillaise" is shown being composed; the viewer then observes it going through the Assembly, then to crowds in the streets, until everyone is involved in singing it. When the film was first exhibited in France, audiences stood up and joined in spontaneous singing of the song that has become their national anthem.[16] Only music has such an effect on people. As such it involves both *purposive* and *effective* dimensions of political behavior.[17] Purposive dimensions involve a sense of explicit intention, an instrumental usage by which one or a few people somehow influence or attempt to influence the ideas or behavior of others. Musically, formal protest songs (such a labor-organizing song as "Talkin' Union" is a good example) would clearly meet tests of explicitness, though functions of any popular culture example might change over time.[18] Thus "La Marseillaise" was transformed from a song written in 1792 to inspire resistance to German intervention against the French Revolution, to an international anthem of revolution, to the official national anthem of France.[19] However it has been used, throughout its history it has proven to be highly effective politically in terms of its instrumental utility.[20] This function arises out of the unique ability of music seemingly to create a kind of spontaneous collective identity or facilitate the investment of people's psychological energies.

Effective dimensions of political behavior, by contrast, exert an influence, whether intended or not. The use of "Tracks of My Tears" in the film *Platoon*, as mentioned earlier, might be an example. Any popular music or any aspect of popular culture may serve a multiplicity of uses. Once a song or recording is created, it is "set free" for use by anyone, including a Charles Manson, who could take a song from the Beatles and perversely twist it in his cultish murder of several people.[21] More recently, in a 1987 election eve rally Britain's Conservative prime minister Margaret Thatcher stood before several thousand Conservative youths who joined together to sing a rewritten text of John Lennon's "Imagine," heretofore considered an anthem of utopian visionaries.[22]

Political dimensions may be expressed less than consciously. Music is used, for example, in ways that mark identity or group boundaries. Groups are known by the music they take as their own.[23] In another way, black spirituals and gospel music have been interpreted as political protest with revolutionary implications, quite apart from the lack of overtly expressed political consciousness of practitioners.[24]

It has long been a matter of debate whether the intentions expressed or "encoded" in any song are received by those hearing it. The ways any musical performance, song, or recording functions politically is a complex matter of analysis and attribution growing out of its essentially interactional character.[25] The meaning of any song, indeed any artifact in popular culture, is determined by the multiplicity of uses it receives. Popular music speaks to wider publics who may experience the information, feelings, and situations in it as their own, may accept only part of what they hear, or may reject or largely reinterpret the song to accord with their own belief systems. The imagery in music (i.e., "substitute imagery") helps people to define themselves, to establish an identity. Popular songs are especially often used in creating "a particular sort of self-identity, a particular place in society."[26]

Personal political implications are evident as well in the ability of music to provide the public with "a way of managing" the intersecting dimensions of their "public and private emotional lives."[27] Thus much of popular music is composed of love songs, which relate to the shared experience of most people and, more significantly, to one of the most important functions of popular music—its ability "to give shape and voice to emotions" that ordinary people have but find difficult to express with coherence and without embarrassment.[28]

As such popular music has wider significance through the interrelation of individual and social situations—personal categories becoming political categories. Because of this property—shared by other forms of popular culture—any music may potentially serve significant critical and even radically transformative functions. The degree to which it does so depends significantly on the dynamic interaction between the work itself and the way it is received. There is what Stuart Hall has termed a "double-stake" or dialectic in popular culture. On one side is an effort to contain the interpretation of meanings to those encoded into any element by its creators while simultaneously on the other side is an effort by those receiving it to invest that element with meaning that may "resist" that encoded by its creators.[29]

The implication is that there probably is no authentically autonomous popular culture as such. But neither is popular culture imposed upon the public by powerful media and culture industries. Cultural domination exists and has real effects, but there are important points and moments of resistance and even supercession of dominant intentions.[30] Defining the popular requires the search within any period for "forms and activities which have their roots in the social and material conditions of particular classes" but, more significantly, express a "continuing tension (relationship, influence, and antagonism) to the dominant culture."[31] In other words, popular culture is a *process* within which tensions and conflict exist over things preferred and those to be transformed. This may encompass things on the surface apparently purely personal to broader conceptions of society. Both are evident in all varieties of popular music. The observer is confronted here with the problem of musical "signification," that is, the appropriate methods by which to determine the meanings attributed and the ways people use popular music, especially in political senses.[32] Analysis becomes especially complex when one considers the many ways popular music is mediated: First, what precisely is "the message"? Second, does the audience "get" the message? Do they understand the meaning attributed by creators (to the extent it can be said there is explicit attribution)? Third, how do they "use" it? A fourth problem involves how the initial message is structured or inflected by the systems of production and transmission or diffusion.

Popular music is one of a variety of cultural commodities (serving as a commodity in both the senses of "value" Marx distinguished in *Capital* as "use" and "exchange" values[33]). People use these cultural commodities to define their identities and define, as well, a particular subculture or personal style. This common procedure involves "subverting and transforming these things, from their given meaning and use, to other meanings and uses."[34] Music can be so utilized because, among other things, it is a commodity. In the varieties of its popular forms, music serves as an item of exchange; it serves its audience through a multiplicity of its own real and potential functions, especially through its ability to contain the investment of a range of interpretation and assignment of meanings.[35]

This process is not without its built-in inequalities, which might seem to be overwhelmingly on the side of the large corporations of the culture and mass media industries. Yet even they must operate within the constraints of market forces, though exercising tremendous market power through shaping available products and advertising.

How is popular music a valid indicator of social attitudes or behavior? Although explicitly stated intentions are significant indicators of the artist's intended meanings, whether people are listening to them and hearing what they are saying is another matter. Content should never be assumed to be equivalent to effect. For example, if one listens repeatedly to a live recording of Bruce Springsteen performing "This Land Is Your Land," apparently before an audience somewhere in California,[36] one can hear a voice choked with emotion and sadness. Yet the greatest live audience reaction seems to occur at the line "from California to the New York island." At the word "California" a great cheer erupts from the audience. Why? Similarly, from this writer's experience, during a concert by Simon and Garfunkel (part of their 1983 "Reunion" tour) in the Pontiac, Michigan, Silverdome before about 40,000 persons, at the line of Paul Simon's song "America,"[37] which mentions Michigan and the city Saginaw (Saginaw, Michigan, is about 70 miles away on I–75), the audience rose from their seats and broke into tumultuous cheers when the names were spoken. What did they hear? What did it mean to them? It could signify a simple validation of their identity, as "Yes, we are here! We exist!" But it also suggests a good deal more: the desire for a feeling of community, one of the "utopian longings" to which mass popular culture responds.[38]

Such events also suggest the salience of an underlying desire for a "sense of place," again part of unexpressed deeper and utopian longings and a related psychological "quest for community."[39] The desire for this sense of place seems much more easily evoked from audiences, and invoked in writing songs, than are responses to more elaborate and complex statements concerning the failure of the promise of America (for example, as clearly intended by the composer Woody Guthrie[40] or especially the performer Bruce Springsteen in his spoken introductions to and performance of "This Land Is Your Land"). Such more complex political associations may be made, but probably for smaller segments of the audience in accord with their own ideological systems.

Popular music significantly gratifies personal desires. It would not be "popular" if it didn't, but it does so through providing imagery that permits the audience to utilize it in a manner simultaneously containing and fulfilling wishes through fantasy, strategically arousing fantasies within "symbolic containment structures." The ambiguity of these structures (in this case, popular songs) gratifies "intolerable, unrealizable, properly imperishable desires only to the degree to which they can again be laid to rest."[41]

There is a significantly political dimension in daily life, in ordinary experience, but it is one always in tension. The audience responses noted suggest that people want to feel a "part of something" in a world of increasingly mediated and homogenized experience, in which there is a decreasing sense of authentic existence and "sense of place."[42] The rapidity of social transformations U.S. society has experienced over this century has shattered and emptied out thousands of small communities—emptied out thousands of "little worlds"[43]—leaving behind a palpable nostalgia, like the roots of trees "free" from the soil. The longing for a past located somewhere and connections to a place that is real seem important desires to which popular music has continually spoken and which give popular music part of its appeal as a utopian critique of a present-day existence that has grown increasingly rootless.

Music functions as *expressive* and *instrumental* political behavior (in addition to the purposive and effective dimensions noted earlier); these lie along a continuum of expressive to instrumental uses. Expressive uses meet significant individual and group needs. Any performance by an individual might be considered an expression or objectification of that person's personality. The performance is a part of and says something about that person. The great jazz tenor saxophonist John Coltrane once said, "When I know a man's *sound*, well, to me that's *him*!"[44] But simultaneously the performance might be said to change the performer; it is, in psychological terms, individually developmental. Performers perfect their art through playing or singing and may in the process "say" something. As will be seen in Chapter 4 in the case of the blues, it is often said the music itself carries a meaning—what Ben Sidran termed a "galvanization of meaning and pitch."[45] The simultaneity of joy and sorrow may be found there, as heard in a classic blues such as Bessie Smith's version of "Empty Bed Blues" and as expressed theoretically with such literary beauty by Albert Murray in *Stomping the Blues*.[46] Bringing it to consciousness requires significant sensitization for the uninitiated who, nonetheless, have *felt* those elements originally encoded with meaning for as long as blues-influenced American popular music has been heard. This "message" in the music, this meaning embodied or encoded in any popular cultural symbol is, of course, given in part by struggles over meaning in what Hall terms the "social field into which it is incorporated."[47]

Expression may be utilized instrumentally as an explicit form of political action designed to move publics. Determining how, or if, this movement is effected is not easy. The empirical literature on mass media effects, especially in the areas of advertising and propaganda, reveals the contested reality of popular music. The most commonly understood, intuitive explanation would hold that music is "injected" in some way into the hearer. This simplistic explanation, growing out of early fears of the effects of propaganda, has been termed the "hypodermic needle" hypothesis. This assumes "(implied or explicit) values expressed . . . are (a) clear to a majority of listeners, (b) subscribed to by a large proportion of listeners, and (c) likely to influence the attitudes and behavior of the uncommitted. The theory further assumes a 'direct hit' for messages broadcast by the electronic media and directed at an undifferentiated target audience."[48] The actual path of any communication is significantly more complex and indirect and subject to the creative imagination of those receiving it.[49] And yet there is evidence that continued exposure to television, particularly in areas without conflicting sources of information such as foreign affairs, exerts significant influences on opinion. More recent work by George Gerbner and associates suggests powerful associations may exist between opinions and heavy television viewing.[50]

Musical meanings are established in a process of dialogue over the "text" between performer and audience. Efforts to establish meaning through apparent substantive lyrical content is a fallacious but common practice among critics. Actual popularity of any music is a product of a variety of factors beyond those deduced from apparent substantive lyrical content. Although there is often little correspondence between intended and imputed messages,[51] there do remain important conventions in ordinary language and at more formal levels of philosophical discourse concerning characterization and attribution of meanings and functions of music by critics and other external observers. The dynamics here are complex, depending significantly upon the situational location or perspective of the observer.

Three significant usages can be applied to describe creators, performers who use music, and the audience receiving them: conservative/hegemonic; negotiated; and emancipatory.[52]

A listener who takes directly the message intentionally encoded in a song (to the extent there is such intent) may be said to be operating within the "dominant" code, whatever the particular content of that code might be.[53] This is "perfectly transparent" communication. Any of the three perspectives set out in the following sections could be decoded "correctly" in this way. Either conservative or emancipatory message content might be completely accepted, partially accepted, or largely opposed. The typologies refer provisionally to ideological uses along a conservative (right) to emancipatory (left) traditional continuum.

CONSERVATIVE/HEGEMONIC USES

The notion of conservative/hegemonic carries implications of maintenance of the status quo, that is, the existing relations and distribution of power and values in a society, and its existing and established traditions, institutions, and "way of life." Plato called attention to this function of music as an agent for indoctrination or reinforcer of elements of the status quo in *The Republic* when Socrates said the Guardians must guard against "music contrary to the established order. . . . They must beware of change to a strange form of music, taking it to be a danger to the whole. For never are the ways of music moved without the greatest political law being moved."[54] Music is seen here as reinforcing the "hegemony" of the existing social order. "A hegemonic viewpoint . . . defines within its terms the mental horizon, the universe of possible meanings, of a whole sector of relations in a society or culture; and . . . carries with it the stamp of legitimacy— it appears coterminous with what is 'natural,' or 'taken for granted' about the social order."[55]

The concept of hegemony, which originated in the work of Antonio Gramsci,[56] has become over the last two decades so widely used in analysis of mass culture as to itself become a matter of contestation. One commonly understood definition sees hegemony as "a ruling class's (or alliance's) domination of subordinate classes and groups through the elaboration and penetration of ideology (ideas and assumptions) into their common sense and everyday practice; it is the systematic . . . engineering of mass consent to the established order."[57] Other conceptions stress the degree to which hegemony is an outcome (always provisional and subject to contestation) of a process.[58] Raymond Williams stressed this dynamic nature of the hegemonic: "A lived hegemony is always a process. It is not, except analytically, a system or a structure. It is a realized complex of experiences and limits. . . . Its internal structures are highly complex. . . . It has continually to be renewed, recreated, defended and modified. It is also continually resisted, limited, altered, challenged by pressures not at all its own."[59]

In Plato's classic conception, the hearing of certain modes of music was intended to develop in hearers the proper respect for the eternal order established in his utopian vision. A "correct" sort of self-discipline and respect for law and order would be the result. The right sort of music would inculcate an appreciation for "embodied form," serving as a prepolitical condition facilitating creation of a social order in which people would apparently be autonomous but oriented toward rules established by the Guardians.[60] A reference in *The Republic* calls attention to the threat to order posed by musicians who "tease and torture the strings, racking them on the pegs" (undoubtedly in the manner of the blues slide guitarist using a bottleneck or metal slider on the strings).[61] Such unseemly sounds would, it seems, somehow produce unseemly political attitudes!

Observers have primarily seen conservative indoctrination taking place in music at the level of content. Reproduction of dominant ideology or conservative elements of belief is seen as a result of exposure to lyrical content (the hypodermic model). So, the white apartheid regime in South Africa carefully censors the formal lyrical content of songs broadcast on state radio[62] and the conservative Communist regime in Czechoslovakia arrests members of a jazz performance art group. In the United States, members of the Parents Music Resource Center (PMRC) urge the Senate Commerce Committee to demand the Recording Industry Association of America (RIAA) to implement a ratings system to limit exposure of children to lyrics either sexually explicit or carrying implications of commonly practiced "unnatural" sex acts. Others protest such ratings as encouraging a "blacklisting" of certain artists or opening the way to additional forms of censorship.[63] Some see elements of conservative ideology, for example, in contemporary country and western music, inferring from lyrical content a significant affirmation of patriotic sterotypes as well as racist and sexist values; though, from an opposite perspective, these might also be seen as another aspect of the utopian longings and quest for community noted earlier as a general quality of popular culture.[64]

Three significant senses of "conservative" are evident: First, (following Socrates and Plato) in socialization for acceptance of existing forms, as an immanent "conservative bias"; second, in terms of explicit conservative ideological content in lyrics; third, in describing effects of the social relations of consumption, an argument that arises out of the emergence of mass festivals and spectacular concentrations of people in mass concerts over the past 20 years.

What are the effects of such social relations of popular music production and consumption? Are there emancipatory or repressive possibilities in any large concentration of people? What about the ideological messages delivered to them in songs and spoken messages from artists? Does the form or context in which they are received contravene or support ideological tendencies in lyrics? Is the public conditioned by "passively" receiving mass-produced commodified popular culture?

THE "POPULAR MECHANICS OF DOMINATION?"

Certainly in the years since the paradigmatic model, the Woodstock Festival of 1969, rock concerts have become huge spectacles—so large that critic Greil

Marcus, among others, has argued that when a Bruce Springsteen, whose music often chronicles the lives of people turned into objects, appears before an audience of 70,000 to 100,000, whatever is said or sung, however eloquently, is somehow "contained"—virtually swallowed up—by the structure of the event. This view suggests that no matter what a Springsteen or a Michael Jackson might think or say, each is playing out a thesis, that of the "popular mechanics of domination."[65] The whole spectacle in this view is the further reproduction of a kind of conservative hegemony. This was to some degree the view put forward by T. W. Adorno in his early work on radio music and "the culture industry."[66] It continues to be an influential and commonly expressed, if one-dimensional, perspective in analysis of popular culture.

Being in a large arena is not automatically and innately reactionary, however; the effects really depend on the historical context and what perspectives and desires the audience bring to the experience. Indeed, from an alternative perspective, in an age of increasing, though colonized, privatization through home video—where virtually anything public has been regarded as somehow contaminated—any mass gathering might carry some subversive implications.[67] Such gatherings, for some, might have some emancipatory possibilities while reinforcing conservative hegemony for others. One cannot know definitively what the effects on the audience will be by the mere fact of their presence. (The present writer was so moved by the spectacle of a Springsteen concert that he wrote this book!)

NEGOTIATED USES

The negotiated use "contains a mixture of adaptive and oppositional elements. . . . This negotiated version of the dominant ideology is shot through with contradictions. . . . It operates with exceptions to the rule. It accords the privileged position to the dominant definitions of events while reserving the right to make a more negotiated application to 'local conditions.' "[68]

The struggle for existence produces an accumulation of frustration as needs and wants are not fulfilled and desires and dreams are repressed. This frustration is, of course, a product of the "normal" repressions all experience in daily life. It nonetheless holds the potential for explosive, random violence or it can be invested in cultural practices that simultaneously contain and preserve the frustrations so that they may be shared with a wider community. So certain cultural practices are tolerated or encouraged as social expedients. Freud noted the range of them in *Civilization and Its Discontents*.[69] Sex, drugs, alcohol, and religion have served such functions, as have sports and music. Chicago bluesman Carey Bell describes how he used music to overcome the frustrations of his existence:

The worst thing that ever happened to me was in '66 when me and my old lady broke up—my first wife. I'd been married to her since I was seventeen. At that time I dropped out of music and got a day job for two years. Then in 1968 when Reverend King was shot, the riots came in Chicago. I was out on Madison Street watching the crowd on the Saturday after the killing. Oh, that street was full of people! But there wasn't a damn thing left there to steal, not after they burn't up every damn thing. So the firemen were fighting fires, and me and about four or five guys and a bunch of women were standing around. Two squad cars and a paddy wagon pulled up. "Get up against the wall!" So we got against the wall with our hands up. So I said, "What'd we *do*?" And the cop hit me with his damn gun right on the side of the head. And after that when we were getting in the wagon, I laughed, and he kicked me. I didn't like that. Well, while I was in jail thinking about these things, I got more and more disgusted and blue. Finally, I said, "Forget it! I'll quit my job. Shit. I ain't gonna do a damn thing."

I got out of jail that Easter Sunday, and that Monday I went out to the job and picked up my last pay. *Then I went to buy me a gun to kill that cop*. I just felt like the whole world had been dropped out from under me. Then it came to me to go to a music store and buy me some harps. I wasn't gonna *work* anymore, but I could play music. *So I bought the harps instead of the gun,* and I've been playing music full-time ever since.[70]

Although Bell's case is an especially striking example, interpreting what it illustrates is problematical. The experience of playing music (or listening, or attending concerts or club performances) may be seen as a tolerated or legitimate way of expressing accumulated feelings of anger, resentment, sexual desire, personal inadequacy, and impotence. Such feelings provide psychological raw materials that could be mobilized into support for movements to transform the existing order. From one perspective, dominant social authority might tolerate various forms of popular culture originated "from below" as effective safety valves. But even the sanctioned ways provide some free space. Channeling life experience into art is not necessarily a betrayal of politics where the game as played provides few solutions to the needs of subordinate groups.

From another perspective, the "freedom" some see in musical performance and the exercise of creativity in improvisation is highly limited, even illusory. Instead of taking action to change fundamentally the repressive existence of daily life, one is offered a substitute world of music, a "negotiated"[71] form of consciousness, a limited or partial realm of freedom that might better be seen as "a fantasy land, a make-believe sanctuary where the disappointments of the real world can be undone, reviewed, redefined, re-enacted and overcome" (in illusory, "change your head instead" fashion).[72] In this way the activity of the "outsider" subcultures of music might be tolerated as havens for discontented audiences and artists yet function simultaneously as safety valves for the ultimate benefit of the oppressor. Are any personal feelings of power engendered merely that—feelings, rather than perceptions of an altered social reality? Is controversy thus absorbed into the existing social framework? Does music defuse and diffuse potentially revolutionary accumulated grievances and domesticate every form of revolt, subtly transforming threats to fads and then into the most commonplace as one now may hear the protest songs of the 1960s in department store elevators as background music?

Meanings are ambiguous here. For any work effectively to "contain" existing anxieties or fantasies with social and political relevance, these must have "some effective presence in the mass cultural text in order subsequently to be 'managed' or repressed."[73] The results of such activity depend upon historical context.[74] Political functions of music depend upon what is made of it. The ambiguity of such typologies becomes evident in the face of contrary use by oppressed/repressed social groups. Slaveholders in the United States, as will be pointed out in Chapter 3, tolerated and even encouraged the unique individual forms of expression in work songs and field hollers and allowed their slaves to conduct religious services that provided the only places where blacks could raise their voices. Provision of even such tiny spaces of freedom may have unintended consequences. The content of work songs came to have a critical and oppositional character. Collective forms of oppositional consciousness grew under the very eyes of the overseer. As Alan Lomax put it concerning work songs, "Here, right under the shotguns of the guards, the black collective coalesced and defiantly expressed its unity and belief in life, often in ironically humorous terms!"[75] As Eugene Genovese pointed out concerning slave humor, there may be explosive potential, depending on the social situation and its consequences:

Oppressed peoples who can laugh at their oppressors contain within themselves a politically dangerous potential, but the weapons of popular culture also betray a conservative bias. . . . Their more dangerous content remains latent as long as the general conditions of life do not generate a crisis that heightens their critical thrust and points it to political terrain. . . . At those moments the oppressor's legitimacy, which the laughter ironically helps to authenticate by its very playfulness, suddenly faces challenge.[76]

Similarly, the black church, growing out of the religion imposed by the dominant slave-holding society to maintain discipline, came to serve important social and political functions: socially, a place where black men and women could come together to practice a fundamentalist yet millenial Christianity that constituted for them an important free space and refuge from a hostile world. Here, too, life was channeled into an art form—spirituals and gospel—becoming a way oppositional orientations and sense of special identity as an oppressed group were kept alive. In the case of Carey Bell cited earlier, his choice of a cultural form into which to invest his energy should hardly be seen as a betrayal of oppositional politics, especially if the kind of oppositional action would have involved the isolated violence of killing a police officer. Through 20 years after the events described, Bell was able to make a significant contribution to the blues of Chicago, one of the most vital urban "folk" musical forms known around the world. As Raymond Williams pointed out, "No dominant culture . . . exhausts all human practice, human energy, and human intention. . . . There can be areas of experience it is willing to ignore or dispense with: to assign as private or to specialize as aesthetic."[77] In this way "negotiated" responses may take on the more "emancipatory" dimensions considered next.

EMANCIPATORY USES

By ''emancipatory'' uses of popular culture is meant those that challenge dominant institutions. '' 'Emancipatory' signifies emancipation *from* something that is restrictive or repressive, and *for* something that is conducive to an increase of freedom and well-being.''[78] Such a conception, as Kellner describes it, ''subverts ideological codes and sterotypes. . . . It rejects idealizations and rationalizations that apologize for the suffering in the present social system, and, at its best, suggests that another way of life is possible.''[79]

Through history, music has often been fundamental to such an emancipatory process, reinforcing exercise of such human abilities to subvert and transform existing systems. Through affectively empowering emotional changes, music promotes establishment of sustaining relations of community and subculture that are fundamental to creation of an alternative public realm, a kind of cultural free space made of materials taken from thousands of composers and musicians who contribute the essential elements of what is propagated by the culture industries.[80] In the chapters that follow, some of the ways in which people have used and continue to use music to ''squeeze out'' free space in the existing class and power relations of society are explored.

NOTES

1. The term ''substitute imagery'' comes from Allan Gowans, *Learning to See* (Bowling Green, Ohio: Popular Press, 1983), one of the most important theoretical works on popular culture.

2. Amiri Baraka et al., ''The Meaning of Bruce,'' *Spin*, vol. 1, no. 7 (November 1985): 51. As Baraka put it,

What is refreshing and encouraging about Bruce Springsteen is his ability to translate both the form and some of the content of the blues. Springsteen is an American shouter, like the black country blues shouters from Leadbelly on, with an ear to James Brown and Wilson Pickett. . . .

What makes Springsteen so convincing, besides his appropriation of the blues shouter's voice is the nature of his concerns. The often tragic poetry of the blues is packed with reflections on a brutal society in which the singers are victims, lonely, broke, and hungry. Springsteen describes a visible, living America with its obvious flaws, a real world.

3. *Newsweek*, September 12, 1988, p. 76.

4. Plato, *The Republic*, trans. Francis M. Cornford (New York: Oxford University Press, 1945), p. 115.

5. One good example was Peter Shapiro's campaign for the governorship of New Jersey in 1985.

6. Sheldon Wolin, *Politics and Vision* (Boston: Little, Brown, 1960).

7. See particularly her essay ''The Theoretical Subversiveness of Feminism,'' pp. 1–10 in *Feminist Challenges: Social and Political Theory*, ed. Carole Pateman and Elizabeth Gross (Boston: Northeastern University Press, 1986). Also especially relevant is Carol Pateman, ''Feminist Critiques of the Public/Private Dichotomy,'' in *Public and Private in Social Life*, ed. S. I. Benn and G. F. Gaus (New York: St. Martin's Press, 1983), pp. 281–303.

8. The definition of politics as the authoritative allocation of values was put forward by David Easton in *The Political System* (New York: Alfred A. Knopf, 1953).

9. See the debates in S. I. Benn and G. F. Gaus, eds., *Public and Private in Social Life* (New York: St. Martin's Press, 1983).

10. C. Wright Mills, *The Sociological Imagination* (New York: Oxford University Press, 1959). On the emergence of personal politics and the women's movement from the civil rights and anti-Vietnam War movements, see Sara Evans, *Personal Politics* (New York: Vintage Books, 1982).

11. On the basic human needs see the many works of Abraham H. Maslow, especially his original statement, "A Theory of Human Motivation," *Psychological Review* 50 (1943): 370–96. A useful overview of the relevance of the approach to politics was provided in James C. Davies, *Human Nature in Politics* (New York: Wiley, 1963). The approach attained the level of conventional wisdom by the 1980s. See the critique by Daniel Yankelovich, "Stepping Off Maslow's Escalator," in *New Rules* (New York: Random House, 1981), pp. 234–43.

12. See Fredric Jameson, "Reification and Utopia in Mass Culture," *Social Text* 1 (1979): 130–48 and Jameson's *The Political Unconscious* (Ithaca, N.Y.: Cornell University Press, 1981) for a revelatory discussion of the ways mass cultural forms may be utilized to fulfull repressed utopian wishes of the mass public.

13. On political agendas see Roger W. Cobb and Charles D. Elder, *Participation in American Politics: The Dynamics of Agenda-Building* (Baltimore: Johns Hopkins University Press, 1983).

14. Gowans, *Learning to See.*

15. Herbert Marcuse, *Eros and Civilization: A Philosophical Inquiry into Freud* (New York: Vintage Books, 1962), p. xvii.

16. This account is related in Simon Frith, "Towards an Aesthetic of Popular Music," in Richard Leppert and Susan McClary, eds., *Music and Society: The Politics of Composition, Performance and Reception* (New York: Cambridge University Press, 1987), p. 141.

17. Christian Bay, *The Structure of Freedom* (New York: Atheneum, 1965), p. 6.

18. On the formal protest song see R. Serge Denisoff, "Protest Movements: Class Consciousness and the Propaganda Song," *Sociological Quarterly* 9 (Spring 1968): 228–47; and R. Serge Denisoff, "The Popular Protest Song: The Case of 'Eve of Destruction,' " *Public Opinion Quarterly* 35 (Spring 1971): 117–22.

19. Ironically, this anthem of liberation has often been invoked against revolutionary actions, most recently in the Indo-China and Algerian wars. The 1977 Academy Award for "Best Foreign Film" went to the French-African film *Black and White in Color,* directed by Jean-Jacques Annaud, which contains a devastating deconstruction of the *Casablanca*-style patriotic group singalong.

20. On "La Marseillaise" see James H. Billington, *Fire in the Minds of Men* (New York: Basic Books, 1980), pp. 57–60, 158–60. Composed "in feverish inspiration" by Claude-Joseph Rouget de Lisle on the night of April 24, 1792, at the request of the revolutionary mayor of Strasbourg upon hearing of the German declaration of war on France, "La Marseillaise," Billington points out, "rallied a people as had no other song since Luther's *Ein Feste Burg.*" Billington's work is rich and comprehensive in its treatment of cultural and symbolic elements of revolution from the eighteenth to the twentieth centuries, presenting significant insights into the production and functions of

the great revolutionary anthems and songs from "La Marseillaise" to "The Internationale" to the Wobbly (Industrial Workers of the World) songs of Joe Hill.

21. Greil Marcus, *Mystery Train*, Revised Edition (New York: E. P. Dutton, 1982). In their 1988 concert film *Rattle & Hum* U2 assert they "reclaim" the song from Manson prior to their performance of it.

22. Simon Frith, "Brit Beat: On and on and On," *Village Voice*, July 14, 1987, p. 77.

23. For a lucid discussion of this process see Dick Hebdige, *Subculture: The Basis of Style* (New York and London: Methuen, 1979).

24. On the radical implications of black spirituals see, for example, Eugene Genovese, *Roll, Jordan, Roll: The World the Slaves Made* (New York: Pantheon, 1974); and James H. Cone, *The Spirituals and the Blues* (New York: Seabury Press, 1972).

25. On the interactional nature of popular cultural phenomena see Norman K. Denzin and James T. Carey, "Problems in Analyzing Elements of Mass Culture: Notes on the Popular Song and Other Artistic Productions," *American Journal of Sociology* 75 (1970): 1035–1041.

26. Frith, "Aesthetic of Popular Music," p. 140.

27. Ibid., p. 141.

28. Ibid.

29. Stuart Hall, "Notes on Deconstructing 'The Popular,' " in Raphael Samuel, ed., *People's History and Socialist Theory* (Boston: Routledge & Kegan Paul, 1981), p. 228.

30. Ibid., p. 233.

31. Ibid., p. 235.

32. Examination of the range of issues involved in the application of semiotics to music is a highly complex matter. I approach it in essentially a metatheoretical way, recognizing its developments have marked, often revelatory heuristic power but involve so many analytical complexities and variables as to make the approach empirically problematical. For several views on basic issues in applying the approach to music, see essays in Wendy Steiner, ed., *The Sign in Music and Literature* (Austin: University of Texas Press, 1981).

33. Karl Marx, *Capital*, Vol. 1.

34. John Clarke, Stuart Hall, Tony Jefferson, and Brian Roberts, "Subcultures, Cultures, and Class," in *Culture, Ideology and Social Process: A Reader,* ed. T. Bennett et al. (London: The Open University Press, 1981), p. 70. This selection appeared originally in Stuart Hall and Tony Jefferson, eds., *Resistance through Rituals* (London: Hutchinson, 1976).

35. Ibid.

36. Videotaped from an ABC television "20/20" program.

37. "America," copyright 1968 by Paul Simon.

38. Jameson, "Reification and Utopia" and *The Political Unconscious*.

39. "Quest for community" comes from Robert A. Nisbet's book *The Quest for Community* (New York: Oxford University Press, 1953), republished as *Community and Power* (New York: Galaxy Books, 1962). This is a work of interpretive power and insight, especially in its evocation of the alienation that emerges as a central condition of modern life, to which popular music is one response.

40. See the discussion of the meaning the song had for Guthrie as an answer to Irving Berlin's "God Bless America" in Joe Klein's *Woody Guthrie: A Life* (New York: Ballantine Books, 1982).

41. Jameson, "Reification and Utopia," p. 141.

42. "No sense of place" refers to Joshua Meyrowitz's revelatory analysis of the effects of electronic media, *No Sense of Place* (New York: Oxford University Press, 1985).

43. See Marshall Berman's discussion of the tragedy of development and the reference to "little worlds" in *All That Is Solid Melts into Air* (New York: Simon & Schuster, 1982), p. 59.

44. John Coltrane, quoted by Ben Sidran in *Black Talk* (New York: DaCapo Press, 1981), p. 14.

45. Sidran, *Black Talk*, p. 13.

46. Albert Murray, *Stomping the Blues* (New York: Vintage Books, 1982).

47. Hall, "Deconstructing 'The Popular,' " p. 235.

48. Paul M. Hirsch, "Sociological Approaches to the Pop Music Phenomenon," *American Behavioral Scientist* 14 (January 1971): 376. For further discussion of models of effects of mass communication media, see Sidney Kraus and Dennis Davis, *The Effects of Mass Communication on Political Behavior* (University Park, Pa.: Pennsylvania State University Press, 1976).

49. Daniel Czitron provides an excellent analysis of empirical media theory in *Media and the American Mind* (Chapel Hill: University of North Carolina Press, 1982), p. 122–46.

50. Dennis McQuail, in "The Influence and Effects of Mass Media," in *Media Power in Politics,* ed. Doris A. Graber (Washington, D.C.: Congressional Quarterly, 1984), pp. 36–53, questions the literature that suggests effects are limited. Also see George Gerbner et al., "Charting the Mainstream: Television's Contributions to Political Orientations," in *American Media and Mass Culture,* ed. Donald Lazere (Berkeley: University of California Press, 1987), pp. 441–64.

51. Denzin and Carey, "Elements of Mass Culture," p. 1036.

52. The typology was suggested by discussion in Hilde Hein, "Aesthetic Consciousness: The Ground of Political Experience," *Journal of Aesthetics and Art Criticism* 35 (Winter 1976); Raymond Williams, *Marxism and Literature* (New York: Oxford University Press, 1977); and Stuart Hall, "Encoding/Decoding," in *Culture, Media, Language,* ed. Stuart Hall et al. (London: Hutchinson, 1980), pp. 128–38. Especially useful was discussion in Andrea S. Walsh, *Women's Film and Female Experience* (New York: Praeger, 1984), pp. 1–22.

53. Hall, "Encoding/Decoding," p. 136.

54. Plato, *The Republic*, Book IV, 424, b–c., trans. Allan Bloom (New York: Basic Books, 1968), pp. 101–102.

55. Hall, "Encoding/Decoding," p. 137.

56. Antonio Gramsci, *The Prison Notebooks* (New York: International Publishers, 1970).

57. Todd Gitlin, *The Whole World Is Watching: The Media in the Making and Unmaking of the New Left* (Berkeley: University of California Press, 1980), p. 253.

58. See Williams, *Marxism and Literature,* for elaboration of the dynamic view of "the hegemonic." A revelatory exchange on the uses of the concept appeared in *Journal of American History* 75 (June 1988): 115–61. See especially the comments of George Lipsitz, "The Struggle for Hegemony," pp. 146–50, and Mari Jo Buhle and Paul Buhle, "The New Labor History at the Cultural Crossroads," pp. 151–57. Discussion of the relevance of the concept in the study of popular culture is found in Walsh, *Women's Film and Female Experience*, pp. 8–15.

59. Williams, *Marxism and Literature,* p. 112.

60. Hein, "Aesthetic Consciousness," p. 146.

61. Plato, *The Republic,* VII, 531, trans. Cornford, p. 251.

62. For an excellent discussion of South African black music see Jeremy Marre and Hannah Charlton, *Beats of the Heart: Popular Music of the World* (New York: Pantheon, 1985), Chapter 2, "Rhythm of Resistance: The Black Music of South Africa," pp. 34–50. A useful survey of recordings of black music of southern Africa appeared in *The Nation,* November 22, 1986.

63. On the general issue of censorship see the insightful comments of John Street in *Rebel Rock: The Politics of Popular Music* (New York: Basil Blackwell, 1986). On the Parents Music Resource Center (PMRC) and efforts to censor popular music the issues are well stated in many things by Dave Marsh. One example, "Sympathy for the Devil: Has the Record Industry Sold Its Soul to the Devil?" *Village Voice,* October 8, 1985, pp. 13–19.

64. S. I. Hayakawa's "Popular Songs vs. the Facts of Life" was among the first. Reprinted in Bernard Rosenberg and David Manning White, eds., *Mass Culture: The Popular Arts in America* (New York: The Free Press, 1957), pp. 393–403. Later works include Paul DiMaggio, Richard A. Peterson, and Jack Esco, Jr., "Country Music: Ballad of the Silent Majority," and Jens Lund, "Fundamentalism, Racism, and Political Reaction in Country Music," in *The Sounds of Social Change,* ed. R. Serge Denisoff and Richard A. Peterson (Chicago: Rand McNally, 1972). The most incisive profile of the music and its practitioners is Nick Tosches, *Country* (New York: Scribner's, 1985).

65. See Greil Marcus' argument on the role of such pop stars as Michael Jackson and Bruce Springsteen in playing out a thesis of "the popular mechanics of domination," in his "Speaker to Speaker" column, *Artforum,* December 1985.

66. T. W. Adorno, "A Social Critique of Radio Music," in *Reader in Public Opinion and Communication,* enlarged edition, ed. Bernard Berelson and Morris Janowitz (Glencoe, Ill.: The Free Press, 1953). (Later editions do not include Adorno's essay.) Also see T. W. Adorno and Max Horkheimer, "The Culture Industry: Enlightenment as Mass Deception" (orginally written in 1944), *Dialectic of Enlightenment* (New York: Herder and Herder, 1972).

67. I am indebted to George Lipsitz for this perspective.

68. Hall, "Encoding/Decoding," p. 137.

69. Sigmund Freud, *Civilization and Its Discontents* (New York: Norton, many editions).

70. Carey Bell in Robert Neff and Anthony Conner, *Blues* (Boston: David Godine, 1975).

71. The notion of negotiated forms of consciousness comes from Williams, *Marxism and Literature.* For an application to popular music see Dave Harker's analysis in *One for the Money: Politics and Popular Song* (London: Hutchinson, 1980). For general application to popular cultural texts see Hall, "Encoding/Decoding."

72. Hein, "Aesthetic Consciousness," pp. 145. The allusion to "Change your head instead" comes from the Beatles' "Revolution."

73. Jameson, "Reification and Utopia," p. 141.

74. Hall, "Deconstructing 'The Popular,' " pp. 227–40.

75. Alan Lomax, Notes to *Roots of the Blues,* New World Records NW252 (New York: New World Records, 1977).

76. Eugene Genovese, *Roll, Jordan, Roll: The World the Slaves Made* (New York: Random House, 1972), p. 584.

77. Williams, *Marxism and Literature*, p. 125.

78. Douglas Kellner, "TV, Ideology, and Emancipatory Popular Culture," in *Television: The Critical View*, Fourth edition, ed. Horace Newcomb (New York: Oxford University Press, 1987), p. 489.

79. Ibid., p. 489.

80. On the notion of free space see Sara Evans and Harry Boyte, *Free Spaces* (New York: Harper & Row, 1986). The present writer's use of the concept came initially through adapting a notion in Simon Frith's *Sound Effects* (New York: Pantheon, 1982).

2

Community, Free Space, and Utopia in Popular Music

In *The Hidden Dimension* Edward Hall pointed out that human perceptions of the world are "programmed" by the language spoken.[1] Can music, itself a language and composed of language, program or "reprogram" human existence? Because people live in communities, their popular music may become a significant constituent of community—however it is defined, whether spatially, denoting a particular location or milieu,[2] or through a psychological identification.[3]

Music responds both to the increasingly common human experience of the decline of intimate connection to community, to the longings that grow out of increasing velocity of change as thousand of little worlds are "emptied out," in Marshall Berman's memorable phrase,[4] and also to the desires for new forms of community and new "codes of public space."[5]

FREE SPACES

While popular music often provides effectively empowering experiences for its audiences, its effects may be more concretely described in terms of a particular kind of temporal-spatial creation. In a variety of ways, it provides or can be used to create dimensions of "free space." Before discussing this free space, it is important to review certain inherent qualities of sound not usually associated with other phenomena that touch the senses. Live music, indeed any sound, has an evanescent quality. It exists while going out of existence. Recording has created the possibility of capturing such sound and placing it within the hands of the public, who may use it in any way they wish, though there are some broad contextual understandings surrounding the meanings.[6]

Auditory Space

Sound evokes a "sense of space."[7] This is different from that evoked, say, by sight or touch, both of which can be avoided through averting the eyes or withdrawing from reach. But we are limited in our ability totally to exclude or ignore sound. As Edmund Carpenter and Marshall McLuhan observed:

auditory space has no point of favored focus. It's a sphere without fixed boundaries, *space made by the thing itself,* not space containing the thing. It is not pictorial space, boxed in, but dynamic, always in flux, creating its own dimensions moment by moment. It has no fixed boundaries; it is indifferent to background. The eye focuses, pinpoints, abstracts, locating each object in physical space, against a background; the ear however, favours sound from any direction. We hear equally well from right or left, front or back, above or below. If we lie down, it makes no difference, whereas in visual space the entire spectacle is altered. We can shut out the visual field by simply closing our eyes, but we are always triggered to respond to sound.[8]

Sound is dynamic and symptomatic of energy. It does not occur in the absence of activity. Because humans are programmed to respond immediately to it, it "takes over" any physical space in which it is heard. An implication is that this property allows the intentional creation, or furnishing, of "sound space" with musical artifacts (recordings) according to human will and desire. Within certain limits imposed by availability of musical and sound materials, people are free to create spaces in which they program their environment. The "ghetto blaster" or "boom box" may be the most obvious and intrusive example, though it too has significant political implications as socially marginal people struggle to shape their own environments to their needs.

Psychological Freedom

The free space created through sound is identifiable with a basic psychological sense of freedom. This may endure for only a moment. One measure of any music is "its 'presence,' its ability to 'stop' time, to make us feel we are living within a moment, with no memory or anxiety about what has come before, what will come after."[9] This quality defines on a continuing basis those relatively autonomous social enclaves people create through participation in various kinds of music. Whether playing or hearing the music—in bars, clubs, discos, concerts, or even the vast spectacles music concerts could be in the 1980s—popular music serves potentially emancipatory functions if people *use* the setting in particular ways to generate and maintain enclaves of autonomy or free space.[10]

Sometimes, as Todd Gitlin points out on the combined use of drugs and rock music in his book *The Sixties: Years of Hope, Days of Rage,* this can be the search for an *inner space*: "The point was to open up a new space, an *inner* space, so that we could *space out,* live for the sheer exultant point of living."[11] This conception, stressing an essentially psychological dimension, an important aspect of the freedom music may provide or stimulate, its similar to Christian Bay's definition in *The Structure of Freedom*: "Freedom means to me self-expression, or the individual's capacity, opportunity and incentive to express whatever [one] is or can be motivated to express."[12] Similarly, Erich Fromm, in *Escape from Freedom,* stressed that "positive freedom consists in the spontaneous activity of the total, integrated personality"[13] and "full realization of the individual's potentialities, together with [one's] ability to live actively and spontaneously."[14]

Such definitions connote a psychological sense of space in which to act freely and with spontaneity. This space is a product of self-confirming action—it must be taken, and the more it is taken, the greater the feeling that it exists, a feeling political scientists describe by such terms as "efficacy" and "sense of subjective competence."[15] Such practice of taking, even though not marking off in physical terms a precisely measurable quantity of space, contributes to the creation of more identifiable social dimensions of free space through foundation of localities and venues embodying local political-cultural traditions. These can vanish when the wider structural conditions that permit them are changed. Kansas City in the 1930s was the cradle of subsequent jazz and rhythm and blues traditions, but its moment passed with the Pendergast machine, which permitted its existence as a "wide open" town.[16] New Orleans, as the cradle of jazz, saw the music move away toward the end of World War I when the Storyville "red light" district was declared off-limits to troops.

Social Space

Howard Becker in *Outsiders* showed how, through participation in an ongoing community of musicians, jazz and similar musicians are involved in fashioning a kind of social space through which to act in freedom. Such social dimensions constitute an alternative "social code" of space.[17] Simon Frith in *Sound Effects* noted how "creative space" could be achieved by artists in spite of the drive of the corporate system to generate commercial musical "product." Thus "rock was 'squeezed out' of the conflict between commercial machinations and youthful aspirations. If the industry was seeking to exploit a new market, the youthful audience was seeking a medium through which to express its experience, and musicians, who were at the center of this conflict, were able to develop their own *creative space.*"[18] Although Frith's usage is largely metaphorical, it conveys significant psychological dimensions with social implications.

In their book *Free Spaces,* Sara Evans and Harry Boyte develop a social and political conception of free space based on concrete social and political relations, emphasizing "the dynamic character of communal spaces. Under certain conditions, communal associations become free spaces, breeding grounds for democratic change."[19] Developing their perspective from insights of women's history, especially the small-group "consciousness-raising" phase of the late 1960s and early 1970s,[20] from labor history—what E. P. Thompson called the "unsteepled churches" of worker meetings and organizations[21]—the experience of ethnic minorities, and from the example of the functions of the free space created by the black church from the after-sundown functions noted by Eugene Genovese, George Rawick, and a multitude of others,[22] Evans and Boyte make evident that cultural dimensions of free social space are the foundation of broader social dimensions of liberation.

The role of music as discussed here intersects with the approach of Evans and Boyte. Music both creates and reflects forms of community. "Communities give people the interests for which they will risk their lives, family, friends, customary crafts, and ways of life."[23] Music is an important constituent and complement. The music of a people is a social relationship. As Thompson pointed out concerning social class, "The relationship must always be embodied in real people and in a real context."[24] Every form of modern popular music can be traced back to such peoples and contexts.

Music, like any form of art, in its function as an "impulse of opposition" to existing conventions, generates a rich and complex variety of enclaves of autonomy in the world through creation and maintenance of an alternative psychological reality which becomes a different kind of public space, a new little world within the old.[25] If such enclaves are largely psychological—a feeling— are they any the less real? They are inevitably connected to real social situations and organizational forms, serving to engender and reinforce support and morale. In the end this may be the most significant function of music, though R. Serge Denisoff notes eight significant functions.[26]

Popular forms of music such as black gospel, labor songs, the folk anthems of Woody Guthrie, the songs of Bob Dylan, the new urban folk as well as "antifolk" songs of Tracy Chapman and other members of her generation can provide a means to concretize a moment, turning it and all the desires it contains into an artifact—a song, a performance, a recording—that maintains a memory of the "abandoned moment," which, through consciously chosen repetitive rehearings, may return to recharge a part of society with renewed desire for what it represents.[27] In this sense the music people take as their own and "possess" through investment of psychic energies in repetitive rehearing creates resources with which to "remake" a segment of the world, in effect following the words of an old gospel song, "I'm gonna live the life I sing about in my song!"[28]

COMMUNITY

In *No Sense of Place* Joshua Meyrowitz suggested a significant aspect of television as a response to human alienation and longings: It creates a feeling of community. Unlike reading a book, in which more limited numbers of people participate, "television is capable of giving the viewer a sense of connection with the outside world and with others who are watching." Viewing television, people often feel they are merely observing the outside world. Ironically, this ability of viewers to "dissociate themselves from the content of television allows for the most widespread sharing of similar information in the history of civilization."[29] A new public arena is created, the social significance of which comes "less in what is *on* . . . than in the very existence of television as a *shared* arena." In this way, "Americans may gain a strange sort of communion with each other."[30]

Through its functioning as "substitute imagery" music, too, mediates experience, though perhaps not to the same degree as television hookups involving billions of people. It nonetheless creates a commonality of cultural experience that remains part of each individual's cultural heredity. Significantly, through the phenomenon of individual and group repetition of recordings, involvement in music for many is probably more influential than television, creating communities of common musical experience (though the video recorder and repeated viewings of films on video cassettes make similar involvements possible with products of those media).

In the case of television, this form of "communion" has implications for manipulation of the public consciousness.[31] The content of this "shared forum" is created by external elites with their own agendas, given currency by the fact that television is looked to

for the declaration and confirmation of the "reality" of events. Protests, scandals, and disasters that have not been reported on radio and television do not seem to have "happened." . . . When Walter Cronkite proclaimed "And that's the way it is" at the end of every CBS news broadcast, his statement was true to the extent that whatever is perceived simultaneously by so many people *becomes* a social reality—regardless of its relationship to an "objective" reality.[32]

A sense of an historical past is increasingly a product of this created, public collective "communion," like a dream,[33] but one in which *someone else* controls the content. What does the audience make of such constructed dreams?

Acceptance through consumption of television, films, novels, and popular music in which the constructed images are embedded suggests their satisfying qualities. Part of their appeal lies in nostalgia. In its original Greek the term *nostalgia* meant a longing for home to the point of illness. Today's usage connotes a somewhat less pathological condition, but one that is responsive to real underlying needs. Paul Monaco has referred to such nostalgic recollection in mass popular culture as "memory without pain."[34] Nostalgic references and recollections respond to human longings yet mediate and manage them in ways that diminish many associated discomforts.

The phonograph record created the possibility of an audience beyond those present at a particular performance. With the added dimension of radio, the potential hearers of any recording are multiplied many times over. The tape recorder and video cassette recorder have further extended the possibilities for individuals to program their own life-worlds—to create (and be created by) their own musical environments from what is available on recordings.[35]

This phenomenon creates the curious paradox of repetition in which the original text assumes decreasing significance in itself as more meaning is read into or invested in the particular song or album as it becomes a part of the life of the hearer through repetitive hearings. Popular music, as the object of this repetitive hearing, becomes thus the repository of a vast range of private associations, as such becoming "part of the existential fabric of our own lives, so that what we listen to is . . . our own previous auditions."[36]

The original musical creation becomes less significant than the uses made of it. Implied is a dialectical process in which the work created, or original text, lies at one pole, and at the other, what Jameson terms an "aesthetic universe," that is, a "message mass or semiotic bombardment from which the textual referent has disappeared."[37] Other approaches[38] emphasize in addition the important influences of preexisting consensus on meaning and the historical context into which any work is delivered.[39]

Constructed or not, these popular cultural creations and the communities who participate in them take on a social reality by virtue of shared participation. However individualized the interpretation, it is nonetheless very real that images, sounds, performers, are experienced by tens of millions, even billions, of people at the same instant or within a particular historically delimited moment. This raises profound issues of what constitutes "a place," as spatial notions seem overcome by illusions created through common participation in constructed images.

PLACE

A significant point of appeal of much popular music, especially as seen in videos, seems to lie in images of place. Images of performances are constructed to appear to take place "someplace."

Most forms of popular music originally developed through pleasing a live audience. In the blues and jazz, the very development of the art forms has, as Albert Murray noted in *Stomping the Blues*, proceeded in terms of performer-audience interactions, themselves drawing on call-and-response patterns in African culture and later slave work songs. That is similarly the case with black gospel music; it developed and is at its most exciting in live performance, especially in its home, the black church. Social change and technology may have overtaken and eroded these particular sorts of live arenas, and many popular music stars rarely tour; but if the rock videos on MTV are an indication, there will still be a significant amount of studio staging of concert performances to construct the appearance of a live audience and performer-audience interaction. The illusion that there is a real place where the musical interaction occurs seems a significant point in the appeal or salability of the music. Whether it involves associations invoked through an image of Bruce Springsteen sipping whiskey at a local bar, Bob Dylan or Stevie Ray Vaughn performing in one, John Cougar Mellencamp in a poor black neighborhood, or Steve Winwood shown in a black juke joint in "Roll with It," there is a powerful evocation that music of the kinds they perform is organically rooted in some place or authentic locale where an audience of real people, preferably including blacks, are depicted as enjoying it.

An important dimension of the alienation arising out of the disintegration of community relates to separation from physical place and, more broadly, nature itself. People have always identified themselves by where they were born or spent formative years. Yet contemporary U.S. mass culture, homogenized through centralized communication networks advanced by increasingly concentrated postindustrial capital, has so eroded regions and localities that more than ever it really doesn't matter from where one comes if one "fits" the requirements of the particular corporation and larger economic system. Though liberating in one sense, psychologically this erosion may entail great costs; disruption of sense of place is of profound importance in human efforts at self-identification.

At a Simon and Garfunkel "Reunion" tour concert in Pontiac, Michigan, in 1983 I was impressed by the thrill that swept the crowd at the mention of "Michigan" and "Saginaw" in Paul Simon's song "America" (which appeared originally on their 1968 *Bookends* album). Most stood and cheered. A similar response occurred in reactions to Bruce Springsteen's striking performance of Woody Guthrie's "This Land Is Your Land." Springsteen obviously chose to sing the song because, as he said, "it's about a promise that's eroding a little bit every day." But the audience in a version taped off television applauds most at the mention of "California." Place is obviously more salient for them than more complex notions of the erosion of the promise of America. Springsteen's New Jersey identification functions in a similar way; hear, for example, the warmth of the New Jersey audience response to his live version of Tom Waits' "Jersey Girl."[40] These examples represent a range of responses elicited by the simplest mention of a place name and regional identification with a singer (Springsteen) who has moved from the localism of the New Jersey shore to international superstar status at least partially through commitment to universal themes expressed in terms of the subculture of a region. More significantly, all represent a longing for place in a world in which every little personal world is being emptied out.[41]

Alienation from nature—in the vast semiurban regions dotted with elegantly designed but unidentifiably interchangeable air-conditioned shopping malls surrounded by acres of black-topped parking, where air-conditioned cars may be left temporarily in the search for culturally defined desirable commodities—has reached the point where perhaps the majority of the population live where they have little sense of the natural contours of the land and spend virtually their entire lives in enclosed spaces. How do they make sense of themselves and know who they are without some common shared elements of popular culture? Music plays an important role here.

One response to this existence among young men may be the quest for power expressed in "heavy metal" rock. Who are all those people in the Guns 'n'

Roses video? Who bought so many millions of their albums that, phenomenally, they had *two* among the top 50 during 1989? This kind of music is an important phenomenon whether one likes it or not. A most important quality of this form, like many forms of popular music, is that it gives a feeling of power to those who would otherwise feel powerless, here providing "power chords" for essentially powerless people. Lovers of the stirring concert music of Beethoven or Wagner or Stravinsky would understand the creation of affectively moving, even empowering qualities of that music, but they would not appreciate how the use of power chords in heavy metal resonates with a similar creation of affect.[42] Both kinds of music bind their audience in a kind of exhilarating community that, for those who appreciate it, is affectively empowering.

My own unsystematic observations of teenage culture suggest other forms of popular culture function similarly. A large (nearly 6-feet tall) 14-year-old boy, resentful at his mother's not allowing him to drink beer or take a puff from a joint of marijuana circulating at a party, was asked about his favorite movie. *"The Terminator,"* he replied. "I've seen it eight times!"

The film is an antiutopian, postnuclear devastation bleak-future sci-fi tale involving the relentlessly horrifying actions of a virtually unstoppable human replicant killer-robot from the future (played by muscleman Arnold Schwarzenegger) who is beamed back to the present day to eliminate the mother of a future resistance leader. In the process he smashes through walls and, with an amazing array of absolutely powerful firearms (all violently seized from local gun shops) and several vehicles, including a giant semitruck, blows away or drives over virtually everybody in sight. It is not difficult to discern the "substitute imagery" here for a stratum of restive teenagers. Living powerless lives, ordered about by parents, teachers, and shopping center guards, they find vicarious empowerment in the lethal efficacy of the unstoppable robot.

TIME

Humans as "time-binding" creatures find senses of past and future as significant for sense of identity as is the present. As the voluminous literature on the effects of mass media, especially television, suggests, this culture has created a citizenry with an attenuated sense of the past, yet one that can achieve a significant sense of "communion with others" through participation in the simultaneous perception of whatever is *on* the major form of popular culture, television. The same might be said of popular music to the extent that it truly becomes a mass phenomenon.*

---

*What constitutes a "mass" level of participation in popular music? Sales are only a very small portion of audience participation. Radio, and now TV, air play is a better indicator. Music researcher Reebee Garofalo at the 1986 Popular Culture Association Convention said that of the average of 5,000 albums produced each year, only about 10 percent get air play, at most 100 of these are heard by the average listener, and far fewer repetitively heard—in fact, as little as 0.2 of 1 percent of the music produced is closely heard by the average listener.

Popular music shapes memory and organizes sense of time. Frith suggests that "one of the effects of all music, not just pop, is to intensify our experience of the present."[43] One way of measuring the quality of music becomes "its 'presence,' its ability to 'stop' time, to make us feel we are living within a moment, with no memory or anxiety about what has come before, or what will come after."[44] Consequences of the way music organizes a sense of time are evident in how popular music both invokes a generalized sense of the past and evokes particular memories of the past and, sometimes, constructs or structures a new sense of meaning about the past. Those who saw the 1983 film *The Big Chill* experienced the transition from organ playing after the funeral in a small country church to a tune that became the full rendition of the Rolling Stones' "You Can't Always Get What You Want." For many activists of the late 1960s it spoke to disappointment and failed promises. Through its use in the film, however, it could come to have new meanings for a mass audience seeking to fashion their own sensibilities concerning their limited existence.

Popular music affects common conceptions of the past. While it helps to retain or bring back the emotional context and make the memory of the past more genuine, it may be utilized to construct a particular affective image of the past. The use of music in contemporary films set in particular time periods is significant for what it reveals about the functions of music. Sometimes music creates a timeless, though illusory, "1940s" film noir feeling. One example is the use of sultry moans of saxophones in efforts to recreate the atmosphere of 1940s film noir classics (which actually rarely featured that style of jazz saxophone performance but instead used studio orchestras with strings). Examples are the 1987 film *Someone to Watch over Me*, using Gene Ammons' soulful early 1960s tenor saxophone version of the title tune, or the earlier 1984 Alan Rudolph film *Choose Me*, featuring several bluesy selections by jazz tenor saxophonist Archie Shepp.

Use of popular music in Vietnam War films has been particularly effective in evoking or constructing historical memory, especially in Oliver Stone's *Platoon* and Stanley Kubrick's *Full Metal Jacket*. A most successful example was in Hal Ashby's film *Coming Home* (1978), where the Rolling Stones' "Sympathy for the Devil" was used on the soundtrack to devastating effect, evoking and communicating the profound sense of fundamental derangement of all human priorities as Bruce Dern in the role of the Marine officer on rest leave from Vietnam (and obviously on the verge of cracking up) described to his wife (played by Jane Fonda) the madness of the atrocities against the enemy dead committed by men under his command: "*My* men were cutting off ears!"

Music contributes to maintenance of myths about the past, clothing memories in a musical glow in the way the Simon and Garfunkel recordings did in *The Graduate*,[45] a 1968 film directed by Mike Nichols that developed a tremendous cult following with viewers returning to theaters again and again (some for six or seven viewings). The music contributed significantly to the film's profound appeal, which lay in the arresting images of violations of some of the most fundamental conventions, such as the interruption of a marriage ceremony and the quasi-incestuous sexual encounters between the main character (played by Dustin Hoffman) and Mrs. Robinson, his girlfriend's mother. These were set against a pervasive sense of the ultimate emptiness of the existence of the lifestyle portrayed.

Particular songs encode meanings that audiences recognize because of widespread experience of historical context. The 1967 Buffalo Springfield recording "For What It's Worth" conveys the disturbing and confusing social changes of the 1960s: that the "something" that is happening is not clear. Crosby, Stills, Nash, and Young's 1970 "Ohio" relates the killing of students at Kent State University and points an accusing verbal finger at then-president Nixon's policies (and, one may infer, any national administration). Both communicated a portentious sense of the historical moment then and are probably usually so decoded today by those in any way familiar with the historical context.

Phrases from Bob Dylan's songs, asking whether this can really be the end, from "Stuck Inside of Mobile with the Memphis Blues Again," or how it feels, from "Like a Rolling Stone," became parts of the personal vocabulary of many in the 1960s and 1970s, as did the Rolling Stones' "Gimme Shelter," a song about the "relief" obtained through drugs but which could be interpreted as a search for safe harbor against a conservative national regime or simply refuge from "straight" conventional society. Bob Dylan's "Shelter from the Storm" from his 1974 *Blood on the Tracks* album provided a similar addition, stressing the haven provided by women, home, a relationship in a heartless world. The Rolling Stones' "You Can't Always Get What You Want" for many spoke to the failed promise of 1960s movements and the disillusionment of the end of the decade.*

Certain music relates to sense of community through carrying on national symbolism, whether of the United States or the continuity of American life, or of other national traditions. Thus the sound of accordions can be said to symbolize France, bamboo flutes Japan or China, aboriginal instruments the "real" Australia, bagpipes Scotland, the tango Argentina, the *quena* flute the Andean highlands of Peru and Bolivia, and so on. Some of the American "classical" composers of the 1930s and 1940s created works with a particular "sound" that are today utilized as a tool box of film and television score themes. The 1987 multiepisodic ABC television series "Amerika," dealing with a fictional America after an alleged Soviet takeover, had a musical score that might be characterized as recycled, or highly derivative of compositions of the American composer Aaron Copeland. Music for the 1983 nuclear devastation film *The Day After*, shown to a massive television audience, featured interpolations of Virgil Thom-

*Todd Gitlin's *The Sixties: Years of Hope, Days of Rage* is filled with similar examples linking music of the 1950s and 1960s to historical movements, especially effectively demonstrating the linkage of music to personal rebellion, first against 1950s conforming and later, in the 1960s, aligned with more organized expressions of revolt.

son's 1930s classic film score "The River," a distinctly "American"-sounding piece in its themes.

In popular music the sound of steel guitar suggests a rural or "country" theme, an arpeggiated Spanish acoustic guitar connotes Spanish-speaking areas of the southwestern United States or Mexico, a recognizable repetitive chord motif within a particular musical mode is used as an "Indian" theme in westerns. In such ways music may be used by composers to preserve or nurture or evoke or create some sense of the past or to construct or inflect some memory of it. Such themes, while sometimes accidental or unconscious also function to maintain memories, sometimes as nostalgia, and thus contribute to a shared sense of the continuity of U.S. culture, even while reconstructing images of it. All are responsive to the longing for community.

Music is used to construct some sense of collective memory, but what kind of memory is it? How is it used? What are its functions? What images does it maintain? To what ends and in whose interest? Perhaps Orwell's antiutopian projection of a brainwashed future *has* come about in ways more elegant and subtle and yet more *total* than he ever dreamed possible as a synthesized past is processed and *bought*.[46] Yet, as the use of musical examples might suggest, it can also be a "usable" past—a *means of resistance* and *a way to revision the future* through invoking past and presently used cultural materials.[47]

Whatever its basis, Robert Nisbet argued, "loss of a sense of the past is an important matter, if only for its functional necessity to revolt. How can there be a creative spirit of youthful revolt when there is nothing for revolt to feed upon but itself?"[48] To put it another way (with apologies to The Talking Heads for inverting the wording, though probably not the intended meaning of their 1985 song "We're on the Road to Nowhere"), we *don't* know where we're going if we don't know where we have been.

As people find it ever more difficult to establish roots, to have a stake in something material beyond personal possessions, some terrifying images of dehumanization have appeared in popular culture. These might be seen as responses to socially endemic alienation and feelings of rootlessness and dehumanization. Ridley Scott's 1982 futuristic antiutopian film *Blade Runner* featuring "replicants"—human-appearing androids with real flesh—forces us to consider what it is to be genuinely human. So do the flesh-eating zombies aimlessly lumbering through a shopping center in George Romero's 1979 satiric film masterpiece on U.S. shopping center culture, *Dawn of the Dead*.

All dimensions of alienation are part of the wider context of community. What is involved is a series of eroding relations both to social function and social authority. The social changes in our society over the past half century have cut millions of people adrift. There has been, in Nisbet's terms, "a dislocation of the contexts of function."[49] Thus relationships—the extended family, neighborhood, social class—which had a depth and inclusiveness in individual lives because they had some functional significance have become emptied of content.

Popular music, through its qualities as substitute imagery, may give some clue to direction and some sense of one's place in all this increasing change; it may even permit individuals and social groups, indeed, whole strata of society, to create out of available materials their own personal worlds and distinct subcultures—new forms of community—within the existing social chaos.[50] Rap music is but the latest cultural expression of this tendency.

Senses of individual function and social authority are prime requirements of community. Yet as Meyrowitz argues in *No Sense of Place,* both are fundamentally eroding in a society transformed through mass media that show little regard for the distinction between "front region" news (the formal political arena, such as a State of the Union speech) and "back region" information and behavior (such as John F. Kennedy's extra-marital affairs or the detailed published descriptions of Ronald Reagan's intestinal polyps or the frequency of President and Mrs. Ford's sexual intercourse).

The progressing erosion of social authority as dimensions of decline of an older dominant community or as part of the creation of new communities formed through political struggle can be traced musically in the evolution in views of the U.S. presidency and polity. A distinct trend in declining regard for the presidency is evident, say from Woody Guthrie's 1945 "Dear Mrs. Roosevelt,"[51] with its maudlin adulation of the departed president (who, Meyrowitz points out, few Americans knew could not stand without braces on his legs) to Country Joe and the Fish's 1967 song "Superbird," which is utterly contemptuous of President Lyndon Johnson. The contempt evident in the latter song would not have been possible without the broad sense of community created through the antiwar struggle. Similar deep political cultural divisions and radically oppositional conceptions of authority are evident in Gil-Scott Heron's deconstruction of Ronald Reagan, "B-movie" of 1980; the powerful 1981 anti-Reagan song by the group X, "More Fun in the New World"; or the devastating mixes of the 1984 "Bonzo Goes to Washington" EP (using Reagan's own voice from the off-the-cuff soundbite "We start bombing in 10 minutes"). The presidency and Reagan personify evil, "the system," and all that is to be struggled against. The trend continues through Jackson Browne's 1986 "For America," which seethes with righteous indignation over U.S. Central American policy and covert actions there, and from the same year Bruce Cockburn's "People See through You," or from 1987 Stevie Wonder's "Characters," which speaks to the deceptions in the Iran-Contra scandal.

The chapters of *No Sense of Place* discussing "Questioning Authority" and "Lowering the Hero to Our Level" partially illuminate the forces underlying these developments, interpreting them largely in terms of mass media effects, as statuses are homogenized and "front" and "back" region behaviors are merged and brought to light.[52] However, the explanation seems one-dimensional and falls rather flat when contrasted to the fury of the utopian indignation and inspired rage in these musical examples.

The erosion of genuine forms of community leaves significant strata of the population with yearnings for something more, something deeper than sharing consumption patterns. The incredibly varied range of intellectual currents and organized movements seeking spiritual enlightenment and growth that Marilyn Ferguson termed "the Aquarian Conspiracy" in the 1970s and 1980s is evidence of such yearnings.[53] The growth of a whole new category of complementary "New Age" music in the 1980s was a response. Music, potentially, can contribute to such spiritual growth, serving to facilitate a shared sense of identity among spiritual seekers and creating on a personal basis the space to seek "inner space" through meditative isolation.

The impulse toward greater community in contemporary society was evident in the book *New Rules,* where Daniel Yankelovich noted a substantial increase between 1973 (about one-third of a national sample) and 1981 (nearly one half, or 47 percent) in the number of Americans who "felt an intense need to compensate for the impersonal and threatening aspects of modern life by seeking mutual identification with others based on close ethnic ties or ties of shared interests, needs, backgrounds, age or values."[54]

That popular music responds to such a desire, perhaps even "managing" it in some limited ways,[55] does not in any sense diminish the genuine quality of the represented need. The underlying quest for community evident in the initially puzzling crowd responses to lines and place names, as noted earlier, seems reflective of yearning for more deeply rooted solidarity beyond that achieved following a professional athletic team or in the much too common collective 1980s hatred for Libya's Colonel Quadaffi and Iran's Ayatollah Khomeini.[56] As a displaced Michigan resident, I felt a curious sense of affirmation when I heard the Simon and Garfunkel performance mentioned earlier.

The cynical manipulation of utopian yearnings is one of the wider and more significant political realities of the need for roots. One recalls in this connection such cultural interpretations of nazism as Fromm's *Escape from Freedom.*[57] Expressions on the faces of the crowds in Leni Riefenstahl's Nazi documentary, *Triumph of the Will,* evidence the longing for which the Nazis provided one kind of response. Bruce Springsteen suggested in one of his interviews that Americans have a "need" to feel good about their country, but that this need, which he regarded as "a good thing," was being "manipulated and exploited" in the Reagan years.[58]

Although Springsteen's words ring true, the phenomenon has occurred in every national administration as far back as George Washington. Can one counterpose the notion of such an authentic community to the "false" or "manipulated" community sold, for example, in the presidential campaign of 1984? One heard quite clearly, "It's morning in America!" with the implication that like choosing a good breakfast cereal one should reelect Reagan. Springsteen's widely noted response was: "It's not morning in Pittsburgh. It's not morning above 125th Street in Manhattan. Like, it's midnight, and there's a bad moon rising!" Such perceptive social criticism from leading rock stars, less frequent in the early 1980s (some even backed Reagan or Thatcher[59]), increased by the end of the decade, thus continuing the long tradition in social criticism going back to those distinctions between real and "illusory forms of communal life" drawn by Marx as early as 1845 in *The German Ideology*[60] or even earlier to Rousseau's demand in *The Discourse on Political Economy* (1755) for a community one could love with that "exquisite feeling" one experiences only for oneself.[61]

A related form of manipulation occurred with the elevation of the family as an object of utopian longing to absurd levels in the 1988 presidential campaign. With rock singers, a significant element of their appeal lies in sexual attraction, such that their marriages are rarely a part of their constructed public images. They are fashioned as fantasy sexual objects. A different phenomenon seemed to emerge in 1988 with the candidates of both parties—both with Jesse Jackson and Michael Dukakis for the Democrats, and certainly with the George Bush extended clan—they all seemed to have legions of happy, healthy children, the product of those "happy marriages" that in an era of disintegrating families seem to function for the mass audience as little utopias or "haven[s] in a heartless world."[62]

Yet the longing to be treated as a whole person persists. It is simultaneously a reaching toward authentic, whole individuality and a yearning for a community in which that individuality will be honored, nurtured, and permitted to grow. Berman argued in *The Politics of Authenticity* that such a conception was one of the enduring legacies of 1960s politics, yet one that was in no manner unique to that era but rooted in impulses similar to Rousseau's quest for a fusion of individuality and community—for "a common self," a desire for a *community* in which to *be* one's self.[63] One of the quintessential documents of 1960s radicalism, the 1962 Port Huron Statement of Students for a Democratic Society (SDS), looked toward creation of a society in which every person could find "a meaning in life that is personally authentic."[64]

The search for authenticity thus becomes inevitably linked to movements for social transformation and renewed community. It "is bound up with a radical rejection of things as they are. It begins with an insistence that. . . . [existing] social and political structures . . . are keeping the self stifled, chained down, locked up. It argues that only if the old structure is renovated, or if a new one is built from the ground up . . . only then can the self come into its own."[65]

Concrete contemporary expressions of the search for community are evident in numerous social movements in Western Europe and in the United States, committed to "engage and transform the immediate environment—the household, neighborhood, municipality—as part of a grassroots-based radicalism."[66] This effort, as Carl Boggs expresses it, seeks "to recover a sense of community outside the state-regulated and commodified universe." It is dependent upon "a *systematic reorganization of space* to enlarge the realm of (open) public discourse and physical freedom," requiring nothing less than a "new code of space" founded upon "expressive rather than instrumental social relations."[67]

Forms of popular music, like community direct action struggles to which they are sometimes linked, play a significant role, keeping alive collective feelings of efficacy, providing affectively empowering subcultural foundations, and reinforcing local community traditions.[68] The history of popular music in the United States is rooted in such localities and associated free spaces. This dynamic is evident from the time of slavery and the early black churches, through the intensity of musical culture in urban ethnic neighborhoods, whether it was jazz in New Orleans or Harlem, local blues traditions in Houston and Dallas, St. Louis, Detroit, or the "black bottom" of Indianapolis. The tendency was certainly present in the unique fusion of jazz, blues, and rhythm and blues in Kansas City in the 1930s that would influence all subsequent popular music, and in the powerful electric urban black "folk" music that was the Chicago blues of Muddy Waters and others in the 1940s and 1950s, as well as in the black urban working-class blues of John Lee Hooker and others in Detroit in the 1940s and 1950s. Related examples of local traditions may be found in the counterculture rock in the San Francisco Bay Area in the 1960s, "outlaw" country music in Austin, Latino music in East Los Angeles, salsa in New York and Puerto Rico, Tex-Mex in the Mexican and Texas border region, the "Sun" sound of Memphis, contemporary Nashville, the Minneapolis sound in rock, and even the clubs of Los Angeles, and certainly in the incredible diversity of musics in New Orleans and environs in the present day, through the radical black social commentary in the revolutionary sounds of the most contemporary rap.[69]

This grounding in specific locations and styles of the past gives the most contemporary popular music part of its appeal as a utopian critique of a present-day existence that grows increasingly rootless. One can see the dynamic at work in the emergence of the two leading forms of contemporary popular music: rap and the urban folk music of Tracy Chapman, Michelle Shocked, Suzanne Vega, The Cowboy Junkies (with lead vocalist Margo Timmins). It may be that the emergence in 1988 of so many women artists who sang in a post-Baez, Collins, and Mitchell style reflected a reaction to the very disquieting power of rap and a longing for the more comprehensible and positive, if somewhat nostalgic, appeals of a new generation of what Robert Christgau has labeled "folkie madonnas."[70]

But all such popular music, whether rap, roots, or urban folk, utilizes universal themes often expressed in readily identifiable local forms and styles by known personalities. It "works" through embodying widely shared dreams and desires and anxieties, as such creating new kinds of communities linked through common participation in shared cultural imagery.

Historically, the desire for community has been accompanied by attempts to build social organizations that satisfy desires for "relations of communion," for forms of human relationship that, in their communal character, are contrasted with the limited, instrumental nature of human relationships in the larger parent society.[71] For most, the efforts devolve onto fruitless quests for the ideal relationship. For many others, this desire may be partially satiated in the collective communion and dialogue of television and the privatizing mass phenomenon of home video. That this vast audience is much more than a community of inert "couch potatoes" is increasingly evident in critical analyses of television audiences, but such analysis is beyond the scope of this discussion.[72]

Still, all these developments reflect a continuing longing for roots, a quest for free space that is also an authentic community. As it has been for two centuries, popular music in the United States is intimately bound up in that quest.

POPULAR MUSIC AS UTOPIAN PREFIGURATION

The musical experience for composer, performer, and audience may serve as a "prefiguration" of wider utopian social transformation—the utopias of which all people dream[73]—as well as more elaborate conceptions of social revolution. The prefigurative impulse embodies in a movement (and, culturally, in a text) the self-liberatory and transformational ends of revolutionary change.[74] Understood at the widest social level, a *prefigurative politics* attempts to "develop the seeds of liberation and the new society prior to and in the process of revolution through notions of participatory democracy, often grounded in counter-institutions."[75]

Implied in prefigurative political "theory" (theory is used here in a broadly inclusive sense, in whatever forms it appears, including popular culture) is an interaction between consciousness and structural context—out of which comes a "resocialization" of those who participate in particular counterinstitutions or cultural movements.[76] Such forms are seen as conducive to individual, as well as wider social, transformation through engendering freer social relations and facilitating potentials for individual growth sought in wider utopian social visions. Because they exist *prior to* and separate from the creation of such envisioned futures, they prefigure the kind of liberating community sought. They assume the function both of positive social "role models"—teaching by example—but simultaneously changing, empowering, and "capacitizing" those involved in them.[77]

Involved is a vision of uniting of ends and means in a continuing process of transformation, both liberating in itself and serving as a transition toward utopian social reorganization. Although the prefigurative conception was perhaps expressed best in the old slogan of the Industrial Workers of the World (IWW) that "by organizing industrially we are creating the structure of the new society within the shell of the old,"[78] its origins go back to Thomas Jefferson's concern with the benefits of participation in "ward republics"[79] and echo in the present in the vast if often euphoric literature on the benefits of participatory democracy.[80] Certainly Marx's prefigurative projection of the Paris Commune[81] is a paradigmatic example of the vision that continued through the years in the council communism of Anton Pannekoek and others,[82] as well as in the various strands of anarchist thought from Kropotkin through the twentieth century[83] and in Rosa Luxemburg's theory of revolution.[84]

What stands out about such a conception is that although it has initially always been crushed by overwhelming physical powers of its opponents in the short run, it provides enduring political-cultural models that do not die, recurrently resurfacing in the minds of later generations who remember, and are inspired by, the Paris Commune, the Spartacist revolt in Germany, the workers' councils movements in Italy in 1919–20, the agrarian and workers' collectives in Spain in the 1930s, and in Budapest in 1956, and the student-worker revolt in France in 1968. Even the first Soviet sputnik in 1957 carried a ribbon from the suppressed Paris Commune of 1871.[85]

In popular cultural terms, in a diverse variety of texts and movements, perhaps for only a moment (seen in historical terms) an "alternative reality" is created or modeled that serves as a prefiguration of elements of an alternative society perhaps as yet barely conceived. Culturally, some of these impulses came together in the myth that was generated around the Woodstock Festival of 1969.

In the late 1960s questions of the relation of pop music to politics were posed openly. Many sought an explicitly political popular music. If the preeminent 1960s moment was the Woodstock Festival, when 500,000 people converged on a farm near Woodstock in upper New York to revel in themselves and some of the major musical acts of the era, it is because many millions subsequently *made* it into a myth embodying utopian aspirations for a community based upon pleasure and the joy of music. Woodstock became one of the most significant symbols of oppositional popular culture.[86] It was "a rock myth, a fantasy about the possibility of creating a self-sufficient musical community."[87] Its success, John Street argued, in pronounced contrast to the "openness" of Live Aid in 1985, "lay in its exclusiveness, the *barriers* it created between 'them' and 'us.' "[88] But if Woodstock as myth was essentially about "being there," it also offered something more, something beyond the naive simplism of the notion that a huge crowd could assemble peaceably and "be there" together: It offered the possibility of a new kind of community.

Though there is little evidence to offer for its future significance beyond its present symbolic embodiment of the wish-images of many of a generation, it might be seen as a social prefiguration of the free space possible in a postindustrial society dedicated to sensual and communal joys of play. As absurd as it sounds at the end of the 1980s (like a line from Woody Allen's 1973 satiric film fantasy on the future, *Sleeper*), in a distant future Woodstock may resonate among cultural radicals in the way the Paris Commune of 1871 echoes in writings of later visionary social radicals. But that will depend upon evolving perspectives whose outcome is as yet unclear.

EMPOWERMENT

Moments of emotional release, cathartic episodes in concerts in which one "gets outside oneself" in joy, carry both prefigurative and affectively empowering implications. I recall one such moment in Los Angeles in the early 1980s when legendary Kansas City blues shouter Big Joe Turner, back from open-heart surgery and a brush with death (he would die two years later), swung out onto the stage on crutches before a packed house at the Club Lingerie to perform a scorching, uptempo set backed by "honking" tenor-saxman Lee Allen and members of the R & B revival band, the Blasters. Turner sang all his classics— "Cherry Red" and "Roll 'Em" from the 1930s to "Shake, Rattle and Roll" from the 1950s—at tempos faster than anyone had ever heard them, generating an intensity of excitement that produced ecstatic howls, whoops, and shrieks from the crowd and had fortyish men (including the author) bounding and leaping into the air. It was one of the most joyous and *empowering* feelings I have ever experienced. Are there political implications? Or is such music the popular culture equivalent of cocaine—a transitory feeling?

The late sociologist C. Wright Mills (who loved BMW motorcycles) repeatedly used the image of the bureaucrat on a motorcycle—a self-critical reference to the *illusion* of being set free. But there may be more to it than that. More recently, Lawrence Grossman has written that "empowerment is about energy, investment and movement."[89] To speak of empowerment and popular music is to focus on the possibilities provided by musical forms for investment of psychic energies and how, for example, "rock and roll organizes one's ability, need and possibility for investing affectively in the world."[90]

Music that empowers releases human energies as well as invites investment of affective powers. It is not an illusion, nor is it a quantifiable something imposed from without; it is, rather, something *generated from within*, something akin to "the glow" that one could see generated at certain historical moments among those who had returned from revolutionary situations. Although conservatives have cynically sneered for generations at the "I've seen the future and it works" naivete of visitors to the Soviet Union in the early 1920s, those visitors were nonetheless impressed by the sense of purpose and possibility—of open potentiality—they observed. Some of it was communicated in recent years in Warren Beatty's film *Reds*, set in the early period of the Russian Revolution. It was similarly evident in Cuba in the 1959–61 period, before conflict with the United States rigidified the society (but perhaps as late as 1970[91]), and certainly in Nicaragua in the 1980s. The emotional glow evident in the 100,000 sympathetic visitors and volunteer workers who have returned from Nicaragua to the United States led one observer to hypothesize, "If this goes on long enough, Nicaragua just might be able to change *this* country [the United States]."[92] Another euphoric visitor told me that Nicaragua will change, not just the United States, but the world. Such visitors have experienced a sense of empowerment, especially among those who find possibilities foreclosed in the United States. Paris during spring 1871 or 1968 might have provided the same effects. In all these situations one senses open-ended possibility, something lacking for progressives in U.S. political culture since at least the spring of 1970 and perhaps until the 1988 Jesse Jackson campaign; although for others significant hopes were engendered by the massive displays of peace sentiment by the nuclear freeze movement in the early years of the Reagan era, such as the 800,000 or more who marched in New

York City in June 1982, or in the continued principled and vigorous widespread opposition to the United States–sponsored wars in Nicaragua and El Salvador throughout the 1980s.

AFFECTIVE TRANSFORMATION

By being empowered one is energized rather than depressed; one might sense the possibility of enormous and positive changes, rather than being overwhelmed by the immensity of what only apparently cannot be accomplished. As noted earlier, political scientists have used "efficacy" and "sense of subjective competence" to describe some dimensions of the phenomenon. These are psychological constructs related to particular historical contexts, but they have an underlying meaning embodied in the lived experience of individuals who are in a sense affectively transformed.

It is important not to overstate the similarity of the temporary high provided by concerts or songs to the more basic socialization processes that are seen in the literature as affecting psychological senses of subjective competence and efficacy. These more complex characteristics of individuals are conceptualized as the result of complicated patterns of socialization from childhood onward in family, school, and peer interaction, in the workplace, and through the acquisition of general political-cultural norms regarding authority and democratic participation, of which popular cultural elements are but one part, though interactive with other systems. However, none of the socialization literature provided predictive clues to the massive outpouring of activism that swept the United States during the 1960s, nor did it predict the social-cultural explosion in France in 1968. The most perceptive explanations seemed to lie in an explanation stressing "indignation," a phenomenon resulting from socially learned standards that provided a reference point against which authorities' violation of basic values in Vietnam or in domestic racism or sexism might be assessed. Here, popular music played a highly catalytic role in bringing contradictions to consciousness.[93]

Measuring precisely how forms of popular music, or any music, may have empowering qualities becomes a more problematical question. No music alone can organize one's ability to invest affectively in the world, though one can note powerful contributions of music to temporary emotional states which are part of the senses of efficacy and subjective competence. The case of "We Shall Overcome" is a good example. The Highlander Folk School and later Citizenship Schools throughout the South provided organizational contexts within which a song could be used as part of a program of training that developed the capacities of community activists to use a wide range of techniques in the struggle for civil rights. The song used in this context provided a stimulus to, or facilitated, affective investment in the civil rights struggle. Music is not a sufficient cause without such patient, systematic organizational effort. Music may serve catalytically, helping to empower and reinforce the energies of those who have gained real capacities for action. For all the attention directed at her as some sort of uniquely heroic individual who supposedly started the December 1955 Montgomery, Alabama, bus boycott, Rosa Parks was (contrary to conventional understandings) also an empowered individual with capacities produced through a program of systematic empowerment: Her own self-directed civil rights work over many years as secretary to the local NAACP chapter and specific courses of training provided by a growing movement, including workshops at the Highlander Center the summer before the Montgomery bus boycott began.[94]

If a sense of empowerment might seem to be what Bruce Springsteen's concerts consistently provided for his audiences, even if in the mid–1980s many in them didn't hear, understand, or even want to think about some of the sophisticated and oblique cultural criticism of the failure of the American Dream in his lyrics, it is important to clarify precisely in what senses that may be so. A Vietnam veteran interviewed in *Rolling Stone* expressed it thus: "Bruce, he gives you the spirit of living. You want to take on the world and challenge it."[95] I felt the same way, but I also brought to the concert experience and interpretive perspectives to decode meanings or to find those to incorporate into my ideological system. For many in the audience that may be asking a great deal if they cannot find constructive outlets. Affective empowerment in such situations may function as an emotional narcotic.

In spite of the overwhelming spectacles the Springsteen concerts became in the 1980s—forms that some felt swallowed much of the content of the lyrics and the singer's articulate and clearly heartfelt raps—I felt stronger and certainly not emotionally manipulated. But what did I *do* with what I had experienced? Intellectually amazed at 70,000 people at the Silverdome in Pontiac, Michigan, in September 1985 shouting in unison, "Show a little faith," I wanted to know what it meant. Indeed, this book is a reflection of several years of inquiry into political uses of popular music as an effort to understand the power of that concert.

NOTES

1. Edward T. Hall, *The Hidden Dimension* (New York: Anchor Books, 1969), p. 1.

2. Anne Buttimer in "Social Space in Interdisciplinary Perspective," in *Surviving the City,* ed. John Gabree (New York: Ballantine Books, 1973), pp. 15–29, provides an overview of the theoretical conceptions of social space of a diverse variety of thinkers from Emile Durkheim in 1890 through French geographers of the contemporary period. Particularly relevant for this discussion are notions of the geographer Chaumbert de Lauwe, who distinguished social space in terms of familial space and neighborhood space through wider regional conceptions, together with a complementary conception of social milieu with dimensions of geography, technology, and culture (the latter, the traditional "atmosphere" ascribed by inhabitants or perceived by others), p. 21. In practice, social space and social milieu are distinguished by (1) population patterns within a time-space framework; (2) economic-activity patterns; (3) social groupings, relationships, behavior, and attitudes; (4) communications and cultural and spiritual life; and (5) educational level.

3. For a theoretical background concerning the wide range of conceptions of space

in human thought, see John Eliot, *Models of Psychological Space* (New York: Springer-Verlag, 1987). Especially relevant is the discussion in Chapter 1, "Characteristics of Psychological Space," and Chapter 2 "Some Philosophical Ideas about Space."

4. Marshall Berman, *All That Is Solid Melts into Air* (New York: Simon & Schuster, 1982), p. 59.

5. On new "codes of public space" see Carl Boggs, *Social Movements and Political Power* (Philadelphia: Temple University Press, 1986), pp. 47–52; and see especially Delores Hayden, "Capitalism, Socialism, and the Built Environment," in *Socialist Visions,* ed. Steven R. Shalom (Boston: South End Press, 1983), pp. 59–81.

6. Regarding the limits of interpretation see Elizabeth Long, *The American Dream and the Popular Novel* (Boston: Routledge & Kegan Paul, 1985), pp. 55–57. Also see Stuart Hall, "Notes on Deconstructing 'The Popular,' " in *People's History and Socialist Theory,* ed. Raphael Samuel (London: Routledge & Kegan Paul, 1981): 227–240.

7. John Shepard, "Media, Social Process and Music," in *Whose Music?* ed. John Shepard et al. (London: Latimer, 1977), p. 13.

8. E. Carpenter and Marshall McLuhan, "Acoustic Space," in *Explorations in Communication*, ed. E. Carpenter and M. McLuhan (London: Jonathan Cape, 1970), p. 67, as cited by Shepard, ibid., p. 13.

9. Simon Frith, "Towards an Aesthetic of Popular Music," in *Music and Society,* ed. R. Leppert and S. McClary (New York, Cambridge University Press, 1987), p. 142.

10. *Emancipatory* signifies liberation from something restrictive or repressive and for something "conducive to an increase of freedom and well-being." See Douglas Kellner, "TV, Ideology, and Emancipatory Popular Culture," in *Television: The Critical View,* 4th edition, ed. H. Newcomb (New York: Oxford University Press, 1987), p. 489.

11. Todd Gitlin, *The Sixties*: *Years of Hope, Days of Rage* (New York: Bantam, 1987), p. 202.

12. Christian Bay, *The Structure of Freedom* (New York: Atheneum, 1965; originally published by Stanford University Press, 1958).

13. Erich Fromm, *Escape from Freedom* (New York: Rinehart, 1941), p. 258.

14. Ibid., p. 271.

15. On the concept of subjective competence see Gabriel Almond and Sidney Verba, *The Civic Culture* (Boston: Little, Brown, 1965). On sense of political efficacy see Carole Pateman, *Participation and Democratic Theory* (New York: Cambridge University Press, 1970).

16. See Ross Russell, *Jazz Style in Kansas City and the Southwest* (Berkeley: University of California Press, 1973).

17. Howard Becker, *Outsiders* (New York: The Free Press, 1963).

18. Simon Frith, *Sound Effects* (New York: Pantheon, 1981), p. 47. Emphasis added.

19. Sara Evans and Harry Boyte, *Free Spaces* (New York: Harper & Row, 1986), p. 187.

20. On free spaces in the women's movement see Sara Evans, *Personal Politics* (New York: Vintage, 1981).

21. E. P. Thompson, *The Making of the English Working Class* (New York: Vintage Books, 1963), p. 155.

22. Eugene Genovese, *Roll, Jordan, Roll*: *The World the Slaves Made* (New York: Pantheon, 1974); George Rawick, *From Sundown to Sunup* (Westport, Conn.: Greenwood Press, 1972).

23. Evans and Boyte, *Free Spaces,* p. 187.

24. Thompson, *English Working Class,* p. 9.

25. Hilde Hein, "Aesthetic Consciousness: The Ground of Political Experience", *Journal of Aesthetics and Art Criticism* 35 (Winter 1976): 147.

26. R. Serge Denisoff has, more than any other individual, explored the range of functions of music for social and political movements. See his *Sing a Song of Social Significance* (Bowling Green, Ohio: Popular Press, 1983).

27. The notion of the return of the "abandoned moment" was suggested by a comment by Greil Marcus on a Lawrence Grossman paper in *Critical Studies in Mass Communication* 3 (1986). The repetitive rehearing notion comes from Frederic Jameson's "Reification and Utopia in Mass Culture," *Social Text* 1 (1979). But on "repeating" and "composing" also see Jacques Attali, *Noise: The Political Economy of Music* (Minneapolis: University of Minnesota Press, 1987), pp. 87–148.

28. Mahalia Jackson sang the song on her *Mahalia Jackson at Newport* album on the Columbia label, recently avaliable on Columbia Special Products.

29. Joshua Meyrowitz, *No Sense of Place* (New York: Oxford University Press, 1985), pp. 89–90.

30. Ibid., p. 90.

31. Two critical analyses that stress the possibilities for autocratic use of television are Jerry Mander, *Four Arguments for the Elimination of Television* (New York: Morrow, 1978), and Michael Parenti, *Inventing Reality: The Politics of the Mass Media* (New York: St. Martin's Press, 1986).

32. Meyrowitz, *No Sense of Place,* pp. 90–91.

33. The notion of dream state comes from Mander, *Four Arguments.*

34. Paul Monaco, *Ribbons in Time: Movies and Society since 1945* (Bloomington: University of Indiana Press, 1987), Chapter 4, "Memory without Pain." Also relevant here is Fred Davis, *Yearning For Yesterday: A Sociology of Nostalgia* (New York: The Free Press, 1979).

35. See John Mowitt, "The Sound of Music in the Era of Its Electronic Reproducibility," in *Music and Society: The Politics of Composition, Performance and Reception,* ed. R. Leppert and S. McClary (New York: Cambridge University Press, 1987), for an exploration of the importance of reproductive technology when analyzing the social significance of music.

36. Frederic Jameson, "Reification and Utopia," p. 138.

37. Ibid.

38. See, for example, Elizabeth Long, *The American Dream and the Popular Novel* (Boston: Routledge & Kegan Paul, 1985), p. 56–57.

39. On the importance of historical context see Hall, "Deconstructing 'The Popular.' "

40. On the 1986 Columbia album *Bruce Springsteen and the E-Street Band Live, 1975–1985.*

41. On little worlds emptied out see Berman, *All That Is Solid.*

42. I am indebted to George Lipsitz for these perceptive insights on heavy metal music.

43. Frith, "Aesthetic of Popular Music," p. 142.

44. Ibid.

45. Philip Slater's *The Pursuit of Loneliness: American Culture at the Breaking Point* (Boston: Beacon Press, 1970) contains the most perceptive analysis of the appeal of *The Graduate.*

46. Mander effectively argues the Orwellian aspects of television in *Four Arguments.*

47. In this connection see Hebdige's comments in the introduction to *Cut 'n' Mix* (London: Methuen, 1987).

48. Robert Nisbet, *Community and Power* (New York: Oxford University Press, 1960: originally published as *The Quest for Community*, 1953), p. ix.

49. Ibid.

50. See Dick Hebdige's analysis of the subcultural creation process, *Subculture: The Meaning of Style* (London and New York: Methuen, 1979).

51. Bob Dylan and The Band performed the song in a series of memorial concerts in 1968 and 1970 issued on Columbia and Warner Brothers Records.

52. Meyrowitz's discussion in Chapter 10, "Questioning Authority," of *No Sense of Place* illuminates the "Teflon" presidency of Ronald Reagan and its erosion toward the end of his second term but significantly underestimates how those who understand the principles of television may manipulate the medium to produce images effective enough to win elections, as the media staff of Vice-President Bush did so skillfully during the 1988 campaign.

53. On these movements see Marilyn Ferguson, *The Aquarian Conspiracy: Personal and Social Transformation in the 1980's* (New York: Granada Publishers, 1983). See as well the new social sectors involved, in Robert Lindsey, "Spiritual Concepts Drawing a Different Breed of Adherent," *New York Times*, September 29, 1986, pp. 1, 8.

54. Daniel Yankelovich, *New Rules* (New York: Random House, 1981), p. 251.

55. Jameson, "Reification and Utopia." The reference to "managing" popular concerns is drawn from Norman Holland, *The Dynamics of Literary Response* (New York: Oxford University Press, 1968).

56. I wish to thank George Lipsitz for discussion on the Simon and Garfunkel episode, which helped me in rethinking the meaning of this expression of feelings. See Lipsitz, *Class and Culture in Cold War America: "A Rainbow at Midnight"* (New York: Praeger, 1981), for a sensitive look at the relationship of social class and popular culture, and Lipsitz, " 'This Ain't No Sideshow': Historians and Media Studies," *Critical Studies in Mass Communication* 5 (1988): 147–61.

57. See also the discussion of Fromm and the Frankfurt School in Martin Jay, *The Dialectical Imagination* (Boston: Little, Brown, 1973), pp. 88–112.

58. Interview with Kurt Loder, *Rolling Stone*, December 6, 1984.

59. See John Street's perceptive comments on the politics of leading music figures, *Rebel Rock* (London and New York: Basil Blackwell, 1986).

60. See "The German Ideology, Part I," in *The Marx-Engels Reader*, 2 ed., ed. Robert C. Tucker (New York: W. W. Norton, 1978), pp. 146–200. The reference to "illusory forms of communal life" appears on p. 160.

61. See the reference in *Rousseau's Political Writings*, ed. A. Ritter and J. C. Bondanella (New York: W. W. Norton, 1988), p. 73. Sheldon Wolin in *Politics and Vision* (Boston: Little, Brown, 1960) termed this Rousseau's quest for "a common self."

62. See Christopher Lasch, *Haven in a Heartless World* (New York: Basic Books, 1977).

63. Marshall Berman, *The Politics of Authenticity* (New York: Atheneum, 1970), especially pp. 201–228.

64. The Port Huron Statement, available in various anthologies such as *The New Radicals*, ed. Paul Jacobs and Saul Landau (New York: Vintage Books, 1963), pp. 149–62.

65. Berman, *Politics of Authenticity*, p. xix.

66. Boggs, *Social Movements and Political Power*, p. 49.

67. Ibid. Emphasis added.

68. Boggs, *Social Movements and Political Power*, p. 48.

69. Jeremy Marre and Hannah Charlton, in *Beats of the Heart: Popular Music of the World* (New York: Pantheon, 1985), link popular music and locality throughout the world.

70. See the *Village Voice* annual critics poll February 28, 1989. Music editor Robert Christgau suggested, ''The folkie madonna, wise and soulful whether calm or passionate, once again seems a comforting idea to the kind of white former boy disquieted by rap and disco.'' *Voice Music Supplement*, vol. 3, no. 1 (February 28, 1989): 10.

71. Joseph Gusfield, *Community: A Critical Response* (New York: Harper & Row, 1975), p. 97.

72. For several insightful essays on television watching as discourse see Robert C. Allen, ed., *Channels of Discourse: Television and Contemporary Criticism* (Chapel Hill: University of North Carolina Press, 1987).

73. Jameson, ''Reification and Utopia.''

74. On the prefigurative impulse see Raymond B. Pratt, ''Toward a Critical Theory of Revolution,'' *Polity*, vol. II, no. 2, (Winter 1978–79): 172–99.

75. Wini Breines, *Community and Organization in the New Left, 1962–1968* (New York: Praeger, 1982), p. 7.

76. The concept of resocialization is developed in Richard Fagen, *The Transformation of Political Culture in Cuba* (Palo Alto, Calif.: Stanford University Press, 1969), pp. 1–18.

77. For a survey of some of the theoretical issues raised by notions of socialization through participation see Pateman, *Participation and Democratic Theory*. On ''capacitization'' see Paulo Freire, *A Pedagogy of the Oppressed* (New York: Seabury Press, 1974).

78. On the IWW see Melvyn Dubovsky, *We Shall Be All: A History of the Industrial Workers of the World* (Chicago: Quadrangle, 1969).

79. See Hannah Arendt's illuminating discussion of Jefferson and councils in *On Revolution* (New York: Viking Press, 1965), pp. 234–85.

80. The literature on participatory democracy is too large to cite adequately. The best overview remains Pateman, *Participation and Democratic Theory*. A clear-eyed critical survey is provided by Edward S. Greenberg, ''The Consequences of Worker Participation: A Clarification of the Theoretical Literature,'' *Social Science Quarterly* 56 (September 1975): 191–209. Also see Lester Milbrath and M. L. Goel, *Political Participation: How and Why Do People Get Involved in Politics?* (New York: University Press of America, 1982).

81. See Shlomo Avineri's lucid exposition of Marx's vision in *Social and Political Thought of Karl Marx* (New York: Cambridge University Press, 1967), p. 240.

82. A brief exposition of the theory of council communists is Richard Gombin, *The Origins of Modern Leftism* (Baltimore: Penguin Books, 1975), p. 77–117.

83. Peter Kropotkin, *Fields, Factories and Workshops Tomorrow*, ed. Colin Ward (New York: Harper Torch Books, 1975).

84. See Ernst Vollrath, ''Rosa Luxemburg's Theory of Revolution,'' *Social Research*, 40 (Spring 1973): 83–109.

85. On the political difficulties of the prefigurative strategy see the perceptive discussion in Carl Boggs, ''Revolutionary Process, Political Strategy, and the Dilemma of Power,'' *Theory and Society* 4 (1977): 359–93.

86. But also see Sol Stern, "Altamont: Pearl Harbor to the Woodstock Nation," in *Side-Saddle on the Golden Calf,* ed. G. H. Lewis (Pacific Palisades, Calif.: Goodyear, 1972), pp. 321–40. Especially relevant to some of the general questions here considered are the critical exchanges over Leon Rosselson, "Pop Music: Mobiliser or Opiate?" in *Media, Politics and Culture,* ed. C. Gardiner (London: Macmillan, 1979), pp. 40–50, and the response by Gary Herman and Ian Hoare, "The Struggle for Song: A Reply to Leon Rosselson," in *Media, Politics and Culture,* pp. 51–60. Also, Don Hibbard, *The Role of Rock* (Englewood Cliffs, N.J.: Prentice-Hall, 1983) contains an interesting discussion of these issues in "The Rock Revolution: Ruminations and Reflections," pp. 133–49, with extensive literature citations.

87. Street, *Rebel Rock,* p. 79.

88. Ibid.

89. Lawrence Grossman, "Reply to Critics," *Critical Studies in Mass Communication* 3 (1986): 92.

90. Ibid.

91. See, for example, the excitement of sociologist Joseph Kahl after a 1969 visit in the 1970 *Trans-Action* magazine issue on the tenth anniversary of the Cuban Revolution. Kahl's article is entitled "The Moral Economy of a Revolution." It is reprinted in *Cuban Communism,* ed. I. L. Horowitz (New Brunswick, N.J.: Transaction Press, 1970). The electric sense of potentiality of the early years of the Cuban Revolution is best conveyed in Warren Miller's *90 Miles from Home* (Boston: Little, Brown, 1961).

92. Tom Carson, "Besides the Sandinistas," *Village Voice,* May 12, 1987.

93. See Peter Lupsha, "Explanation of Political Violence: Some Psychological Theories versus Indignation," *Politics and Society* 2 (Fall 1971), pp. 89–104.

94. On the origins of "We Shall Overcome" see Frank Adams, *Unearthing Seeds of Fire: The Idea of Highlander* (Winston-Salem, N.C.: John F. Blair, 1975), pp. 75–76, 154–55. On Rosa Parks, the Highlander School, and other movement halfway houses, see Aldon Morris, *The Origins of the Civil Rights Movement* (New York: The Free Press, 1984).

95. Merle Ginsberg, "The Fans . . . ," *Rolling Stone,* October 15, 1986.

3

The Spirituals, Gospel, and Resistance

Religious suffering is at the same time an *expression* of real suffering and a *protest* against real suffering. Religion is the sigh of the oppressed creature, the sentiment of a heartless world, and the soul of soulless conditions. It is the *opium* of the people.

> Karl Marx,
> Introduction to the Critique of Hegel's
> *Philosophy of Right* (emphasis added)[1]

While religion certainly may at times be an opiate, the religion of the oppressed usually gives them the sustenance necessary for developing a resistance to their own oppression. . . . The religion of the slaves kept alive in them the desire and basis for a struggle for freedom.

> George Rawick,
> *From Sundown to Sunup: The Making of the Black Community*[2]

The musical creations of slaves in the United States reveal how music functions as an instrument of expression and as an alternative way of existing—a free space fashioned out of existing materials (in this case, elements of their African cultural heritage and the new religion—the Christianity of the white man—imposed upon them).

In this initial case one can see how music may become a mode of political discourse for any individual or group. Part of the worldwide appeal of American popular music—a music that still bears significant traces of the incorporation, first, of elements of African music and the infusion of the particular adaptations of Christianity by the slaves and, later, especially in the case of "soul," of black sanctified and gospel music—lies in the facility with which it can be heard and used by the audience. It is directed at them and invites their participation, serving simultaneously as expressive behavior for the artists performing and creating it. Its unique facility for being used, its all-pervasive functionality, comes significantly from the central characteristics of the musical tendencies brought by millions of slaves to the New World. In this sense it truly is popular music and a form of popular culture demonstrating that influence of Afro-America Robert Farris Thompson called "the flash of the spirit."[3]

For the slaves music was a central and highly functional element in daily expression and virtually all activities. They picked cotton, planted rice, husked corn, rowed, rocked their babies, cooked their food, and performed virtually "every conceivable task to the accompaniment of song with an intensity and style that continually elicited the comments of the whites around them."[4]

Black music at that time had two additional uniquely significant functions that persist into the present day: From Africa came the cultural practice of songs, stories, proverbs, and word games serving dual roles of maintaining communal values and solidarity while simultaneously providing opportunities for individuals to transcend, at least in symbolic senses, most of the restrictions imposed by environment and society by permitting the expression of "deeply held feelings" that could not be openly expressed under ordinary social constraints.[5] These qualities are equivalent to what was earlier characterized as impulses toward authenticity and community. Both qualities—community and authenticity— would become central to the powerful cultural amalgam of American popular music in the mid-twentieth century.

In creating their version of the spirituals from white hymns of seventeenth- and eighteenth-century English composers such as Dr. Watts and others (usually collectively known as Dr. Watts), black slaves appropriated elements of the culture of those who dominated them to "make" their own world, or at least to *reconstruct* one so far as possible from the fragments of their own cultures shattered by the experience of their forced exile from African homelands.

What were the precise elements of African culture so significant to succeeding cultural forms? In his revelatory *Flash of the Spirit* Thompson suggests, "Listening to rock, jazz, blues, reggae, salsa, samba, bossa nova, juju, highlife, and mambo, one might conclude that much of the popular music of the world is informed by the flash of the spirit of a certain people specially armed with improvisatory drive and brilliance."[6] Those "certain people" were the millions of slaves forceably uprooted from their homelands and brought to the New World.* Thompson describes the particular qualities embodied in the culture they brought with them: "Since the Atlantic slave trade, ancient African organ-

*For estimates of the volume of the slave trade, see Philip D. Curtin, *The Atlantic Slave Trade: A Census* (Madison: University of Wisconsin Press, 1969). Curtin's figures suggesting a volume of ten million slaves taken out of Africa are challenged as excessively low in J. E. Inikori, "Measuring the Atlantic Slave Trade," *Journal of African History*, vol. 17, no. 2 (1976): 197–223.

izing principles of song and dance have crossed the seas from the Old World to the New. There they took on new momentum, intermingling with each other and with New World or European styles of singing and dance."[7] Among those principles are the following:

The *dominance of a percussive performance style* (attack and vital aliveness in sound and motion);

A propensity for multiple meter (competing meters sounding all at once);

Overlapping call and response in singing (solo/chorus, voice/instrument; "interlock systems" of performance);

Inner pulse control (a "metronome sense," keeping a beat indelibly in mind as a rhythmic common denominator in a welter of different meters);

Suspended accentuation patterning (offbeat phrasing of melodic and choreographic accents); and, at a slightly different but equally recurrent level of exposition,

Songs and dances of social allusion (music that, however danceable and "swinging," remorselessly contrasts social imperfections against implied criteria for perfect living).[8]

Black song style, both during long centuries of slavery and today, over 100 years after emancipation, maintains such continuities of antiphony, group nature, pervasive functionality, improvisation (vitally alive today in rap), and strong elements of dance and expressive body movement. All are characteristics closer to West Africa and Afro-American music in the West Indies and South America than Western European musical styles.[9] Indeed, slaves in the United States, following the practices of the African cultures they had been forced to leave behind them, not only assigned a central role to the spoken arts but encouraged and rewarded verbal improvisation, maintained the participatory nature of their expressive culture, and continued to utilize the spoken arts to voice criticism as well as to uphold traditional values and group cohesion.[10]

THE "INVITATION" OF BLACK MUSIC

All these interrelated qualities were infused into American popular culture, creating forms so structured that they invited, and were subsequently themselves invested with, the incredible energies of generations of both white and black artists in a process of widespread interrelation and cross-influencing that is today evident in virtually every performance by every popular U.S. and British rock artist live or on video.

This great musical flowering in the United States has through history been a response to a complex of "concrete needs" basic to human survival.[11] It has been particularly evident to European observers that in the history of America, out of the experience of the repressed black minority arose a series of musics that were relatively independent of white cultural hegemony that can be characterized as crucial elements in a larger "strategy of survival." What is so fascinating is that these forms into which blacks invested so much of their personalities and which served as elements of subcultural strategies of survival were themselves later reappropriated by whites in spectacular ways.[12] Later (as discussed in Chapter 6) rock 'n' roll was reproduced by elements of the white working class[13] as a "hybridized form" of black music, but one *itself* a form, like the African-influenced music that permitted a maximum of individualization of expression while reaffirming group solidarity. How does the music do that?

It can be understood by starting with the first black American music, the spirituals, a music that was part of the subculture of resistance developed first by slaves and continued by later members of the black minority in the United States. The spirituals and, as will be seen in the next chapter, the blues demonstrate with *all* forms of popular music that "song forms and performances are themselves models of social behavior that reflect strategies of adaptation to human and natural environments."[14] The spirituals provide the first example of black music as a music of survival: It has provided as a cultural form a means of survival, "a secret language of solidarity, a way of articulating oppression, a means of cultural resistance, a cry of hope."[15]

Albert Murray poetically evokes the affirmative power of black music as a mode of resisting despair in *Stomping the Blues*.[16] It has become virtually axiomatic among students of popular music that where there is great oppression, there one should look for the development of powerful and beautiful forms of music.[17] Slavery is a root form of oppression. And it, or the social conditions persisting in its aftermath, produced in the spirituals, the blues, and related musical forms a unique cultural creation. That in the United States resistance to oppression took on such largely cultural, rather than more overtly political, forms should be obvious when one considers the relative power relations between dominant and subordinate peoples.[18] These cultural forms have proven to be deeper, more profound, and more enduring than the relatively few large-scale, physically overt revolts that most slaves quite correctly recognized would be suicidal. Originally, the enslaved black minority confronted the politically organized and legitimated cultural power of white slave-owning society, which exercised virtually total supremacy over all facets of existence, though it is now known there were numerous attempts at revolt by slaves. Indeed, day-to-day overt physical resistance was endemic, as is evident in a variety of personal accounts through the centuries of the "peculiar institution" of American slavery.[19]

Many slaves were subjected to hideous physical abuses in addition to the pervasive and systematic efforts to destroy them as normal human beings by making it virtually impossible for them to function freely as individual personalities, family members, or members of ongoing communities.[20] Yet numerous accounts by slaves of their revulsion at their status have been collected that leave no doubt of both their realism and heroism. Although the degree to which there was resistance has over the last century been a matter of some controversy among scholars, the debates around the topic themselves sometimes reveal a good deal more about the ideological perspectives of historians than the phenomenon itself.

Throughout U.S. history there has been a continuity of power by white prop-
erty-owning males in every area of social life. This power was capable of
determining which aspects of the black experience were acceptable to the larger
society and which were not. The slaves in particular lacked the variety of outlets
available in contemporary society and operated only with the merest legitimating
shred of legal protection for their lives, and that functioned largely to the benefit
of slaveholders.[21] For example: "In 1851 a Virginia judge ruled that a master
could not be indicted for beating his own slave even if the whipping and pun-
ishment were 'malicious, cruel, and excessive.' In a similar case, a South Carolina judge declared that 'the criminal offense of assault and battery can not, at
common law, be committed upon the person of a slave.' "[22]

Of course, the slaves did not bear such impositions without some overt forms
of resistance on a day-to-day basis and even in organized formal acts of rebellion.
As James M. Cone put it in his powerful liberationist essay *The Spirituals and
the Blues*: "Black rebellion in America did not begin with the Civil Rights
movement and Martin Luther King, nor with Black Power and Stokely Carmi-
chael or the Black Panther party. Black resistance has roots stretching back to
the slave ships, the auction blocks, and the plantation regime. It began when
the first black person decided that death would be preferable to slavery."[23]
Resistance continued in the form of fleeing to free territory in the North or
Canada and in daily efforts to lighten the work load through shirking work,
damaging crops and machinery, pretending to be ill, and generally disrupting
routine.[24] And, of course, there were the formally organized larger-scale efforts
at revolt of Gabriel Prosser, Denmark Vesey, and Nat Turner and the calls of
David Walker and Henry Garnett for rebellion and resistance among slaves.[25]
But the slaves also had to recognize the reality of the overwhelming power that
confronted them.

Since the end of slavery, there have been some significant political outlets for
black people (the presidential campaigns of Jesse Jackson being contemporary
examples). Nonetheless America's huge black minority have, save for the pitiful
remnants of Native Americans whose social situation is even worse, been the
most exploited and poorly represented social group over the last century of U.S.
politics.[26]

At over 12 percent of the population, blacks are without the numbers, save
for areas in which they are concentrated and thus predominate, to effectively
operate in outright opposition to whites as an organized bloc without some
alliances with disaffected whites or other minorities. More significantly, the
emergence of cultural forms embodying their interests and concerns, which all
minorities produce, embodied qualities of such broad appeal, especially in music,
that they persist over long periods, remaining for those sensitive to their meanings
forms of resistance deeper and more profound and certainly more enduring than
sporadic efforts at physical resistance.[27]

Certainly, these people of color have not been the only critics or opponents
of the larger society. Every generation has seen some form of resistance and
rebellion expressed in cultural form. But cultural forms of resistance have been

exceptionally significant in U.S. society over two centuries precisely because overt, formally organized political forms have been weak or poorly organized or the victims of massive repressive force when they reach the point of possibly altering the overall structure of power and scope of government.[28]

THE SPIRITUALS

Many Americans born around or before World War II at some time in their lives have had the experience of hearing a powerful black singer such as Mahalia Jackson, Marian Anderson, or Paul Robeson (all now deceased) do a concert version of a classic spiritual such as "Didn't My Lord Deliver Daniel, And Why Not Every Man?" or "Deep River" or "Swing Low, Sweet Chariot" or "He's Got the Whole World in His Hands." Today these songs, if heard at all, are heard as one number in a concert by a black classically trained operatic singer such as Leontyne Price. In recent decades spirituals have for the most part, except for the ever-popular eighteenth-century composition by the white Englishman John Newton, "Amazing Grace,"* been supplanted by *composed* "gospel" works, such as Thomas A. Dorsey's 1932 composition "Take My Hand, Precious Lord," sung at the funerals of both the Reverend Martin Luther King, Jr., and President Lyndon B. Johnson.

The titles of the spirituals mentioned above are but a few of the hundreds of "slave songs"[29] fashioned out of parts of English hymns, biblical themes, African-derived performance practice, and slave subculture that have intrigued observers since early in the 1700s.[30] White America first became aware of these spirituals on a broad scale through the 1871 concerts staged by a group of singers from Fisk University in Nashville, the Fisk Jubilee Singers, who sought to raise money for their school, founded by the American Missionary Association (related to the Congregational Church) as one of several schools for ex-slaves. The school had significant white associations: "Taking its name from Union Army General Clinton Fisk, head of the Missionary Association, and housed in an abandoned army hospital barracks, Fisk opened its doors in 1866. In financial straits from the beginning, it was on the verge of bankruptcy in 1870, when George L. White,

---

*Amazing Grace" is immensely popular among black and white audiences and performers and not just in North America. In addition to recorded versions by Aretha Franklin (Atlantic Records two-disc set, *Amazing Grace*) and by other artists such as Joan Baez and Judy Collins, including memorable public performances such as Joan Baez's at the 1987 Chicago Folk Festival, a Scots bagpipe version had wide currency in recent years. See Anthony Heilbut, *The Gospel Sound: Good News and Bad Times*, rev. ed. (New York: DaCapo Press, 1985), pp. xxi–xxiii, for an analysis of the particular appeal of the hymn to the black audience, especially the lines

> Through many dangers, toils and snares,
> I have already come.
> 'Twas grace that brought me safe thus far
> And grace will lead me home.

A terrifying white racist use of the song is portrayed as a scene in Costa-Gavras' 1988 film *Betrayal*.

the treasurer of the university, who was also the director of its choir [and a white man] proposed a concert tour to raise funds.''[31] (Here one sees an important and recurring element of black popular music in the United States—associations with white facilitators or partners of one sort or another over the years who have felt its power and heard its message, from John Hammond in the 1930s to Jerry Wexler and numerous others in the 1960s and 1970s.[32]) The Fisk Jubilee Singers went on to become something of a sensation among audiences in the North, even eventually traveling to England. By the conclusion of their first tour they raised over $150,000 for the school (a substantial amount at the time). They also stimulated the development of similar groups of singers at other locations.[33]

Although their singing style was carefully controlled and modulated, reflecting the ''refinements'' of formal education, and anglicized beyond all recognition, they were still called primitive and savage. Henry Ward Beecher, a leading abolitionist, warned friends in England, ''You will hear from them the wild slave songs, some of which seem like the inarticulate wails of breaking hearts made dumb by slavery.''[34]

What was in the nature of the spirituals that they may be considered so politically significant as the first cultural form of both resistance and an affirmation of identity developed by oppressed blacks in U.S. history? In a chapter of *The Souls of Black Folk* (1902) entitled ''The Sorrow Songs,'' W. E. B. Dubois called them ''the most beautiful expression of human experience born this side the seas'' and the ''greatest gift of the Negro people.'' They were, in spite of efforts of some to paint a picture of enslaved or postslavery blacks as resigned or even content with their situation, ''the music of an unhappy people, of the children of disappointment; they tell of death and suffering and unvoiced longing toward a truer world.''[35] It is the latter quality that makes them of particular interest here, for these cultural forms provide the first significant opportunity for analysis and exposition of the ways political meaning may be taken from or be embodied or concealed in popular music.

As Stuart Hall and associates[36] emphasize, meaning is made by those who use music, ''actively constructing a specific selection of things and goods *into* a style . . . [a process which involves] subverting and transforming these things, from their given meaning and use, to other meanings and uses.''[37] Given the travail of the slaves this might seem to understate the way that meaning is encoded in or stamped on specific examples of musical forms through a process of investing meaning and making disparate elements one's own.[38] This is a complex question of analysis.

There are several aspects of the music to consider. In analyzing it externally in terms of form and function, one must be sensitive to the internalized dimensions as well, for these songs were never merely, as Lawrence Levine put it, ''uninternalized anodynes.'' This was music that people lived and felt! One can appreciate to what degree only by being sensitive to and conscious of the system under which they lived.

From external analysis of this early form, one hopes to be able to say more about other, later, forms as well. As Levine indicated concerning his own inquiry, "The subject of slave religious music has produced a large and varied literature, the bulk of which has focused upon matters of structure and origin."[39] The question of origin is significant insofar as it bears on the *process* by which a subordinate or oppressed group creates music as a means of resistance. Thus the literature that attempts to determine the "genuineness" of slave creation by sorting out the proportion of raw material originated by whites, which is part of literature on similarities and differences in white and slave music seeking the "true" origins of the spiritual stretching back over 150 years, is less relevant. That it continues to generate significant interest is evident in a variety of works.[40] Such questions of origin, however, although of scholarly interest, are secondary to use and function. Certainly similarities between white and slave religious expressions existed. George Pullen Jackson's work[41] over a half century ago was important in making the similarities explicit, but his research was based on published examples, not on performance style.[42] More significantly, even more important systematic differences were evident: "Even when melodies of a white and black spiritual are similar, the texts are . . . quite often disparate. Thus it was not uncommon for whites to have sung of Jesus: 'O when shall I see Jesus/ And reign with him above,' while to a markedly similar tune blacks sang of the Hebrew people: 'O my Lord deliver'd Daniel,/O why not deliver me too?' "[43]

Moreover, black spirituals, in marked contrast to most white spirituals, contained the most vivid sorts of biblical imagery, a "compelling sense of identification with the Children of Israel" and a "tendency to dwell incessantly upon and to relive the stories of the Old Testament."[44] These particular characteristics persist, though in substantially diminished form, in only a portion of modern black gospel.[45] However, they are still evident in many of the immediate pre– and post–World War II recordings of the greatest gospel singers and groups such as Sister Rosetta Tharpe[46] or Mahalia Jackson.[47] The major differences between black or "soul" gospel and white forms in the 1980s seem to lie less in the lyrical and thematic content than in the more rhythmic and dynamic performance styles, as a viewing of such films/videos as *Gospel* and *Say "Amen" Somebody* make clear.

Another approach, seeking to avoid the direct conflict of attribution of origin, has emphasized the cultural "syncretism" involved in the creation of the spirituals; that is, a number of conditions existed that allowed slaves to retain what Levine calls "the integrity of their own musical heritage." There were, for example, analogies between African call-and-response patterns and the Anglican practice of a leader "lining out" hymns (calling out a line of hymn text before it is sung). Slave masters encouraged religious practices of the kinds *they* approved, largely led by white preachers counseling obedience. Also, slaves lived in relative cultural isolation, which helped retain elements of style.

But much more important is the process of *signification,* the taking of cultural elements and making them one's own completely separate from the intentions of creators. As previously suggested, "All commodities [songs included] have a social use and thus a cultural meaning; they are . . . cultural *signs*. They have already been invested, by the dominant culture, with meanings. . . . They 'mean' only because they have already been arranged, according to social use, into culture codes of meaning which *assign meanings to them.*"[48] The potentially revolutionary implications of this for cultural resistance lie in the fact that "it is possible to expropriate, as well as to appropriate, the social meanings which they seem 'naturally' to have; or, by combining them with something else, . . . to change or inflect their meaning. Because the meanings . . . are socially given . . . their meaning can also be socially altered or *reconstructed.*"[49] This perspective is directly relevant to the manner in which the slaves created their own religion and music out of elements of that their masters tried to impose on them. The process is evident in succeeding forms of popular music.

If the use to which the cultural elements are put is the significant factor, extremely complex questions of origin of the spirituals and associated vast scholarly literature are largely irrelevant for understanding the consciousness of slaves. Levine made this evident in noting that "it is not necessary for a people to originate or invent all or even most of the elements of their culture. It is necessary only that *these components become their own*, embedded in their traditions, expressive of their world view and life style."[50] No clearer examples exist than in the spirituals.

The literature on slave religion and spirituals is itself extensive, with such works as John Lovell's encyclopedic *Black Song: The Forge and the Flame* demonstrating how one could spend a good part of a lifetime on aspects of the topic.[51] Lovell suggests the spirituals should be considered a form of "folk" music. Folk music is often defined as music transmitted as part of an "oral" and largely rural culture, in contrast to the formally written forms of European literature society.[52] It is music transmitted to a "folk community." Lovell characterized it thus:

Every folk song, verse, and melody is the product of a folk community. The community supplies its themes and its subject matter. . . . Within the community and nowhere else, are its conventions, its social, moral, theological, and legal principles, its open and hidden prides and prejudices. Many of these run counter to established law and custom in the larger society. . . . Folk music, both old and contemporary, is representative of the people's ancient traditions as well as an indicator of their current tastes.[53]

How is such a community defined? Certainly a people of common background and shared characteristics over several generations—class, ethnicity, origin—provide the basis of a common set of values and interests. The slaves provided such a community through two common experiences: "The African tradition shared by all those who inspired, composed, and sang the songs; and the American experience of slavery."[54]

Religious Free Space

The spiritual is inextricable from the unique adaptations to Christianity made by the slaves. One should be aware of the historical insights of Eugene Genovese, George Rawick, and others into the unique religious life-world of slaves and later free black people. They created an area of cultural freedom in an environment otherwise inhospitable to their very existence as human beings. Hall has been cited as saying, "We live in a world where marginality has *at last* become a productive space."[55] Yet over a century *before* the engaging musical creations arising out of contemporary marginality, slaves—the most oppressed of social groups and certainly the most marginal (though economically significant to their owners through labor)—were able to fashion powerful and enduring social and musical forms under the very eyes, whips, and guns of the overseers and owners.[56]

In *From Sundown to Sunup*, Rawick considers the ways in which these human beings who made a mass forced migration to North America to be worked from dawn to dusk and beyond were able to salvage some vestige of personality and community. They were able to do so because they did have at night and on weekends "a life outside of work in the time that was, or that they *made,* their own. That life was important in creating and recreating the slave personality and the slave communities. . . . Only if we understand this side of the slaves' lives can we understand how their personalities were kept from destruction, how they developed and built their communities."[57] This space they created for themselves permitted a process of self-recreation that was "consistent not only with the ability to work but with the ability to *struggle against* the social conditions and relations of that work."[58] In a most significant sense, "the ability of any group of men and women to fight against their own oppression" is directly linked to "the social 'living space' they manage to carve out for themselves both at work and at home." And the slaves provide no better example of this interplay than in their use of religion and its related music, the spirituals. Indeed, the weight of evidence suggests in slave culture the virtual transcending of sacred-secular distinctions in the meager free spaces they were able to create in their own time. Because they came from an African cultural background that saw a holy and sacred dimension to all activity, for them "religious activities were areas of considerable potential creativity and social strength. The slaves in the New World used religion as the central area for the creation and recreation of community."[59]

Because independent forms of activity were discouraged or even banned, slaves engaged in unique forms of oppositional creativity through religion and music. Rawick's study of interviews with thousands of ex-slaves and his survey of nineteenth-century observations finds "an attempt on the part of the masters to superimpose a formal religion on the slaves . . . as a form of social control."[60] But the slave masters' religion never seemed to gain the total adherence of the slaves, who continued to carry on prayer meetings at night. "What contemporaries referred to as the 'African cult' not only did not disappear, it continued to flourish with great creativity and strength."[61] When speaking of slave religion, Albert Raboteau points out in *Slave Religion*, one must consider how slaves "kept in touch with what Paul Radin has described as 'an inner world' where they could 'develop a scale of values and fixed points of vantage from which to judge the world around them and themselves.' In this inner, religious world the primary value and fixed point was the will of God. And in opposition to the slaveholder's belief, the slave believed that slavery was surely contrary to the will of God."[62]

In surveying a number of works on slave religion, one finds numerous cases indicating a strong belief among slaves that their masters were surely going to Hell because they were slave owners and inflicted such misery on the lives of slaves. It is no accident that the slaves identified so strongly with the Hebrew Children and the various Old Testament prophecies of the destruction of Israel's enemies. Raboteau relates the account of a New England governess who was astonished at the violence of the biblical metaphor summoned by a normally mild-mannered slave housekeeper in outrage after a beating given her daughter:

Thar's a day a-comin'! Thar's a day a-coming'. . . . I hear de rumblin' ob de chariots! I see de flashin' ob de guns! White folks' blood is a-runnin' on de ground like a riber, an' de dead's heaped up dat high! . . . Oh, Lor'! hasten de day when de blows, an' de bruises, an' de aches, an' de pains, shall come to de white folks, an' de buzzards shall eat 'em as dey's dead in de streets. Oh, Lor'! roll on de chariots, an' gib de black people rest an' peace. Oh, Lor'! gib me de pleasure ob livin' till dat day, when I shall see white folks shot down like de wolves when dey come hongry out o'de woods!"[63]

Most slaves would never permit a white person to hear such sentiments, nor would they even express them openly. And herein lies the roots of the double and hidden meanings that are a central aspect of black music in America. Slaves lived in a world where their government and "God," as defined by most denominations at the time, seemed to condone their condition.

Masters believed that Blacks who sang spirituals worked more efficiently and obediently. The introduction of Old Testament stories signaled the attempt of masters to rid slaves of African beliefs while teaching them a new doctrine of servility. The slaves, however, used the Bible stories to retain aspects of their traditional religions in the form and structure of their songs. Masters gave slaves a special catechism, hoping to teach Blacks to look for rewards in heaven through obedience to their overlords here on earth.[64]

The texts of such catechisms included passages like the following:

Q: What did God make you for?

A: To make a crop.

Q: What is the meaning of "Thou shalt not commit adultery?"

A: To serve our Heavenly Father and our earthly master, obey our overseer, and not steal anything.[65]

Like the Liberation Theology thinkers of the mid-twentieth century,[66] the slaves found a powerful countervailing critical message in Christianity and the stories of the Old Testament and they used it: This critical message was fashioned into a sometimes simple, always very powerful populist theology of hope and resistance.[67] But it was one that often had to conceal its meaning to avoid detection and suppression.

One slave characterized his feelings thus: "Got one mind for the boss to see; got another for what I know is me."[68] Deception thus became a subtle form of resistance. It was evident in a wide variety of songs that conveyed one meaning on the surface and another to initiates.[69]

The manner in which this process functioned was in the adoption in black preaching style and song of what Levine terms "the apocalyptic visions and heroic exploits of the Scriptures." This was particularly true in the case of slave spirituals, which "were informed not by the Epistles of Paul but by the history of the Hebrew Children. . . . The essence of slave religion cannot be fully grasped without understanding this Old Testament bias. . . . Daniel and David and Joshua and Jonah and Noah, all of whom fill the lines of the spirituals, were delivered in *this* world and delivered in ways which struck the imagination of the slaves."[70]

Several spirituals were used to alert slaves to the imminent presence of a "conductor" who would lead them North on the "underground railway."[71] Harriett Tubman, a former slave who had escaped, returned 19 times to lead over 300 others to freedom. Her presence was supposedly announced by the singing of this spiritual:

> Dark and thorny is de pathway
> Where de pilgrim makes his ways
> But beyond dis vale of sorrow
> Lie de fields of endless days[72]

Thus signaled, those desiring aid knew an underground "conductor" was near and that preparations should be made to get ready to leave on the "railway."

The Spirituals as Utopian Statements

The process by which slaves made meaning from existing cultural materials is evident in a wide range of sources, all of which confirm the powerfully political sense in which functioned these musical creations of what E. J. Hobsbawm would call "prepolitical" people.[73] The significant point here is that no people could create "a music as forceful and striking" as that of the slaves without feeling it as a total expression of their personalities. Such expressions, within the reality of their lives, were not necessarily ineffective means of opposition or escape. One must impose twentieth-century conceptions of formally organized political movements on these cultural forms of opposition to doubt that slaves were able to fashion determinate areas of free space through their unique adaptations of music and religion. What more meaningful ways of opposition did they have, given the realities of power?[74]

The spirituals suggest music may function in a profoundly utopian way, seeking to transcend the existing order.[75] Where there are no formally organized ways of creating alternatives, music *is* that space, that realm of freedom only in concrete historical-sociological transformations; certainly Marx's view would demand that kind of change, as would Marcuse's later formulations. Yet who is to say that it is, in any transcendent or eternally valid sense, less meaningful as a mode of human struggle against oppression than most of the ill-fated, formally organized political and revolutionary movements of human history? The stream of music begun by the slaves has certainly proven to be more enduring and more influential in daily life than any political organizations they or other later movements for change were able to establish in the United States.

GOSPEL: "THE GOOD NEWS"

The incomparable energy and emotional fervor that so many observers of slave musical performances saw persists in the contemporary period in black gospel music. It is alive in the composed, usually vibrantly up-tempo creations and performance practices to which former bluesman Thomas A. "Georgia Tom" Dorsey (who became the stern patriarch "Professor" Dorsey) made such a contribution from the early 1930s to the 1980s, when he was still active, and which gave such great singers as Sam Cooke and Aretha Franklin to the mass popular music audience in the 1960s.

Gospel is at once the most influential and yet least-known American popular music. Anthony Heilbut, its best historian, has described it as "the most important black musical form since early jazz."[76] Both the music and the church it came out of are impressive creations of an oppressed minority who used the music as a mode of psychological "revitalization." For half a century the nation has, in Heilbut's words, "nurtured unacknowledged a cultural form as imposing as jazz, and a life style as peculiarly native as the hippie's."[77]

The influence of gospel is everywhere in popular music. The beat and dramatic qualities and much of the group interaction in rock and every form of black popular music come from gospel. The expectations of listeners, whether in response to elaborate rock "symphonies" or even to ads for detergents have been formed by gospel. Indeed, the interbeat tension and anticipation of climaxes one associates with rock derive directly from the gospel church. Dance steps expressive of the novelty of physical freedom, evident in the very latest rap videos in 1989, come from the "shout" or "holy dance of victory" in the gospel church (though whether performers are even remotely conscious of it is unclear). Earlier, the hymns that sustained sit-ins in the 1960s, the shouts that energized marches, the "brother and sister" rhetoric of the movement days of the 1960s—all came from the gospel church.[78]

To these one could add the vocal styles of nearly all post–World War II blues performers, all the soul singers (most of whom started singing in gospel), and, as a consequence, many of the white rock performers of the 1960s and 1970s and 1980s.

Gospel, too, had its roots in the era of slavery and, perhaps more significantly, in the revitalizing pentecostal and sanctified churches of the black masses who were not integrated into middle-class life and its churches in the decades after Emancipation. The religious frenzy that emerged in what would later be called hard gospel was first demonstrated by the slaves; it was actually seen by very few whites, however, because it was carried out after dark, "from sundown to sunup," as Rawick put it.[79] It was part of that world made by slaves in their cultural "strategy of survival" in an environment hostile to their very existences as separate individuals. Those secret meetings provided a sense of autonomy and community, "not merely a community unto themselves but a community with leaders [the black preachers] of their own choice."[80] Indeed, "the frenzy . . . brought the slaves together in a special kind of communion, which brought out the most individual expressions and yet disciplined the collective."[81] Concerning this social collective, two qualities were significant, first for slaves and later for the millions of black people who made the church central to their community: "The slaves' wildest emotionalism, even when it passed into actual possession, formed part of a *system* of collective behavior, which *the slaves themselves controlled*. The slaves may have been driven wild with ecstasy when dancing during their services, but never so wild that their feet would cross without evoking sharp rebuke" (the crossing of the feet was considered sinful). In addition, "the slaves' behavior brought out a determination to assert their power and the freedom of their spirit."[82] Both these qualities are evident in the social life of the black churches that arose as genuine "religions of the oppressed," in Vittorio Lanternari's terms,[83] in the depressed social and economic realities that followed the onset of the segregation era.

By a decade after the end of the Civil War, the failure of Reconstruction to alter in any fundamental way the status of blacks in the South was clear. In the early 1870s there had been some participation in the politics of southern states, though no black person was a governor during Reconstruction, nor were blacks a majority in any state senate. Indeed, only in South Carolina, where blacks constituted about 65 percent of the population, did they ever control the lower house of a legislature.[84] If, briefly, blacks and whites had worked out political alliances in North Carolina and Virginia in the 1870s and 1880s,[85] and as late as the 1890s in one area of Texas where the People's Party was biracially organized,[86] by the end of the decade a process of effective disenfranchisement was underway and all the patterns associated with segregation and "Jim Crow" began to emerge.[87]

It is difficult to imagine the dread and despair that black people who had hoped for so much from Emancipation must have felt as their formal legal rights were gradually taken from them in the rising national tide of racism that swept much of the country, rolling into the United States Supreme Court between 1873 and 1898.[88] These developments and their implications were profiled by C. Vann Woodward in his popular and widely circulated *The Strange Career of Jim Crow*. In the 1873 *Slaughter House Cases* and in 1876 in *U.S.* v. *Reese* and *U.S.* v. *Cruikshank*, privileges and immunities previously recognized as federally protected were curtailed drastically. More appalling was the continuation of the trend in the 1883 *Civil Rights Cases* in which the restrictive parts of the Civil Rights Act were virtually nullified as the Court found the Fourteenth Amendment gave to Congress the power to restrain only states, but not individuals, from racially discriminatory actions and overt segregation. As early as 1877 in *Hall* v. *de Cuir*, the Court ruled a state could *not prohibit* segregation on a "common carrier." From there it was easy to rule in 1890 in *Louisville, New Orleans, and Texas Railroad* v. *Mississippi* that a state could require such segregation.

The nadir of Negro rights was reached when in *Plessy* v. *Ferguson* (1896) the Supreme Court said that "legislation is powerless to eradicate racial instincts," laying down the notorious "separate but equal" rule that would justify segregation for over half a century. This was followed incredibly by *Williams* v. *Mississippi* of 1898, which approved the Mississippi plan that would effectively deprive Negroes of the right to vote. Thus, from the highest court in the land, a legal road was established for segregation and disenfranchisement through a variety of devices such as literacy requirements, poll taxes, and outright intimidation and terror. This would be followed by wholesale expulsion of blacks from a number of higher-status job categories throughout the South.[89] The economic effects on black living standards were as appalling as political disfranchisement. As William Harris relates the situation, the nadir of black economic status had arrived: "Conditions worsened in both agriculture and industry as white landowners, industrial managers, and white workers, particularly unionists, combined to relegate blacks to unemployment or casual labor. This worsening of status of blacks was an index of their utter powerlessness in the South."[90]

Woodward pointed out one dimension of this utter powerlessness: "The effectiveness of disfranchisement is suggested by a comparison of the number of registered Negro voters in Louisiana in 1896, when there were 130,334, and in 1904, when there were 1,342. Between the two dates the literacy, property, and poll-tax qualifications were adopted. In 1896 Negro registrants were in a majority in twenty-six parishes—by 1900 in None."[91]

To secure the submission of blacks and divert the (correct) suspicions of poor whites that they too might suffer from disfranchisement, a massive campaign of white supremacy, Negro hating, and racial chauvinism was instituted that had boys who hadn't been born when U. S. Grant was buried marching in the shirts of their fathers while novelists ground out glamorous stories of the Ku Klux Klan. Sensational stories of Negro crime, rape, insolence, and insurrection were spread to terrify further the already cowed black population. Lynchings were not uncommon, and mobs roamed at will through colored neighborhoods. Shortly after the 1898 election 400 white men led by a former congressman prowled through Wilmington, North Carolina, setting fires and killing several black people.[92] Similar mob scenes would occur in succeeding years, culminating in four days of anarchic violence by whites after Hoke Smith's white-supremacy victory in Atlanta in 1896. There, mobs roamed the city looting, killing, and lynching defenseless blacks.[93]

These were clearly the kinds of times foretold by those famous lines of "Amazing Grace":

> Through many dangers, toils and snares
> I have already come.
> 'Tis grace hath brought me safe thus far
> And grace will lead me home.

For those who knew them, those lines could ever after evoke memories of such terrible times and the centuries-long struggle for genuine freedom that would continue in the race riots of 1919, the Klan oppressions of the 1920s, the economic deprivation of the Great Depression, and the struggle to survive in great urban centers after the tremendous migrations out of the South of the 1940s and 1950s.

The Black Church and the Rise of Gospel

The qualities of fervor and emotionalism and self-assertion that were wild, yet disciplined, and demonstrated a carefully controlled set of mutually nurturing social relations seen earlier in slave religion eventually contributed to producing the tightly knit black churches that later gave the nation such inspiring and eloquent preacher-politicians as the Reverend Martin Luther King, Jr., and Reverend Jesse Jackson. These qualities would continue to serve as central points of organization in the black urban community.

In *The Negro Church in America* E. Franklin Frazier described the social functions of the church in the transition from slave status to urban existence in the mid-twentieth century. In the first decades after slavery the churches served as the social nucleus of all Negro existence, including economic ventures, which began in and were centered around them. As a Negro middle class developed and some integration into the social life of the urban environments of the North took place, the church, at least for the middle class, served to integrate less effectively social and economic life for that segment of society.

Working-class, or lower-class, Negroes, as Frazier pointed out, "reacted to the cold impersonal environment of the city and of the large denominational churches by joining the 'storefront' churches and the various cults."[94] And although a certain "external conformity to the patterns of American culture" developed, "the masses of Negroes . . . continue[d] to be influenced in their thinking and especially in their feelings and sentiments by the social heritage of the Negro which is represented by the Spirituals and the religious orientation towards the world contained in the Spirituals."[95] With the Europeanization of the Negro church, the great mass of less-integrated lower-status black people began to seek other ways to "satisfy their deepest emotional yearnings."

The gospel song movement thus arose, in Frazier's view, "out of the revolt of the lower strata against the church and the growing secularization of Negro religion . . . [as] an accommodation between traditional Negro religion and the new outlook of Negroes in the new American environment."[96]

While former bluesman Thomas A. "Georgia Tom" Dorsey and Sallie Martin are usually given credit for starting the modern gospel song movement in a formal way in the 1930s, Dorsey related to Anthony Heilbut, "In the early 1920's I coined the words 'gospel songs' after listening to a group of five people on Sunday morning on the far south side of Chicago. This was the first I heard of a gospel choir. There were no gospel songs then, we called them evangelistic songs."[97] Dorsey probably heard singers from one of the sanctified or Holiness denominations.

Well before the astute entrepreneurial developments of Dorsey and his associates that made him a successful businessman, and before the development of the Dorsey mystique celebrating him as the "originator" of gospel, the "sanctified" churches of the end of the nineteenth century played a significant role in cultural revitalization of a black community at the very bottom of American society economically and suffering from the psychological stigma and social isolation caused by the spreading racism of Jim Crow segregation. The increasingly mobile and dissatisfied black lower class was fertile ground for what A. F. C. Wallace termed a "revitalization movement."[98] Black people revitalized their lives with music. This was also the era of the emergence of the blues, a secular music of expressive individuals directed at the social collective outside the churches (discussed in detail in the next chapter).

Gospel in its purest, or "hard," variety exerts a tremendous magnetism that in part comes from the pulsating rhythms that are a fundamental quality. "The foundation of this rhythm was in the dance beat that was popular at the turn of the century, ragtime."[99] Prior to gaining the name "ragtime" in 1897 with the appearance of William Krell's "Mississippi Rag,"[100] ragtime piano was referred to as "jig piano," apparently derived from jig dances that surfaced in the mid-1890s in two very popular forms of music, the ragtime piano compositions of Scott Joplin and others and the dance bands such as Buddy Bolden's.[101]

Simultaneous with the emergence of this rhythm was the Holiness movement. As Joseph Washington points out in *Black Sects and Cults,* "The Holiness movement seemed to be a sufficient answer for desperate blacks, for it broke out like wild fire among the masses. It grasped the Reverend C. P. Jones in Selma, Alabama, and in 1894 this Baptist preacher left to found the Church of Christ Holiness U.S.A."[102] And it shook others as well, leading to the foundation in an old gym in Lexington, Mississippi, of the Church of God in Christ (COGIC) by Charles Harrison Mason of Memphis, who had been expelled from the Baptist Church for his preaching that salvation was impossible without "holiness," or the presence of the Holy Spirit. Like a number of fundamentalist Pentecostal sects, Reverend Mason's espoused literal interpretation of the Bible, faith healing, and uniquely utilized dance rhythms to help the congregation reach a euphoric state in which they would be more receptive to the Holy Spirit. This admission of dance, frowned upon by so many denominations as sinful, required bringing itinerant guitarists and other musicians into the churches to accompany the singing.[103] That these Pentecostal sanctified and Holiness churches provided the main arena for the practice of what eventually became the highly emotive and rhythmic hard gospel of the mid-twentieth century seems clear.[104] Denominations such as the COGIC, which claimed nearly a half million adherents around 1970, are still significant sources of the music. Counting white pentecostal influences, Heilbut suggests 20 million Americans have been exposed to Holiness influences.[105]

Women and Gospel

Women have played a unique role in the development of this particular musical form, which from its earliest moments has permitted almost unlimited artistic freedom in the context of a tradition extending back over two centuries. The church was once the only place black people could raise their voices, and certainly for most of the time from Emancipation to World War II, it provided the only morally acceptable public arena for the artistic self-expression of the masses of black women. Indeed, "gospel alone among folkloric forms—or, for that matter, most forms of high art—allows women to be peerless artists, not by denying the facts of their womanhood, but rather by declaring and exploiting them. The gospel singer can be sensual and erotic, can testify out of experiences that only a poor black woman would undergo, yet need not make herself ridiculous or pathetic."[106]

The sexual politics of gospel are fascinating. Women have been the greatest singers in the tradition—Sister Rosetta Tharpe, Roberta Martin, Mahalia Jackson, Clara Ward, Dorothy Love, Bessie Griffin, Willie Mae Ford Smith, and so many others—a fact that suggests something of a matriarchy. Yet it is one that must contend with a predominantly male corps of preachers, reflecting a sexual division of labor that appears remarkably sexist yet still provides free spaces for the development of artistic creativity and a remarkable range of self-expression. In the so-called Golden Age of Gospel (from the mid–1940s into the 1960s) and even in the present period, one sees from both men and women an awe-inspired regard for the improvisational abilities of women singers, but along with it adherence to a rather strong preference for male preachers.[107] There is a genuine albeit strictly delimited area of freedom in the black church and in the gospel tradition for women. Within that, virtually any vocal activity and such extreme expressions of emotion from women in the audience as "falling out" (fainting) are accepted as a perfectly normal part of the gospel experience.

In a radio interview with Studs Terkel, Heilbut suggested that perhaps the greatest of the male gospel quartets, the Soul Stirrers, achieved their unique sound through the efforts of the founding father of the group, R. H. Harris, to absorb and incorporate the unique improvisational singing that women had first contributed to the genre.[108] Male quartets had been active in black churches since the 1890s, but in the 1930s the Soul Stirrers changed the predominant preoccupation with vocal technique in performance of spirituals and jubilees then popular. The Soul Stirrers were, as Heilbut pointed out in the notes to a collection of their recordings,

distinguished by their serenely composed background harmonies. 'We were raised up on shape-note music,' (Roy) Crain recalls—which means that pure tonality was prized rather than the moaned slurs common to other quartets. But the moans and slurs were provided in almost folkloric fashion by R. H. Harris. Harris' limpid melancholy tenor with its frequent flights into falsetto evoked several musical forms: a bit of cowboy yodeling, some traits of pop crooners like Bill Kenney, above all a relentless fervor and melismatic fluency that sprang wholly out of the Dr. Watts hymns he heard as a child in his family's Methodist church. To these elements he added his unique rhythmic sense, what he calls "delayed time," a capacity to sail across bar lines, to bounce irregularly off a syncopate background, to be at once rhythmically playful and deadly serious.[109]

The Soul Stirrers, of course, would go on to influence two generations of male black singing groups through Harris' development of the techniques of dual lead singers and the falsetto lead, allowing a constant a capella backing by a quartet while one of the lead singers (the other being one of the quartet members) improvises against the background they provide. This became, and remains, the basic style of scores of gospel quartets from the 1940s through the present.[110] And it was instrumental in shaping the sound of scores of black and white male popular singing groups over the past 50 years.

Gospel has also been the subcultural base from which some of the greatest popular singers have emerged and has been the ground from which have sprung important elements of rhythm and blues and, of course, the whole soul genre (not discussed here because it is treated so definitively by Peter Guralnick in *Sweet Soul Music*).[111] In the mid–1940s one of the best gospel singers, Sister Rosetta Tharpe, did numerous gospel-influenced novelty numbers with Lucky Millender and his orchestra.[112] The Golden Gate Quartet became a popular nightclub act, eventually moving to Paris, where their successors continue to operate. Clara Ward became a popular Las Vegas act and the Staple Singers moved wholly into the popular field in the late 1960s, remaining active to the present. Two of the most significant and influential popular singers of the past 25 years, Sam Cooke and Aretha Franklin, both came out of church-related gospel singing. Indeed, Franklin continues to pay homage to her gospel roots. But they were only two of the scores who made the transition.*

Political Implications of Gospel

Gospel music is performed by an elect group whose numbers are declining; but that does not set it apart from the other forms of black music—blues, rhythm and blues, jazz, and soul. It is also different: It is a way of life, but that is so for the practitioners of other black musics as well. It is also art merged with life. Heilbut sees it as somehow unique in this aspect, although I have talked with too many blues and jazz performers over a decade to see the difference. It is different in being "a ministry of the Word," however. As such, it seeks to "save" souls. If nothing else, by the example of ecstatic involvement in the music.

Gospel is also self-expression in the context of what Heilbut terms "the spiritual moment." In fact, in gospel the feeling of community is the message: "It's this feeling of a community caught up in the spiritual moment that turns gospel into a 'foretaste of glory.' "[113] There is a prefigurative dimension to the gospel experience that is more than ecstatic social psychology. In its creation of a new, free space in a world of trouble, it is also political. It is a means of achieving some psychological release, yet it also has an other-worldly dimension in that it is directed to God. In discussing Afro-American musical adaptation, John F. Szwed drew a useful distinction, suggesting that "church music is directed *collectively* to God; blues are directed *individually* to the *collective*."[114] He was writing of the older spirituals and hymns, but the distinction is a useful one. I would suggest the emphasis on individually expressive virtuosity in gospel embodies both these dimensions with the gospel singers singing to the collective, inviting their participation through feeling, with the whole process directed toward God. As the great gospel song writer W. Herbert Brewster remarked, "A gospel song is a sermon set to music. It must have sentiment and doctrine, rhetorical beauty and splendor."[115]

The presidential campaigns of the Reverend Jesse Jackson have demonstrated another important political dimension of gospel. Jackson's 1984 campaign used the gospel church as its organizational base. By stressing their universal plight, Jackson was able to unite ecumenically Baptists, Methodists, Pentecostals, and Spiritualists. Typical Jackson rallies began with sung or shouted local choir performances, after which the reverend would "speak." His delivery and cadences were pure "church." Indeed, Jackson's most common phrases, Heilbut discerned, "came from songs every gospel lover knows, for example 'Movin'

---

*Among the others: Little Richard, Dinah Washington, B. B. King (King made only one gospel album but was strongly influenced by Sam Mccrary of the Fairfield Four), Johnnie Taylor (Sam Cooke's successor in the Soul Stirrers), Lou Rawls (formerly with the Pilgrim Travelers), Wilson Pickett, Billy Preston, Cissy Houston, Della Reese, and David Ruffin.

on up,' and 'Weeping May Endure for a Night.' "[116] As Heilbut notes, such phrases were employed years earlier by the Reverend Brewster also to political effect. In a Jackson rally then or in 1988, as I was able to observe both in the Michigan and Montana primary campaigns, it appeared revivalist modes of expression were being reenacted in political context. Whether the "old forms" were retained because of loyalty or gratitude or their "sheer expressive convenience" (Heilbut), there was an unmistakable effort to use those forms to express and assert a new, secular, but nonetheless empowering and liberatory political message.[117] These merged impulses remained evident throughout Jackson's 1988 presidential campaign through his spell-binding address to the Democratic National Convention filled with biblical allusions and vivid rhetoric still reflective of the gospel church.

RELIGION AS OPIATE?

There is an inaccurate tendency to identify the gospel community and church with a kind of political quiescence or conservatism. Some sociologists have attempted, through manipulation of data from political attitude surveys, to demonstrate that the religion favored by black people caused them to be politically passive, as did Gary Marx in a standard formulation: "It has long been known that the more fundamentalist sects such as the Holiness groups and the Jehovah's Witnesses are relatively uninterested in movements for secular political change."[118] The basic notion implied in Marx's approach is the old and simplistic "pie in the sky" criticism of religion as opiate, inaccurately identified with the much richer and complex analyses of the functions of religion in works of Karl Marx. Some of the most significant relationships between religion and politics were simply not considered by Gary Marx in his study. For example, the latter study classifies the proportion of "militant" Negroes by denomination, as Table 3.1 indicates.

This study, based on a national sample of black persons, failed to point out both that the overwhelming percentage of black people belonged to the more fundamentalist denominations, and 70 percent of the *total number* of "militants" in Marx's own samples were from the more fundamentalist or predominantly black churches (a result, seen in the second column of Table 3.1, I obtained by repercentaging Marx's data). This absolutely fundamental connection to the black church would not be surprising to anyone familiar with the origins of the civil rights movement or the extensive literature that has developed concerning its origins, especially Aldon Morris' *The Origins of the Civil Rights Movement*,[119] which begins with the black church as the absolutely fundamental source and institutional *center* of the movement!

As Heilbut points out in his study, those who engage in gospel's expressive musical statements about "dangers, toils and snares" and "death disrobing us all" have always known exactly what kind of existence they live. Although the vivid, millenial imagery of the spirituals is not usually evident in the Dr. Watts–

Table 3.1
**Percentage of Black Political "Militants" among Black Members of
Major Denominations vs. Percentage of Total Black Political "Militants"
from Largely "White" vs. Largely "Black" Churches in a National
Sample**

Denomination	Percentage of Black Members of Denomination in Sample "Militant"	Denominational Militants Recomputed As Percentage Of All "Militants" (n=560) in Sample of Blacks By Religion	
Episcopalian	46% (n=24)	4.3%	
			(Black "Militants" From So-called "White" Churches = 30.4%)
United Church of Christ	42% (n=12)	2.1%	
Presbyterian	40% (n=25)	4.5%	
Catholic	40% (n=109)	19.5%	
Methodist	34% (n=142)	25.4%	
			(Percent of Total Of All Black Militants From "Black" Churches =69.64%)
Baptist	32% (n=142)	25.4%	
Sects and Cults	20% (n=106)	18.9%	

Source: Basic data taken from Gary T. Marx, "Religion: Opiate or Inspiration of Civil Rights
Militancy among Negroes?" *American Sociological Review* 32 (February 1967): 64–72,
recomputed and rearranged by the present author for this table.

style hymns, the language still speaks to the often desperate aspects of black
life. It is no wonder, then, that people return to a hymn such as "Amazing
Grace."[120] The reasons for this are clear: Although civil rights and other legislation ostensibly to aid black people reappears in each historical era, the social
conditions for the "gospel poor" have hardly changed.[121]

A song such as "Amazing Grace" continues to resonate with the black experience. No song so consistently moves black congregations. Dorothy Love
Coates explained what the song meant to her: "Look, we didn't have any money,
and how much luck is the white man gonna let you have? The Government just
started waking up to the fact we're here, and nobody's fooled they care. So now
tell me, if it wasn't *grace* that brought us safe thus far, show me what did it."[122]

Black gospel reflects the social conditions of existence and the consciousness
of its audience. It is an expressive music that is sung for a people at the bottom

of a society that has persistently excluded them. It is the only music that speaks consistently of the imminence of death and the only popular music that contains the promise of its transcendence. Although it may have passed its golden age and may no longer be a primary route for individual expression for a younger audience, the social conditions that produced it, and thus the psychological need for it, still persist.

NOTES

1. Karl Marx, "Contribution to the Critique of Hegel's *Philosophy of Right*: Introduction," (1844) in *The Marx-Engels Reader,* ed. Robert C. Tucker, second edition (New York: W. W. Norton, 1978), p. 54.

2. George Rawick, *From Sundown to Sunup: The Making of the Black Community,* vol. I of *The American Slave: A Composite Community* (Westport, Conn.: Greenwood Press, 1972), p. 33.

3. Robert Farris Thompson, *The Flash of the Spirit: African and Afro-American Art and Philosophy* (New York: Random House, Vintage Books, 1984).

4. Lawrence Levine, *Black Culture and Black Consciousness* (New York: Oxford University Press, 1977), p. 6.

5. Ibid., p. 7.

6. Thompson, *Flash of the Spirit,* p. xiii.

7. Ibid.

8. Ibid.

9. Levine, *Black Culture and Black Consciousness,* p. 6.

10. Ibid.

11. The notion of black popular music as a strategy of survival was powerfully expressed by Iain Chambers in "A Strategy for Living: Black Music and White Subcultures" in *Resistance through Rituals*, ed. S. Hall and T. Jefferson (London: Hutchinson, 1976), pp. 157–66. Also see Chambers' more recent work *Urban Rhythms* (New York: St. Martin's Press, 1985).

12. Ibid. Eugene Genovese probably preceded Chambers in his usage of the concept "strategy of survival." See *Roll, Jordan, Roll: The World the Slaves Made* (New York: Pantheon, 1974), pp. 587–99.

13. See George Lipsitz, *Class and Culture in Cold War America* (New York: Praeger, 1981), especially Chapter 10, " 'Ain't Nobody Here but Us Chickens': The Class Origins of Rock and Roll"; Chambers, *Urban Rhythms,* is also relevant throughout.

14. John F. Szwed, "Afro-American Musical Adaptation," in *Afro-American Anthropology: Contemporary Perspectives*, ed. N. E. Whitten, Jr., and J. F. Szwed (New York: The Free Press, 1970), p. 220.

15. Chambers, "Strategy for Living," p. 161.

16. Albert Murray, *Stomping the Blues* (New York: Vintage Books, 1982).

17. As an example see Robert Christgau's evocation of Murray's insight in his review essay on Paul Simon's *Graceland* album, "South African Romance," *Village Voice,* September 23, 1986, pp. 71–73ff.

18. Genovese provides perhaps the finest and most succinct judgment on this cultural resistance, *Roll, Jordan, Roll,* pp. 587–99.

19. See Marion D. De B. Kilson, "Towards Freedom: An Analysis of Slave Revolts

in the United States," pp. 176–78, and Vincent Harding, "Religion and Resistance among Antebellum Negroes, 1800–1860," pp. 179–200, in *The Making of Black America: Essays in Negro Life & History*, vol. 1, ed. A. Meier and E. Rudwick (New York: Atheneum, 1969). The most complete account of the daily life of the slaves may be found in the multiple volumes of *The American Slave: A Composite Autobiography*, ed. George Rawick (Westport, Conn.: Greenwood Press, 1972). See especially Rawick's interpretive summary in vol. 1, *From Sundown to Sunup: The Making of the Black Community*.

20. E. Franklin Frazier, *The Negro Church in America* (New York: Schocken Books, 1963), pp. 1–6, describes the methods of destroying remnants of African culture and resocializing the slaves upon arrival in North America.

21. Genovese, *Roll, Jordan, Roll*; James Lovell, *Black Song: The Forge and the Flame* (New York: Paragon Books, 1986); Rawick, *The American Slave*; Herbert Aptheker, *American Negro Slave Revolts* (New York: International Publishers, 1943, 1966).

22. Lovell, *Black Song*, p. 145.

23. James M. Cone, *The Spirituals and the Blues* (New York: Seabury Press, 1972), p. 24.

24. Kenneth M. Stampp, *The Peculiar Institution* (New York: Vintage Books, 1956), pp. 108–109.

25. Harding, "Religion and Resistance." Also see the discussion among Aptheker, Eugene Genovese, and others over the extent and frequency of slave revolts in *In Resistance*, ed. G. Y. Okihiro (Amherst: University of Massachusetts Press, 1986). For further discussion also see August Meier and Elliott Rudwick, *Black History and the Historical Profession, 1915–1980* (Urbana: University of Illinois Press, 1986).

26. The economic state of black America at the end of the 1980s remains heavily stamped by the experience of slavery. So more sobering evidence is needed than the special tissue of *Journal of Black Studies* 17 (December 1986) containing devastating commentaries on the economic situation of black people in America: the Center on Budget and Policy Priorities report "Falling Behind: A Report on How Blacks Have Fared under Reagan," p. 148–72; Joe Feagin, "Slavery Unwilling to Die: The Background of Black Oppression in the 1980's," pp. 173–200; and Sidney M. Wilhelm, "The Economic Demise of Blacks in America: A Prelude to Genocide?" pp. 201–254. Clearly, the roots of the blues are not hard to find!

27. Genovese, *Roll, Jordan, Roll*, pp. 587–621; Levine, *Black Culture and Black Consciousness*, throughout.

28. That is the thesis of Alan Wolfe's provocative work *The Seamy Side of Democracy: Repression in America*, second edition revised (New York: Longman, 1978). Also see E. J. Hobsbawm, *Revolutionaries* (New York: Meridian, 1973), on the weakness of political forms in the United States resulting in cultural forms of opposition, in contrast to France.

29. Miles Mark Fisher, *Negro Slave Songs in the United States* (Secaucus, N.J.: The Citadel Press, 1978; orig. pub. 1953).

30. The vast literature on the slave songs and spirituals is covered most comprehensively in John Lovell, *Black Song: The Forge and the Flame* (New York: Paragon House, 1986).

31. Arnold Shaw, *Black Popular Music in America* (New York: Schirmer Books, 1985), p. 1.

32. Peter Guralnick in *Sweet Soul Music: Rhythm and Blues and the Southern Dream*

of Freedom (New York: Harper & Row, 1986) shows how the white partner remains a significant element of what we call black music. See especially pp. 5–6.

33. See Lovell, *Black Song*, p. 402–425.

34. Quoted in Viv Boughton, *Black Gospel* (London: Blandford Press, 1985), p. 13.

35. W. E. B. Dubois, *The Souls of Black Folk* (New York: Fawcett World Library, 1961; orig. pub. 1902), p. 182–183.

36. Hall's work occurs largely in group contexts. See, for example, John Clarke, Stuart Hall, Tony Jefferson, and Brian Roberts, "Subcultures, Cultures, and Class," in *Culture, Ideology and Social Process: A Reader*, ed. Tony Bennett et al. (London: The Open University Press, 1981), pp. 53–80; and Stuart Hall and Tony Jefferson, eds., *Resistance through Rituals: Youth Subcultures in Post-War Britain* (London: Hutchinson, 1976).

37. Clarke et al., "Subcultures, Cultures, and Class," p. 70.

38. That this does not, ironically, always have "progressive" political implications was made abundantly clear when John Lennon's "Imagine" was appropriated by young Conservatives who sang a rewritten text of it at an election eve rally for Conservative candidate Margaret Thatcher.

39. Levine, *Black Culture and Black Consciousness*, p. 19. Also see Dena J. Epstein, "A White Origin for the Black Spiritual? An Invalid Theory and How It Grew," *American Music* (Summer 1983): 53–59.

40. Shaw, *Black Popular Music in America*.

41. See the discussion in Epstein, "A White Origin?" and Levine, *Black Culture and Black Consciousness*.

42. Epstein, "A White Origin?"

43. Levine, *Black Culture and Black Consciousness*, p. 23.

44. Ibid.

45. Ibid., pp. 174–89. By 1947 a study of songs in use among sharecroppers on a Mississippi Delta plantation found that only 19 percent of the songs in active use were spirituals. See Samuel Adams, "The Acculturation of the Delta Negro," *Social Forces*, 26 (1947): 203–204. A decade later Harry Oster found that in Louisiana, spirituals were "no longer a natural spontaneous part of the repertoire of most folk Negroes." Notes to Arhoolie Records 2013, *Angola Prison Spirituals* (cited by Levine, *Black Culture and Black Consciousness*, p. 471).

46. Sister Rosetta Tharpe, *Gospel Train*, MCA 1317.

47. See particularly her performance of the classic spiritual "Joshua Fit the Battle of Jericho" on the album *Mahalia Jackson at Newport, 1958*, Columbia Special Products JCS 8071.

48. Clarke et al., "Subcultures, Cultures, and Class," p. 70.

49. Ibid.

50. Levine, *Black Culture and Black Consciousness*, p. 24. Ironically, there may be some significant insights here concerning what has loosely been termed the white "rip-off" of black music.

51. Lovell, *Black Song*.

52. See the *Folk Music Source Book*, ed. Larry Sandberg and Dick Weissman (New York: Alfred A. Knopf, 1976); Roger D. Abrahams and George Foss, *Anglo-American Folksong Style* (Englewood Cliffs, N.J.: Prentice-Hall, 1968); Harold Courlander, *Negro Folk Music, U.S.A.* (New York: Columbia University Press, 1963). Charles Keil in his

Urban Blues (Chicago: University of Chicago Press, 1966) demonstrates the essentially oral and folk character of modern electric urban blues, as does Ben Sidran in *Black Talk*.

53. Lovell, *Black Song,* p. 129.

54. Ibid., p. 136.

55. Jeremiah Creedon, "Stuart Hall: A Cultural Theorist Who Plays by TV Rules," *In These Times,* September 23–29, 1987, p. 20.

56. Alan Lomax makes this point in his perceptive annotation to the New World Records collection *Roots of the Blues, NW 252.*

57. Rawick, *From Sundown to Sunup,* p. 32.

58. Ibid.

59. Ibid., p. 32.

60. Ibid., p. 33.

61. Ibid.

62. Albert Raboteau, *Slave Religion* (New York: Oxford University Press, 1978), p. 309.

63. Ibid.

64. Mary A. Livermore, *My Story of the War* (Hartford, Conn.: 1889), pp. 260–61. Cited by Raboteau, *Slave Religion,,* p. 313.

65. Charshee Lawrence-McIntyre, "The Double Meanings of the Spirituals," *Journal of Black Studies* 17 (June 1987), p. 384.

66. On Liberation Theology in Latin America see Phillip Berryman, *The Religious Roots of Rebellion* (Maryknoll, N.Y.: Orbis Books, 1984). Cone's *The Spirituals and the Blues* is written from the perspective of black liberation theology, his major area of specialization.

67. This theology is expressed most succinctly in Cone, *The Spirituals and the Blues.*

68. Ibid., p. 27.

69. Harold Courlander, in *Negro Folk Music, U.S.A.*, argues that if double meanings were as common as some suggest, "if songs of the type of 'Steal Away to Jesus' [supposedly advocating running away] and 'Go Down Moses' are to be considered conscious disguises for political, temporal meanings, a large part of the religious repertoire must be placed in the same category. Every reference to crossing the Jordan could be interpreted to mean escape to the North; every battle of the Israelites might be read to mean the battle for Negro freedom," p. 43. That is precisely the point! Levine, *Black Culture and Black Consciousness* finds such similarities to be no accident: "There was always a latent and symbolic element of protest in the slave's religious songs which frequently became overt and explicit" (p. 51).

70. Levine, *Black Culture and Black Consciousness,* p. 50.

71. For a brief account of the Underground Railway and the activities of Harriet Tubman, see John Hope Franklin, *From Slavery to Freedom: A History of Negro Americans* (New York: Vintage Books, 1969), pp. 253–59.

72. Eileen Southern, *The Music of Black Americans: A History* (New York: W. W. Norton, 1971), pp. 129–30.

73. See his *Primitive Rebels: Studies in Archaic Forms of Social Movement in the 19th and 20th Century* (New York: W. W. Norton, 1959).

74. Levine, *Black Culture and Black Consciousness,* p. 51.

75. Karl Mannheim, *Ideology and Utopia: An Introduction to the Sociology of Knowledge* (New York: Harcourt Brace, 1936).

76. Anthony Heilbut, *The Gospel Sound: Good News and Bad Times* (New York:

DaCapo Press, 1985), p. xxix. Heilbut's work is the most comprehensive study of this powerful music and its major practitioners.

77. Ibid., p. x. Also see Viv Boughton, *Black Gospel: An Illustrated History* (London: Blanford Press/New York: Sterling Publishing, 1985). This work contains a number of photographs of performers never previously published.

78. Ibid.

79. Rawick, *From Sundown to Sunup*.

80. Genovese, *Roll, Jordan, Roll,* p. 238.

81. Ibid.

82. Ibid., p. 239.

83. In *The Religions of the Oppressed* (New York: Alfred A. Knopf, 1963) Vittorio Lanternari said:

A religious phenomenon may be explained only in so far as it is possible to trace its historical origin and development and to analyze it systematically in relation to concrete secular conditions. The conditions may be described as the *existential experiences* to which human society is bound at any given historical moment, and which in turn give rise to cultural *exigencies* which apply likewise to that particular moment. (p. vi)

The declining conditions of existence of black America from 1890 onward provide such a background.

84. Peter Carroll and David W. Noble, *The Free and the Unfree: A New History of the United States* (New York: Penguin Books, 1979), p. 285.

85. Ibid., p. 292.

86. See William H. Harris, *The Harder We Run: Black Workers since the Civil War* (New York: Oxford University Press, 1982), p. 35. Harris provides an excellent overview of the economics underlying the social status of black America in the decades in which blues, gospel, jazz, and ragtime had their origin.

87. C. Vann Woodward's *The Strange Career of Jim Crow: A Brief Account of Segregation* (New York: Oxford University Press, 1957) provides a succinct overview of the political and cultural climate in his chapter "Capitulation to Racism," pp. 49–95. Harris, *The Harder We Run,* provides a more detailed overview of social and economic trends and extensive bibliographical background.

88. See Woodward, *Strange Career,* pp. 52–54.

89. Described by Harris in *The Harder We Run*.

90. Harris, *The Harder We Run,* p. 29.

91. Woodward, *Strange Career*, p. 68.

92. Ibid., p. 69.

93. Ibid., pp. 68–95.

94. Frazier, *The Negro Church in America*, pp. 72–73.

95. Ibid., p. 73.

96. Ibid.

97. Heilbut, *The Gospel Sound,* p. 27.

98. A. F. C. Wallace, "Revitalization Movements," *American Anthropologist* 58 (April 1956): 264–81.

99. Bernard Klatzko, record notes to Herwin 202, *Bessie Johnson*.

100. Guy Waterman, "Ragtime," in *The Art of Jazz,* ed. Martin Williams (New York: Grove Press, 1960), pp. 11–31. Rudi Blesh and Harriet Janis, *They All Played Ragtime,* 4th ed. (New York: Oak Publications, 1971), was the standard history for many years

until Edward Berlin, *Ragtime: A Musical and Cultural History* (Berkeley: University of California, 1980). Also see John Edward Hasse, ed., *Ragtime: Its History, Composers and Music* (New York: Schirmer Books, 1985).

101. Klatzko, record notes to Herwin 202, *Bessie Johnson.*

102. Joseph R. Washington, Jr., *Black Sects and Cults* (New York: Doubleday, 1972), especially pp. 58–72, "Holiness and Pentecostal Sects." A publication in "The C. Eric Lincoln Series on Black Religion," this is a good brief overview of black fundamentalist sects. Also see J. Milton Yinger, *The Scientific Study of Religion* (New York: Macmillan, 1970), pp. 324–30, "Religious Movements among American Negroes."

103. The excitement and fervor of these proceedings comes through on some of the recordings of the 1920s and 1930s reissued on records as Herwin 202, *Bessie Johnson;* Herwin 203, *God Give Me Light, 1927–31;* Herwin 204, *Blind Joe Taggart: A Guitar Evangelist, 1926–31;* Herwin 206, *The Rural Blues—Sacred Tradition, 1927–31;* Herwin 207, *Whole World in His Hands;* and Blues Classics BC17 and BC18, *Negro Religious Music,* vols. 1 & 2, "The Sanctified Singers—Part I & II"; and BC19 *Negro Religious Music,* vol. 3, "Singing Preachers & Their Congregations." The latter contains numerous examples of the ecstatic quality of sanctified services which moved from spoken portions easily into song, then to moaning and back.

104. See the illuminating discussion of the modern Holiness church and its influence on gospel in Heilbut's *Gospel Sound,* pp. 173–89.

105. Ibid., p. 174.

106. See ibid., p. xiii and p. 328.

107. See the George Neirenberg film *Say 'Amen' Somebody* for some insight into the struggle between male attitudes and female efforts at self-expression in the gospel community.

108. See the magnificent recorded anthology of the work of R. H. Harris and the Soul Stirrers (which Harris left in 1950) plus selections from groups Harris influenced—The Five Blind Boys of Mississippi and the Sensational Nightingales—assembled by Anthony Heilbut on Spirit Feel Records SF1001.

109. Anthony Heilbut, notes to Spirit Feel SF1001, *Father and Sons.*

110. See Heilbut's account of the Soul Stirrers in *The Gospel Sound,* pp. 75–93.

111. Peter Guralnick, *Sweet Soul Music: Rhythm and Blues and the Southern Dream of Freedom* (New York: Harper & Row, 1986).

112. Lucky Millinder and His Orchestra with Sister Rosetta Tharpe, *Lucky Days,* MCA Records.

113. Heilbut, *The Gospel Sound,* p. xix.

114. Szwed, "Afro-American Musical Adaptation," p. 224.

115. Quoted by Heilbut, *The Gospel Sound,* p. 98.

116. Ibid., p. 331. These may be heard to great effect in Jackson's stirring remarks of July 27, 1987, at the New Bethel Baptist Church, Detroit, Michigan, as released on Aretha Franklin's 1988 Arista album *One Lord, One Faith, One Baptism* (AL–8497).

117. Heilbut, *The Gospel Sound,* p. 331.

118. Gary T. Marx, "Religion: Opiate or Inspiration of Civil Rights Militancy among Negroes?" *American Sociological Review* 32 (February 1967): 64–72.

119. Aldon Morris, *The Origins of the Civil Rights Movement* (New York: The Free Press, 1984).

120. Heilbut, *The Gospel Sound,* p. xxiii.

121. Ibid.

122. Ibid., p. xxii.

4

The Blues: America's National Song Form

The Blues ain't nothin' but a botheration on the mind.

Otis Spann

The blues man is in a sense every man: the country bluesman is an archetype
of the migrant laborer; . . . the urban blues artist, something of an ideal man
or prototype for his generation.

Charles Keil, *Urban Blues*[1]

Every successful country singer I know has a humble background, . . . and
the colored blues have been a part of their musical heritage. *Every one of
them, bar none.* Elvis will tell you himself that where he got his style is
from the colored blues singers.

Johnny Cash, quoted by Shelton, *No Direction Home*[2]

It has often been said that the blues is America's national song form.[3] What
about the blues continues to amaze and inspire each new generation? Culturally,
the "blackest" of black music, its roots lie in the dim past of black culture; but
its appeal may have much to do with the fact that it is a personal expression of
the frustrations in the first generation of black freedom in this country.

In a white culture in which contending versions of possessive versus expressive
individualism have occupied a central place, as Robert Bellah and associates
expressed it in *Habits of the Heart*, the blues has exerted a particular and peculiar
appeal to successive generations of whites who find it speaks to some of their
most basic psychological needs.[4] Greil Marcus has argued that "like all art
forms, rock and roll rises up when it can catalyze the desires of an era."[5] The

blues, the major constituent element of rock 'n' roll, remains resonant with meaning for each generation of whites because the form has, for nearly a century, persistently catalyzed some of the most basic existential and expressive needs of a society of increasingly atomized individuals. The blues expresses unfulfilled longings present society does not effectively meet and perhaps never can.

The blues is a music of individuality created by and for a generation of supposedly emancipated, but increasingly frustrated, independent black people who knew they were "somebody" in spite of the repressive social realities they encountered. The music continues as one of the wellsprings of American popular music because today it meets some of the same needs for whites as it originally did for blacks.

To recognize the continuing significance and centrality of the blues in popular music is to recognize the importance to whites of this "black" music's central qualities. Successive generations of white mediators, after much initial reluctance to record the music as performed by the black people who created it,[6] have appreciated its market appeal and ultimate sustaining powers. As Richard Goldstein, one of the quintessentially hip white pop and rock culture critics of the late 1960s once wrote, "The blues matters because it's always there when you need it—those 12 bars inviolate, self-contained, eternal. Blues is the humus of American music."[7]

The cultural components—those elements of the "flash of the spirit" discussed in the previous chapter—that produced the unique synthesis that is the blues lie in the past centuries of the black experience—in worksong and field hollers—and thus there is a certain irony in the fact that music first produced by black people out of their own unique experience and creative subjectivity should be so dependent on white "gate keepers." But the music is also an expression of the indomitable drive and irrepressible energy of a people who could seize any opportunity for creative expression available to them. Subsequently, several generations of black artists have developed a variety of blues styles and subcultures in such centers as Memphis, Atlanta, St. Louis, Los Angeles, and, especially, Chicago. American society still shows pronounced inequality and endemic racism, but cultural outlets for black expression have so proliferated and preferences changed to such a degree that, today, blues music meets the needs of a biracial, but significantly white, audience.

Increasingly, some of the most dynamic blues interpreters are white women and men. Moreover, that the music comes through, as does most of our popular music, with the distinguished exception of Motown, largely through generations of white "mediators" (record company owners and executives, talent scouts, producers, writer-composers, agents, and critics) demonstrates an important exploitation factor at work here—the phenomenon known in some contexts as "white rip-off."[8] Probably *most* bands and performers, white and black, make very little out of their records (and only a minority get recorded), and they most probably spend more on their careers than they ever get back. While there are extravagant rewards for those few who succeed, for every Michael Jackson,

Bruce Springsteen, Madonna, or Whitney Houston there are thousands of local and regional artists and bands who operate at subsistence level. Within the blues, as evident from scores of interviews, only a handful of artists approach the incomes of the second tier of highly paid pop/rock stars. Most are lucky to come off the road not owing money.

Peter Guralnick's examination of the soul phenomenon, *Sweet Soul Music*, suggests that without the facilitating role of white "friends" of the music, much of the public enjoyment of such cultural forms would never take place.[9] Atlantic Records producer Jerry Wexler has confessed, "We did what we dug. We were fans of the music we recorded, fans who had the rare privilege of making records that we liked and enjoyed. And the weird thing is that we made money—lots of money—out of doing our thing."[10] That it was also the *artists'* thing, too, is sometimes lost. Nonetheless, one must recognize that there have been several generations of white entrepreneurs who have really loved the music and have done everything they could to further public exposure and acceptance of the "message" of the blues.

What is that message? Above all else, those who know the blues appreciate its simplicity of form, its potent directness, its imagery, and its capacity to capture and fuse hard realism with exultant sensuality to create a cultural practice providing that cathartic emotional release so central to effective artistic achievement in popular culture. These qualities make the blues a fundamental resource of much of American popular music.

SECONDARY EMBODIMENTS OF THE BLUES

The blues exists in many forms today. The most obvious of these is rock music. Wherever one turns in the popular music world, one hears elements of the blues: in the gritty rhythm and blues of the latest Michael Jackson album and videos; in the performance gyrations of legions of heavy metal rockers; in every guitar lick on MTV; in Bob Dylan and the scores of those derivative of him; in the country music that stems from Jimmie Rodgers' white blues of the 1920s; in the powerful fusion of blues and Tex-Mex and blues-influenced western swing out of the Southwest; in the unique fusion of Cajun and blues and rock 'n' roll coming out of New Orleans and the Louisiana area; in every guitarist who owes so much to B. B. King and T-Bone Walker (and that means too many to mention).*

But the blues also exists today as a basic, distinct, distinguishable style of

---

*Throughout the English-speaking world one sees on occasion graffiti declaring "Clapton is God!"—this in reference to the British guitar virtuoso. But Clapton has said, "Some people talk about me like a revolutionary—that's nonsense. All I did was copy B. B. King." Who created B. B. King? King, as a Memphis disc jockey, heard all the rhythm and blues recordings of the 1940s and mentions Lonnie Johnson, T-Bone Walker, and Django Reinhardt as guitar influences and took his vocal style from the black church. He was especially influenced by the singing of Sam McCrary of the Fairfield Four.

music with a significant public. To appreciate the vitality of the music one has only to stand with over 100,000 fans at the Chicago Blues Festival in Grant Park, Chicago (over 600,000 people attended events at the 1988 festival[11]), or try to crowd into one of the scores of Chicago blues clubs, or attend the concerts of any of the blues societies that exist all across the nation, or visit the annual San Francisco or Sacramento Blues Festivals, or watch the growth of the Blues Foundation in Memphis, or read the growing number of blues publications, or listen to the proliferation of blues recordings issued yearly on labels such as Alligator and Rounder.

BEGINNINGS

Although literary references to "feeling the blues" go back several centuries, there is general agreement that the music, as one can recognize it today, began in the Deep South, perhaps in a levee camp or, more likely, on a plantation in Mississippi, about 1890. Actually, a situation of what might be termed poly-genesis probably existed, given the wide distribution of the cultural components of blues style throughout the South.[12] The blues began in many places where individuals sang about themselves, played guitar with a knife blade, or blurred, embellished, or "bent" notes when singing. There are journal entries from the 1830s describing "extra-ordinarily wild and unaccountable" songs.[13] William Cullen Bryant in South Carolina in 1843 commented on the "singularly wild and plaintive air" sung by slaves husking corn.[14] Others, such as W. C. Handy, who heard references to "the blues" as early as 1892, described the emotional impact of the strange sounds produced by a knife blade applied to guitar strings by an old Negro guitarist sitting in a train station in Tutweiler, Mississippi, in 1903.[15]

The banjo and fiddle were in wide use throughout the nineteenth century, but they soon gave way to the guitar, which provided, Paul Oliver suggests, "a warm and deep resonance" that we today associate with the blues.[16] (I have heard recent recordings of five-string banjo played with a bottleneck that demonstrate that the commonly played instrument could well have been used for country blues sounds far earlier.) Nonetheless, those who sought out black music in the South and Border States immediately after the Civil War do not report what today is called blues until the last decade of the nineteenth century.[17]

The first so-called blues recordings were actually done by whites, many of them specialists in Negro dialect material. It was nearly a decade after the first blues "craze" in 1914–15 (W. C. Handy published the "Memphis Blues" in 1912 and the "St. Louis Blues" in 1914) that practicing black country "folk" bluesmen began to be recorded.[18] This required overcoming company resistance to recording black artists. Initially, several black women singers were recorded singing vaudeville versions of the blues. It all happened because white entrepreneurs, finally made aware of the 14 million black persons of the potential "race" market, reluctantly decided to do it.

Part of what today is known as the blues began as a stereotype of blacks created by whites. As with a good deal in black culture in the United States, the forms and stereotypes that whites initiated and fostered were eventually transcended by black artists, though it took over a decade, Charles Keil has suggested, "to adapt the white stereotype, work it through, master it and turn it into a black identity."[19] When that was done, what an identity it was and remains! There is really nothing in American music to equal the impact of the arresting, often stunning sounds of the great black blues singers and shouters: Ma Rainey and Bessie Smith—the first queens of the blues; Big Joe Turner and Jimmy Rushing—shouters out of Kansas City; Son House, Robert Johnson, Muddy Waters, Howlin' Wolf, B. B. King, Elmore James—all born and raised in Mississippi; Blind Willie Johnson and Blind Lemon Jefferson out of Texas; and more.

HISTORICAL DEVELOPMENT

Roots of the blues existed throughout the Deep South.[20] The first firm accounts of music that seems to be the blues come from the period, which coincides with the adulthood of the first generation of blacks born after Emancipation.[21] Here were people cast adrift from the well-defined if brutally oppressive social roles established during slavery. The subsequent course of development of the music follows the migration patterns of blacks out of the old Deep South toward northern cities, where local blues subcultures would flourish around every major black community.[22] As blacks moved off the land, they brought the blues to urban areas—to Memphis, Atlanta, Houston, Dallas, St. Louis, Cincinnati, Indianapolis, and especially the objective of the greatest number of migrants, Chicago. New York, though the recipient of most of the southeastern migrants, was much more a jazz center in spite of that fact. The white folk movement of the 1960s would arise there with significant black influence and participation of numerous black "folk" bluesmen from the Piedmont region in its earlier formative years.

Later, local traditions developed around Kansas City, really one of the greatest musical melting pots, spawning most of the best saxophonists and the shouting vocals basic to rhythm and blues and the new jazz art, bebop.[23] During and after World War II, Detroit, Los Angeles, and the San Francisco Bay area became important centers of the music because of the massive influx of black workers.[24]

BLUES TYPES

Distinctive types of music were associated with each era of migration.[25] All blues styles were fashioned from the "basic resources" of call-and-response patterns in worksong and church music, plus, Keil suggests, "field hollers, peddlers cries, songs from children's games, the chanting style used by most Negro preachers, marching band music, country dance music, as well as the content and phrasing of everyday Southern Negro speech."[26]

Country Blues

These resources were fashioned into the various forms of southern country blues with such common characteristics as relatively unstandardized forms (varying bar lengths, for example), "strong-beat" phrasing, and spoken introductions and endings played by individuals who accompanied themselves on unamplified acoustic guitars. There were significant variations among the country blues styles that were carried via predominant migration patterns and routes.

Mississippi Country Blues

Most familiar because of its strong influence on Chicago blues and the subsequent rock of the Rolling Stones is the "Delta" style, originating in the region of Mississippi south of Memphis between the Yazoo and Mississippi rivers,[27] with its "drones, moans, bottle-neck techniques, and 'heavy' texture."[28] Individuals associated with this style include Charley Patton (sometimes called the "Founder of Delta Blues"), Son House, Bukka White, Robert Johnson, Muddy Waters (in his earlier years; in his later years he simply added instruments and amplification to create the modern Chicago urban blues), and John Lee Hooker (who, after migrating to Michigan, would apply heavy, if primitive, overamplification to create the Detroit style in the post–World War II period).[29]

Texas Country Blues

Another rich country tradition existed in Texas, where the country blues tended to feature single-string playing, more relaxed vocal qualities, and "lighter" texture (though one of the greatest of all bluesmen, the rough-voiced gospel-shouting slide guitar genius Blind Willie Johnson shared many elements of the so-called Delta style).[30] Individuals in this school include Blind Lemon Jefferson, Mance Lipscomb, and Lightnin' Hopkins.[31]

The "Piedmont" Tradition

The southeastern states and East Coast region constituted the regional basis of the other major country blues tradition, sometimes known as the Piedmont tradition, that would influence later schools. Performers in this area showed the closest relation to white folk traditions and a pronounced ragtime influence. Among the important performers from the region are Blind Willie McTell, Buddy Moss, Blind Boy Fuller, Brownie McGee and Sonny Terry, and the Reverend Gary Davis, who would influence later generations through his incredible ragtime technique and his teaching guitar during the years of the second Folk Revival in the 1950s and 1960s.[32]

The first generation of black migrants (in the years before World War I) seemed particularly influenced by ragtime.[33] Vigorous ragtime and related piano and

Table 4.1
Demographic Changes in the South and among the Black Population in the United States, 1900–1960

```
-------------------------------------------------------------------
Net Loss Through Migration From The South
1900-10            180,500
1910-20            453,800
1920-30            773,400
1930-40            347,500 (depression)
1940-50          1,597,000
1950-60          1,457,000
Changes In Black Population Distribution In The South and U.S.
          1900           1960
South     89.7           59.9
  urban   15.4           35.0
  rural   74.4           24.9
U.S.(outside South)
          10.3           40.1
  urban    7.2           38.2
  rural    3.1            1.9
-------------------------------------
```

Source: U.S. Census Data, in Rowe, *Chicago Breakdown*, pp. 26–28.

guitar styles developed into distinctive local, early urban blues traditions in a number of cities. It was really in the period of the massive migration of the 1940s and 1950s that the distinctive styles of electrified country blues from Muddy Waters in Chicago and John Lee Hooker in Detroit developed, while the migration patterns to the West Coast from Texas and other areas of the Southwest produced distinctive jump or swing blues and a greater emphasis on rhythm and blues stylings. Aaron "T-Bone" Walker out of Texas, who moved to Los Angeles in the 1930s, originated a unique electric guitar style based on single-note runs that was taken up by B. B. King in Memphis and, through King's commanding national influence, by most subsequent Chicago bluesmen and a generation of rock guitarists as well.[34]

DEMOGRAPHIC FACTORS

Trends in the blues reflected the profound demographic changes taking place in the nation as both blacks and whites moved off the land out of the South. These changes are evident in Table 4.1. In 1900, 77.5 percent of the black population lived in rural areas, 22.6 percent in urban areas. By 1960 only 26.8 percent of the black population of the nation lived in rural areas, whereas 73.2 percent were located in urban areas.

CHANGING APPEAL

There have been few blacks in managerial positions in the recording industry from its earliest days. For the most part whites controlled all recording of the blues and other "race" records (though they received significant amounts of mail from black consumers who urged local favorites to be recorded). Whites also managed sales to the black "race" market. Those who have written about this powerful music of black artists have almost exclusively been whites, with the notable exceptions of writers Albert Murray and Leroi Jones/Amiri Baraka and Ralph Ellison.[35]

One should not, however, underestimate the significance of the free space the recording industry provided for black artists during the first decade of blues recording. Lawrence Levine goes so far as to suggest that not only did the Negro market exist, "it was able to impose its own tastes upon the businessmen who ran the record companies."[36] Those who ran the companies, researchers such as John Fahey and Samuel Charters found, really did not understand much about the music and, consequently, gave virtually complete artistic freedom to those they recorded. The objective of the companies was maximization of sales. The artists brought to the various recording studios were considered to be the best judge of what would sell in their regions. Accordingly, virtually no restrictions on content were imposed.[37]

Indeed, Fahey points out, "virtually anyone who could make any kind of musical sound could make at least one audition record for Paramount, Vocalion, or Victor."[38] The consequence of these essentially nondirective and wide-open practices was a quite effective documentation of local country blues tradition in Mississippi in the late 1920s and early 1930s. Literally hundreds of southern black artists were thus allowed the freedom to audition, be recorded, and have records issued of numbers they had been singing for decades.[39]

This phenomenon would be repeated over the history of the recording industry, though perhaps without such striking degrees of openness, thus demonstrating the cultural freedom possible within a system essentially treating popular culture as a commodity for sale. Since the aims of companies have been to sell recordings, they have been willing to provide a significant degree of access to whatever they thought might sell. In this manner a significant degree of creative free space was essentially "squeezed out" of a system with certainly no formal ideological commitment to providing it. The net result of this system is that between 1927 and 1962 "the commercial recording industry did an infinitely better job of collecting, preserving and making available to the public" native folk music, especially *black* folk music, than did American scholars of folk music.[40]

Over the years of the development of mass media there has been a growing tendency to assume that popular cultural commodities are somehow imposed on a passive mass of consumers. The practices of the early years of the "race" recording industry would suggest a significant variation from this supposed pattern so far as initial access is concerned. However, that virtually no trace of most of the masters of these recordings remains is another side (the "back" of the "unseen hand") of capitalist culture. The situation is similarly the case with popular film art, where works of historical importance and once wide circulation have been allowed to deteriorate because of declining market demand.[41]

Through the twentieth century, as greater and greater cultural opportunities for black musical forms have developed and the black population has become more urbanized, hip, and sophisticated, the appeal of the blues has declined among black consumers, who show a preference for other forms of music. Big Bill Broonzy, who made several transitions during his career from his birth in Scott, Mississippi, in 1893 to his death from lung cancer in Chicago in 1958, found during his reversion to popular "folk" blues in the 1940s and 1950s that blacks in his audience would sometimes say, "Bill, why do you sing them songs about pickin' cotton . . . them days is gone forever." If there was a significant message to the blues, black audiences already knew it; whites were just beginning to hear it.

Over the last 30 years the market for the blues, both performed and recorded, has increasingly been among a stratum of educated whites. Like all music the blues fulfills important social, psychological, and expressive political functions, but these have been increasingly for a white audience. But why should the blues exert such fascination for several generations of whites? What do the blues express?

INTERPRETING THE "MEANINGS" OF THE BLUES

Charles Keil suggested that concepts of the blues, of what it means to be a Negro or black, serve as a series of almost naturally occurring "projective tests." In his view, "white liberals, black militants, and others of varying pigmentation and persuasion hear in the blues, essentially what they *want* to hear, find in the blues ethos what they expect to find."[42]

But a particular kind of content has also been invested in the blues. It speaks to, for, and about unmet needs and represents a catalyzation of the desire for a kind of freedom as yet unfulfilled, and perhaps not even fully conceived, yet one that invites participation and experience of its particular *feeling*. Contemporary audiences may appreciate the good feelings generated by the music, interpreting the music as party music. However, blues texts speak with many voices. Because of limits imposed by their own experience, most listeners may fail to appreciate the other voices present in the music—the memories that went into the music in its formative period. Appreciating the more sophisticated expressive uses of the form requires sensitization to the voices that resonate in the history of the blues—voices of the first generation of "free" blacks in the often frustrating and depressing aftermath of Emancipation. The contemporary audience must be initiated into the tradition out of which the music arises and the individual histories that the music embodies, otherwise the multivocality of the blues "message" will be only partially heard.

Richard Wright once said:

The most astonishing aspect of the blues is that, though replete with a sense of defeat and down-heartedness, they are not intrinsically pessimistic; their burden of woe and melancholy is dialectically redeemed through sheer force of sensuality, into an almost exultant affirmation of life, of love, of sex, of movement, of hope. No matter how repressive was the American environment, the Negro never lost faith in or doubted his deeply endemic capacity to live. All blues are a lusty, lyrical realism charged with a taut sensibility.[43]

No better example of what Wright was talking about exists than the "Empty Bed Blues," as sung by Bessie Smith, which combines the stark realism of the recognition of her abandonment by her lover of the night before with a succeeding verse, accompanied with the robust and bawdy trombone of Charlie Green expressing the most exultant and apparently unrepressed sexuality and extolling her lover's sexual prowess.[44] This expresses the essential dualities and expressive, sometimes disconcerting, ambiguities in the music that permit and embody both joy and sorrow, realism and expectations.

Thus Kansas City shouters Jimmy Rushing and Big Joe Turner could sing to women lines that said they were beautiful, but that they also had to die someday. Or T-Bone Walker could sing he loved his woman, but that she hurt him all the time. David Evans in *Big Road Blues* refers to these examples of *contrast* in the blues as a "basic structural principle in folk blues."[45] In Blind Willie McTell's 1927 "Death Cell Blues" one hears his lament he is charged with murder, but that he never harmed a man. Some writers have criticized traditional country blues for apparent incoherence of stanzas, failing to see that there may be an underlying "emotional association." This view has been expressed by Samuel Charters and Harry Oster.[46] The greatest of the classic blues of whatever regional or local tradition have an elusive quality in their lyrics and, musically, convey a simultaneity of feeling that may be their most significant legacy to subsequent popular music, especially rock 'n' roll.

BLUES FORM

To speak of blues form is to do so in a somewhat more expansive sense than the precise technical definition of 12 (and often 8 or 16) bars or measures of music, the blues scale, and the particular "blue notes." These are usually set as a progression of three chords through 12 bars: the tonic (I) in the first four; the subdominant (IV) in the second four bars; and the dominant (V) in the concluding four measures, repeating the progression through each chorus.

In his exposition of the essential technical elements of the blues, Arnold Shaw captures the elusive quality that fuses meaning and feeling. As he points out in his effective discussion in *Black Popular Music in America,* the scale utilized in the blues, containing a flatted third and seventh, "puts it outside the major-minor diatonic system of Western music."[47] These flatted notes are actually "bent" or partially flatted, which give the blues its sound. Perhaps most significant about this construction (and perhaps one of the factors responsible for the unique appeal of the "sound" of the blues) is the peculiar kind of "tension" generated by playing these blue notes against or over major chords.

Better than other technical discussions, Shaw points out how misleading it is to speak of the blues as *sad*-sounding music, suggesting that the moaning, or "cry," of the rural bluesmen might be mistaken for sadness, but because the three chords used are resolute major chords, there is no way the overall mood of the music itself can be considered sad.[48] Rather, the hearer senses *tension* arising from "the paradoxical or ambiguous relationship between the chords and the flatted melodies."[49] This tension musically is as characteristic of the blues as it was in the lives of those who created the music. It is here that one finds "secrets" of the meaning and appeal of the music to generations of hearers and performers, particularly in the free space within the form for exercise of the creative imagination.

In *The Poetry of the Blues* Charters pointed out how the blues became a significant *poetic* form through development of the three-line (AAB), 12-bar (four measures of music per line) form, reflecting the poetry of West Africa, which allowed the singer to set out a line, then repeat it while thinking of a rhyming line, in this way, it would appear, inciting the expectations of listeners, who are in effect "invited" to "receive" the succeeding line.[50] A call-and-response pattern, probably in the case of the blues, derivative of worksong under slavery (but originally African in origin) is thus established.

The form combines individual expressiveness and communal group context. The singer directs the song expressive of individual feelings toward the audience, who take those feelings as their own—the phenomenon of substitute imagery. As "Lil Son" Jackson once put it, "If a man sing the blues it come more or less out of himself, if you know what I mean, see. He's not askin' no one for help. And he's not really clingin' to no one. But he's expressin' how he feel."[51] The blues singer speaks *individually,* but does so toward a collective audience.

THE BLUES AS EXPRESSIVE COMMUNICATION

The blues, Ben Sidran pointed out in *Black Talk*, is a form of communication that is a "galvanization of meaning and pitch" into a single kind of vocalization that contains multiple voices.[52] It has never been, Gunther Schuller saw in *Early Jazz*, "art music." It was, and remains, in his view "an essential *mode of expression,* through which a minority could render its suffering,"[53] and, one must add, happiness. Thus one should hear the music, not as sad, but as a way of laying sadness to rest. Nor should the analyst underestimate the insight of the blues into the highly complex and varied dimensions of human suffering, together with the sheer joy and often sensual exultation, the music can provide.

The blues is a manifestation of an "oral" subculture opposing the "literary" modes of thinking characteristic of white American society. As "modes of perceptual orientation," oral and literate culture have radically different views of what constitutes "practically useful information." Thus, oral cultures employ only the spoken word and its oral derivatives, including musical representations of basic vocal styles. As Sidran puts it, "To paraphrase McLuhan, the message is the medium.'' The oral tradition encourages a greater degree of emotional, and perhaps even physical, involvement in the environment, which in turn allows for a more developed sense of community as well as a heightened collective awareness and even "collective unconsciousness."[54]

The advantages of the oral mode are manifest in the ability of groups to carry out spontaneous, even improvised, activity. In this cultural mode music is one of the most legitimate outlets for blacks—indeed, in some periods it has constituted virtually the *only* outlet. It is this concept of music as a larger cultural expression that makes it so powerful. The vocalized tone and rhythmic approach allow for nonverbal, often unconscious, communication. This African and black cultural tradition thus constitutes a negation of the entire European tradition rooted in a pattern of structure and regularity.[55]

In another context, Ernest Borneman effectively conceptualized this phenomenon in technical terms as follows: "While the whole European tradition strives for regularity—of pitch, of time, of timbre and of vibration—the African tradition strives for precisely the 'negation' of these elements."[56] In language, he suggests, "the African tradition aims at circumlocution rather than at exact definition. The direct statement is considered crude and unimaginative; the veiling of all contents in ever-changing paraphrases is considered the criterion of intelligence and personality."[57] In music, Borneman points out, "the same tendency towards obliquity and ellipsis is noticeable: no note is attacked straight; the voice or instrument always approaches it from above or below, plays around the implied pitch without ever remaining on it for any length of time, and departs from it without ever having committed itself to a single meaning."[58] Timbre is thus "veiled and paraphrased by constantly changing vibrato, tremolo, and overtone effects. The timing and accentuation finally, are not 'stated,' but 'implied' or 'suggested.' "[59]

In oral culture, Sidran suggests, music is created by the group as a whole and the individual is integrated into the society at such a basic level of experience that individuality in fact "flourishes in a group context." Rhythm plays a major role in this process; it not only creates and resolves tension but "conveys information." Whereas the literate culture stores information through writing, oral culture stores it through physical assimilation, thus itself constituting a "matrix of information." Within the music, therefore, the subject-object dichotomy is eventually transcended so that performer and listener enter into the same process. Ideas and acts are unified. The process of communication becomes the very process of building community.[60]

Within the blues one especially sees "the semantic value of intonation contouring." Hence the "blue notes," the melisma or vocal smears, the cries and moans of field hollers and gospel songs and, later, the unique sound of the great saxophonists—all carry a "nonverbal kind of information." There is a certain "galvanization of meaning and pitch" into a single vocalization. Musically, this is expressed by the unique "voice" of each instrument or vocalist culminating in development of an individualized "sound."[61]

This quality of blues, moreover, is inseparable from a specific context. If, initially, the message carried was one of resignation, there was a longing for escape, freedom, even resistance and revenge. This intonational communication was intensely emotional—more basic even than speech![62] The use of cries and the melismatic approach was "a means of bringing out the individualism in an otherwise destroyed personality." It all began when slaves, through music, expressed themselves as individuals.[63]

Herein lies part of what might be regarded as the "revolutionary" character of black music. The origination of unique cries was something beyond "mere stylization." It was the basis on which a mass of people could, together, commit themselves to action while retaining individuality. Because this action took place in the face of some of the most overt kinds of oppression, such as denial of political rights, murder, and lynching, music was a social act of great subversive power within black culture. To the extent each person was involved in the music, each was involved in a process of transformation. From this perspective, then, black music should be seen as revolutionary. This is so if only because the music retains an African perceptual and communication approach. Black music took on an oppositional or countercultural meaning as slaves created in their worksongs and then in spirituals an immense "culture of resistance" under the very eyes of their masters.[64]

The result was that in a society otherwise atomized, musical forms helped provide outlets for group action relatively free from the influence of otherwise dominant whites. The essentially revolutionary aspects of the vocalization expressed by a leader and encouraged by the responses of a chorus—the basic antiphonal pattern of almost all Afro-American music—were central to these songs, which were also significant social actions because they were actions taken *together* by black people during an era when other sorts of mass activity were outlawed. Thus, music became not simply a leisure activity but a way of life. Particularly in periods of the most oppressive forms of cultural suppression, music was a social means of physical and emotional self-affirmation.[65]

The blues has been a most significant source for subsequent black music and most white popular music over the past century. Jazz in its various forms is perhaps best seen as resulting through the merging of circus and minstrel bands with the blues tradition: "a product of a peculiarly black voice (blues) in a peculiarly white context (Western harmony)." The blues tradition, first and foremost, has been an idiom of simultaneous individual expression and social activity. It has been and remains today, through a structure that invites improvisation and spontaneity, a music of freedom.[66]

PSYCHOLOGICAL ROOTS

If it is now clear that the blues was a product of the era after Reconstruction in which blacks were formally freed from the land, it needs to be emphasized that, as noted in the previous chapter, they found themselves increasingly repressed on every side in economic terms. This situation produced a condition of growing psychological tension and thwarted personal expectations as the promise of Emancipation gave way to the harsh realities of racism and Jim Crow legislation. Out of these conditions the blues arose as an intensely personalized music. That is evident in the earliest secondary accounts from Mississippi and Texas and in the recordings of the major figures of country blues. Their songs expressed an increasingly rich and complex creative subjectivity, evidence that the free space of the music allows for the creative expression of the performer's personality and of the innate artistic powers of the most oppressed members of the society.

The music created was a response to a new kind of thwarted individuality for those who performed and heard the music.[67] Writers on the effects of slavery once tended to stress the atomization of individuals and the crushing of spirit that the system intentionally sought. However, rather than asserting the inevitability of some indelible "mark of oppression,"[68] a more powerful legacy might be "a disposition to confront the most unpromising circumstances and make the most of what there is to go on, regardless of the odds" while "finding delight in the process . . . [and] forgetting mortality at the height of ecstasy."[69] Rather than dwelling on what was done to the creators of the blues, it might be far more fruitful to consider what they did with what was done to them, to consider how they seized from their apparently limited and oppressive world the opportunities to create a music that persists through generations, remaining one of the most significant of world musics, informing and influencing much of the popular music of recent decades. There is an important *political* lesson here: Oppressed people fight with what they have and enter arenas to which they have access. In the case of black people in the United States, to engage in cultural action is rational and effective action, given the context in which they had to work.

As young black people of each generation encountered the brutal reality of a racist society, however less overt the racism was, it was a kind of shock that could have produced in many a psychic wounding of character and withdrawal, as black children found beyond a certain age they were no longer acceptable playmates; they could not drink from "whites only" water fountains; or, as Martin Luther King's young daughter found out in the mid-twentieth century, they could not visit a widely advertised amusement park simply because of the color of their skin.[70] But the predominant response has been an affirmation: the creation of a profound alternative culture of resistance. In the years since the first generation of supposedly emancipated blacks produced the blues, there have been many political and social expressions of resistance.[71] Some have moved toward radical political activism.[72] Yet black music remains perhaps the most profound and affirmative cultural embodiment of that resistance. As such, it may constitute a more enduring political response than more formally organized movements.

As an important affirmational response to psychological needs that racism sought to deny, the blues communicated expectations, desire, indignation, joy, and sensuality in a fusion of enduring power and appeal. This attribute of the blues as a form of communication lies in the fact that the blues "allow[s] some things to be sung that could not otherwise be expressed."[73] The blues is *ritualized* to a high degree, with forms and conventions that function psychologically, John F. Szwed notes, with the intention of "easing or blocking" the stress associated with what A.F.C. Wallace has termed "transformation of state."[74] Ritual events help to restore a sense of social equilibrium under conditions that produce individual psychological stress.[75] Thus comes the old notion that the blues eases the "troublin' mind." A large number of songs embody those words, the best known being Richard M. Jones' 1926 formalization of traditional materials into the blues "Trouble in Mind," which itself has since become a part of the oral folk tradition.[76]

The St. Louis bluesman Henry Townsend, interviewed by Paul Oliver, demonstrated acute insights into the psychological mechanisms involved in the appeal of the blues:

There's several types of blues—there's blues that connects *you* with personal life—I mean you can tell it to the public as a song, *in* a song. But I mean, they don't take it seriously which you are tellin' the truth about. They don't always think seriously that it's exactly *you* that you talkin' about. At the same time it could be you, more or less it *would* be you to have the feelin'. You express yourself in a song like that. Now this particular thing reach others because they have experience the same condition in life so naturally they feel that what you are saying because it happened to them. . . . Because people in general they takes the song as an explanation for *themselves*—they believe this song is expressing *their* feelings instead of the one singin' it.[77]

The blues serves a cathartic function, providing a means of psychological release through the substitute imagery, which is an important way that popular music functions to meet the needs of the mass audience.

Another psychological approach to the blues conceives the music as the return of all that society has repressed in the minds of people seeking their fullest individuality. Herein probably lies another reason for the appeal of the blues among a stratum of college-educated, but alienated, intelligentsia as well as among significant numbers of radical intellectuals who find themselves "outsiders" in American society.

Proceeding from a surrealist-psychoanalytic perspective Paul Garon, in *Blues and the Poetic Spirit*, hears the blues as a form of poetic revolt against all the repressions of society: "As a creative activity operating on a most unusual level of mental functioning, the blues is also *psychologically* and *poetically* significant." For Garon, "the blues is the musical and poetic expression of working-class black Americans, and as such it has served and continues to serve a specific function in a specific social context." He regards the blues as "the poetic voice of a people distinctively victimized by the whole gamut of the repressive forces of bourgeois/Christian civilization." In this view, the blues can play a significant role in releasing the human mind from the repressions *all* experience as humans in civilization.[78]

Garon aims to move beyond the "one dimensionality" he saw in other studies of the blues "to illuminate the thread of poetry and revolt which runs through the blues."[79] Using a critical psychoanalytic perspective, he focuses on the relation of the unconscious or "primary processes" and the "secondary processes" or more "rational" mental functions as he sees these, and the effects of psychological repression, in the music. A psychoanalytic approach, fused with critical insights from Marxist, surrealist, and even anarchist approaches, the effort is to illuminate music of some of the most consciously expressive members of an oppressed social minority who elaborated a way of "speaking their minds" that has become a world music.

The notion of repression refers basically to "that process whereby something (an idea, a memory, etc.) is rendered incapable of reaching consciousness." Political analogies lie in "various forms of punitive domination and external restraint, many of which, when institutionalized (e.g., in the family), become almost indistinguishable from their psychological counterparts."[80]

Central to this position is the "poetic act," embodying "the necessities of revolutionary fervour which, for humanity, represent indispensable ingredients of the struggle for freedom. For the surrealists, this implies a dynamic fusion between the concept of revolt and the concept of poetry." Poetry, in this view, "seeks to engage the imagination in a constant thrust towards other occluded aspects of reality."[81]

By its predilection for first-person presentation the blues is "a self-centered music, highly personalized, wherein the effects of everyday life are recounted in terms of the singer's reactions." This unique personal level of presentation in an especially vivid manner of feelings, images, and desires usually unstated may intensify the appeal of the blues to its audience.[82]

Psychological repression is contested and often overcome in blues imagery as repressed desires become openly expressed. This phenomenon of repression and the energies expended on it reveals a tremendous human potential, evident in "*fantasy* and the possibilities realized by the image."[83]

Seen in this way, many puzzling and (to some) even offensive aspects of blues expression are more easily understood. Garon's approach, while bewilderingly eclectic, becomes significantly revealing in discussion of aggression and sexuality, recognizing the common obstacle in love relationships of "the inability to confront one's own aggression, as well as one's own sexuality." He suggests that "the contradiction between love and hate exists only in the conscious mind, however, and in the unconscious the two coexist side by side and simultaneously."[84]

IMAGES PROJECTED TO OVERCOME REALITY

Sociological interpretations fail to understand the status of such "contradictory impulses in mental activity." If one interprets the blues solely as "a *sociological* statement on black life in America,'' there is a failure to account for all the contradictions in lyrical content.[85] David Evans in *Big Road Blues* refers to the principle of contrast in blues lyrics.[86] Meaning is not expressed in a linear manner. The great blues singers are ''reporters'' and perhaps the most vital sense of their reporting lies in their manner of reporting the mental processes.

Garon emphasizes strongly that it is less the oppressive social and economic conditions of black life in America than ''*the effects of these conditions on the mind*'' that are expressed in the blues. In other words, ''what the songs contain may be 'reflections' of reality, but they might also contain images projected with the purpose of *overcoming* reality.''[87]

Understood in this manner, some of the many expressions in the blues threatening violence, usually against women, might be understood from another, perhaps clinical perspective; but they are still not easy to hear. One singer sang he felt like shooting his pistol in his woman's face. Another, Big Maceo Merriweather, in his ''32–20 Blues'' (1945), related how he walked all night carrying his 32–20 pistol, looking for his woman who was out with another man. Big Joe Turner in one song (''Nobody in Mind,'' 1940) suggested he would cut his woman's head, just like he would chop a block of wood. And, most recently, Albert Collins suggested he might have to hit his woman with a brick. For all the violence expressed in such examples, they are the product of a stratum of individuals who were substantially less secure economically than the women they sang about, who had steady work as domestics, even in the depths of the Depression. The audience for the songs was in perhaps worse economic straits than the singers.

The blues might be seen as a kind of ''spontaneous intuitive critical method.''[88] Through free association and expression of some of the most passionate inner feelings, ''the imaginative possibilities'' of existence are hinted at. Nowhere is this more evident than in the treatment of sexuality and eroticism. This is the first thing that strikes many listeners about the blues. As a teen-ager first hearing records of blues shouters Jimmy Rushing and Big Joe Turner, I found lines suggesting all female bodies are similar in the dark, or explicitly asking a woman how she wants her ''rollin''' done to be stunning in their directness.[89] Writers such as Samuel Charters have extolled this quality. Charters once remarked concerning his initial attraction to the black blues tradition, ''White culture had developed . . . defensive hypocrisy toward so many elements in its life, from sexuality to more personal mores. In the black expression I found directness, an openness and an immediacy I didn't find in the white.''[90]

Garon presents a similar directness and immediacy. He suggests, ''The search for erotic love lies at the core of the blues—indeed at the core of all authentic poetry—just as sexuality lies at the core of every individual.'' To those who stress an obsessive preoccupation with sexuality in the blues (usually expressed in far more subtle terms than in contemporary rock lyrics), Garon counters with the notion that ''all *humanity* is preoccupied with sexuality, albeit most often in a repressive way; the blues singers, by establishing their art on a relatively non-repressive level, strip the 'civilized' disguise from humanity's preoccupation."[91] Here the interpretation of the erotic goes beyond the merely sexual toward the more expansive conception in Marcuse's *Eros and Civilization*.

The blues in this interpretive reading hints at "new realities of non-repressive life, dimly grasped in our current state of alienation and repression" revealed by the imaginative possibilities suggested in "the character of sexuality as it is treated in the blues."[92] Previously unimaginable dimensions of desire are thus evoked that poetically transcend existing morality. Yet the truths revealed are not simply imaginative, though the imagination revealed might be considered striking. The blues deals with the frustration of sexuality, but this frustration is paradigmatic for the whole condition of human existence. It is surely no accident that uneducated black blues singers become poetic tribunes not just of a repressed social minority but for those who feel "the dynamic interrelationship of projected gratification and actual frustration," which is "the key to the essence of the blues."[93]

Herein perhaps lies the appeal and critical power of the music and a basis of its continuing attraction to generations of educated whites: "What is possessed is not wished for—what is not possessed is wished for."[94] This capacity for fantasy, which allows the listener to come to grips with frustrations and repressed desires, creates a cultural form embodying simultaneously reflective and projective potential: "The capacity for fantasy becomes the crucial function in the ability to finally overthrow reality and the displeasures that accompany it, to unleash desire in truly non-repressive situations of gratification and joy."[95] The blues becomes, then, in these special senses, a *revolutionary* force.

THE BLUES AND THE POLITICS OF AUTHENTICITY

One appeal of the blues is in its expression of the feelings of people seeking to realize an authentic individuality in a world that seems organized either to frustrate it or appropriate that meager selfhood which people are able to achieve. For nearly 100 years the blues has existed as the expression of the individual. The music serves as a projection of the sufferings, aspirations, and thoughts of each singer. Each song becomes a direct expression of immediate experience. The poetry of the blues expresses the innermost thoughts and minute daily experiences of the singer, who gives voice to feelings, thoughts, and desires shared by an audience of countless thousands over the generations. Through the recordings of classic singers, which some in each generation rediscover, one is again reminded of that capacity of art, Marcus suggested, "which makes moments into artifacts" and "has the power to turn moments of desire into memories of that which has been abandoned . . . [and] charge social practice with regret, which can be transformed into new desire, or, alternately, cooped up in museums."[96]

This quality of the blues as the expression of unique individuality captured the minds of attentive members of a generation and was infused into rock, making the central quality of the blues the most important aspect of mass popular musical culture, at least as critics have chosen to make judgments on that phenomenon. As one-time critic (and later manager of Bruce Springsteen) Jon Landau argued, "The criterion of art in rock is the capacity of the musician to create a *personal, almost private universe* and to express it fully."[97] Indeed, Simon Frith suggests that "it was this sense of *individual creation* that first distinguished rock from other forms of mass music."[98] In fact, because the Beatles wrote their own songs, they were, like the first blues singers, free people—free from Tin Pan Alley both in ideological and economic senses. Of course, they were preceded in this by Chuck Berry, who for several years before the arrival of the Beatles wrote his own subtle but humorous and obliquely socially critical lyrics.[99] With Bob Dylan, who drew heavily on the blues, and a few others, a model of popular musical art as personal confession and the authentic expression of feeling was established, such that by the late 1960s "self-consciousness became the measure of a record's artistic status."[100] This central criterion of good rock as subjective expression comes directly from the blues.

The blues is fundamental to subsequent rock music (and a significant component of country as well as other styles). As John Lennon once put it, "The blues is a chair, not a design for a chair or a better chair. . . . It is the first chair. It is a chair for sitting on, not . . . for looking at or being appreciated. You sit on that music."[101]

NOTES

1. Charles Keil, *Urban Blues* (Chicago: University of Chicago Press, 1966), p. 152.

2. Johnny Cash, quoted by Robert Shelton, *No Direction Home: The Life and Music of Bob Dylan* (New York: Ballantine Books, 1987), p. 460.

3. Russel Ames, *The Story of American Folk Song* (New York: Grossett and Dunlap, 1955), pp. 258–59; Marshall Stearns, *The Story of Jazz* (New York: New American Library, Mentor Books, 1958), pp. 75–81; Alan Lomax, Notes to New World Records NWR 252, *Roots of the Blues* (New York: 1977).

4. Robert Bellah et al., *Habits of the Heart* (Berkeley: University of California Press, 1986).

5. Greil Marcus, "Critical Response," *Critical Studies in Mass Communication* 3 (1986), p. 80.

6. See the discussion of the role of Perry Bradford in seeking the first blues recording by a black artist in Levine, *Black Culture and Black Consciousness*, p. 224.

7. Richard Goldstein, *Goldstein's Greatest Hits* (New York: Tower Publications, 1970), p. 208.

8. See Steven Chapple and Reebee Garofalo, *Rock and Roll Is Here to Pay* (Chicago: Nelson-Hall, 1977), especially Chapter 7, "Black Roots, White Fruits."

9. Peter Guralnick, *Sweet Soul Music* (New York: Harper & Row, 1986).

10. Jerry Wexler, interviewed by Arnold Shaw, *Honkers and Shouters* (New York: Collier Books, 1978), p. 411.

11. Steven Rosen, "Popularity of the Blues Makes for a Busy Time for Festival Producers," *New York Times,* July 6, 1988, p. 22.

12. See Jeff Titon, *Early Downhome Blues: A Musical and Cultural Analysis* (Urbana: University of Illinois Press, 1977), p. 29. Also Bill C. Malone, *Southern Music—American Music* (Lexington: University Press of Kentucky, 1979), p. 42.

13. Paul Oliver, *The Story of the Blues*, (New York: Chilton Books, 1969), p. 9.

14. Ibid.

15. Ibid. p. 26.

16. Oliver, *Story of the Blues*, p. 27.

17. See Lawrence Levine's discussion of the field work of Lefcadio Hearn and others, *Black Culture and Black Consciousness* (New York: Oxford University Press, 1978), p. 301.

18. See Robert M. W. Dixon and John Godrich, *Recording the Blues* (London: Studio Vista, 1969); Dixon and Godrich, *Blues and Gospel Records, 1902–1942*, 2nd rev. ed. (London: Storyville Publications, 1986); Oliver, *Story of the Blues*, p. 6–30.

19. Charles Keil, "True Blues" (Review of Robert Palmer, *Deep Blues*, and Samuel Charters, *The Roots of the Blues*), *New York Times Book Review*, September 27, 1981, pp. 15, 22.

20. See Oliver, *Story of the Blues*; Robert Palmer, *Deep Blues* (New York: Penguin Books, 1982); David Evans, *Big Road Blues: Tradition and Creativity in the Folk Blues*, (Berkeley: University of California Press, 1982), for good discussions of the origins of the blues.

21. See Evans, *Big Road Blues*, p. 40.

22. One of the best brief accounts of the migration appears in Mike Rowe, *Chicago Breakdown* (New York: Drake Publications, 1975); reprinted as *Chicago Blues* (New York: DaCapo Press, 1981).

23. See Ross Russell's *Jazz Style in Kansas City and the Southwest* (Berkeley: University of California Press, 1973).

24. George Lipsitz in *Class and Culture in Cold War America: "A Rainbow at Midnight"* (New York: Praeger, 1981) makes the strongest and best case for the working-class origins of the blues and rock 'n' roll.

25. Charles Keil presents a useful taxonomy of 29 types of blues styles in his *Urban Blues* (Chicago: University of Chicago Press, 1966), Appendix C, "Blues Styles: An Annotated Outline," pp. 217–24.

26. Keil, *Urban Blues*, p. 222.

27. The Delta style is covered in rich detail in David Evans' *Big Road Blues*.

28. Keil, *Urban Blues*, p. 217.

29. See Pete Lowrey's informative notes to the Atlantic reissue album of Hooker's recordings, *Detroit Special*, Atlantic SD7728.

30. On Texas country blues see Paul Oliver, *Story of the Blues*, pp. 36–41, 135–138; Samuel Charters, *The Bluesmen* (New York: Oak Publications, 1967), pp. 165–210.

31. Blind Lemon Jefferson's best recordings are available on Yazoo Records 1069, *King of Country Blues*. This two-record anthology was created out of the very badly worn copies still extant of the initially poorly recorded Paramount 78s; it reproduces the vocals and guitar of Jefferson with a clarity never previously available on early LP transfers. Lipscomb has several albums on the Arhoolie label. Hopkins made hundreds of recordings, showing great consistency from his first recordings for Gold Star in 1946 (reissued on Arhoolie 2007, *Early Recordings*) through the 1970s. Blues Classics 30, *Houston's King of the Blues*, featuring early 1950s recordings is especially fine. Also

recommended is Candid 9010, *Lightnin' in New York*, done in the 1960s featuring Lightnin' on piano in addition to guitar.

32. On the Piedmont tradition see Bruce Bastin, *Cryin' for the Carolines* (London: Studio Vista, 1971). Bastin's original research continued and his findings, revised and substantially expanded, were published as *Red River Blues: The Blues Tradition in the Southeast* (Urbana: University of Illinois Press, 1986). Bastin's work contains numerous citations of relevant recordings.

33. The most important recent works on ragtime are Edward Berlin, *Ragtime: A Musical and Cultural History* (Berkeley: University of California Press, 1980) and John Edward Hasse, ed., *Ragtime: Its History, Composers and Music* (New York: Schirmer Books, 1985). Bastin's *Red River Blues* provides the best information on the influence of ragtime in the Piedmont tradition.

34. See Pete Welding's illuminating esssay on Walker's influence on all subsequent guitarists in the Blue Note double album *T-Bone Walker: Classics of Modern Blues* (BN-LA–533-H2).

35. Albert Murray, *Stomping the Blues* (New York: Vintage Books, 1982); LeRoi Jones (Amiri Baraka), *Blues People* (New York: Morrow, 1963, 1971); Ralph Ellison, *Shadow and Act* (New York: Signet Books, 1966), part 2, "Sound and the Mainstream."

36. Levine, *Black Culture and Black Consciousness*, p. 228.

37. See John Fahey's informative discussion of the recording environment experienced by Son House, Charley Patton, and others in *Charley Patton* (London: Studio Vista, 1970).

38. John Fahey, *Charley Patton*, p. 14.

39. Fahey, *Charley Patton*, p. 14. Levine, *Black Culture and Black Consciousness*, p. 228.

40. Fahey, *Charley Patton*, p. 15.

41. I am reminded of the recent "reconstruction" of the 1937 film *Lost Horizon* directed by Frank Capra. I recall seeing the film again and again sometime around 1950 in a small theatre in Lansing, Michigan. Yet in the 1987 reconstruction, parts of scenes that I remembered from my childhood seemed lost; in their place were inserted stills to fill in film lost from the once numerous prints. We do indeed live in a throw-away society.

42. Charles Keil, *Urban Blues*, p. vii.

43. Richard Wright, "Forward" to Paul Oliver, *The Meaning of the Blues* (New York: Collier Books, 1963), p. 9.

44. Bessie Smith, "Empty Bed Blues" on Columbia double album CG 30450.

45. Evans, *Big Road Blues*, p. 146.

46. Ibid.

47. Arnold Shaw, *Black Popular Music in America* (New York: Schirmer, 1986), p. 113.

48. Arnold Shaw, *Black Popular Music*, p. 114.

49. Ibid.

50. Samuel Charters, *The Poetry of the Blues* (New York: Avon Books, 1970), p. 25.

51. Lil Son Jackson, interviewed by Paul Oliver in *Conversation with the Blues* (New York: Horizon Press, 1965), p. 165.

52. Ben Sidran, *Black Talk* (New York: DaCapo Press, 1981), p. 13.

53. Gunther Schuller, *Early Jazz* (New York: Oxford University Press, 1968), p. 36. For technical discussions of blues form see Evans, *Big Road Blues*, pp. 15–105; Lawrence

O. Koch, "Harmonic Approaches to the 12-Bar Blues Form," *Annual Review of Jazz Studies* 1 (1982):59–72.

54. Sidran, *Black Talk*, pp. 2–3.

55. Ibid., pp. 3–6.

56. Ernest Borneman, "The Roots of Jazz," in *Jazz*, ed. Nat Hentoff and Albert J. McCarthy (New York: DaCapo Press, 1978), p. 17.

57. Borneman, "Roots of Jazz," p. 17.

58. Ibid.

59. Ibid.

60. Sidran, *Black Talk*, pp. 8, 11.

61. Sidran, pp. 13–14.

62. Sidran, pp. 14–16.

63. Sidran, pp. 13–14.

64. Sidran, pp. 14–16. Also see Alan Lomax's discussion of cultural resistance in worksong in his notes to the New World Records collection *Roots of the Blues* (NWR 252).

65. Sidran, *Black Talk*, pp. 16–17.

66. Ibid., p. 34.

67. See the important insights of Shaw on the psychology of the blues in *Black Popular Music in America*, pp. 106–115.

68. The reference is to the psychiatric analysis of the effects of racism on the structure of the black personality by Abraham Kardiner and L. Ovesey, *The Mark of Oppression* (New York: W. W. Norton, 1951). This formulation, which stressed the overwhelming nature of the oppression experienced, the sense of failure and impotence in a crushed and psychologically crippled people, was heavily criticized from the time of its publication. For an excellent brief critique and related critical references see Alexander Thomas and Samuel Sillen, *Racism and Psychiatry* (New York: Brunner/Mazel Publishers, 1972), pp. 45–56.

69. Albert Murray, *Stomping the Blues*, pp. 69–70.

70. See the poignant account of this incident in Stephen Oates' biography of King, *Let the Trumpet Sound* (New York: Harper & Row, 1982), p. 181–182.

71. For an overview of some of these movements, see August Meier and Elliott Rudwick, *From Plantation to Ghetto*, rev. ed. (New York: Hill and Wang, 1970).

72. An excellent study of the operation of these mechanisms is Loren S. Weinberg, "The Political Socialization of Community Activists," Ph.D. Dissertation, Department of Political Science, University of Colorado, Boulder, 1982.

73. John Szwed, "Afro-American Musical Adaptation" in *Afro-American Anthropology*, ed. N. E. Whitten and J. F. Szwed (New York: The Free Press, 1970), p. 225.

74. A. F. C. Wallace, *Religion: An Anthropological View* (New York: Random House, 1966), p. 106.

75. Szwed, "Afro-American Musical Adaptation," p. 223.

76. *The Book of the Blues* (New York: MCA Music, 1963), pp. 195–96.

77. Henry Townsend, interviewed in Paul Oliver, *Conversation with the Blues* (New York: Horizon Press, 1965), pp. 164–65.

78. Paul Garon, *Blues and the Poetic Spirit* (London: Eddison Bluesbooks, 1975), pp. 15–16. Reprinted in the United States by DaCapo Press, New York.

79. Ibid., p. 18.

80. Ibid., p. 19.

81. Ibid., pp. 20–21.

82. Ibid., p. 33.

83. Ibid., p. 66.

84. Ibid., p. 72.

85. Ibid.

86. Evans, *Big Road Blues*, p. 146.

87. Ibid.

88. Garon, *Blues and the Poetic Spirit*, p. 9.

89. Jimmy Rushing with Count Basie, "Jimmy's Blues," on Columbia LP *Count Basie Classics*, (CL 754 o.p.), partially rereleased on the Pausa label as *Basie's Best*; Big Joe Turner with Pete Johnson and His Orchestra, "Tell Me Pretty Baby," on Arhoolie R2004, *Jumpin' the Blues*.

90. Samuel Charters, "Preface" to revised edition of *The Country Blues* (New York: DaCapo Press, 1975), p. ix.

91. Garon, *Blues and the Poetic Spirit*, p. 66.

92. Ibid., p. 67.

93. Ibid., p. 67.

94. Garon, p. 67.

95. Garon, p. 67.

96. Greil Marcus, "Critical Comment," *Critical Studies in Mass Communication* 3 (1986).

97. Jon Landau, cited by Simon Frith in *Sound Effects: Youth, Leisure, and the Politics of Rock 'n' Roll* (New York: Pantheon, 1981), p. 53.

98. Frith, *Sound Effects*, p. 83.

99. Berry's socially critical vision is evident in the 1988 film *Chuck Berry: Hail, Hail, Rock and Roll*. The confrontive stance informing his music is revealed when he stands in St. Louis in the lobby of the theater to which he was denied admission as a black child and recalls how his ancestors were *sold* from the steps of the courthouse a few blocks away. A few hours later thousands of his fans would pay a lot of money to see him play in that very theater.

100. Ibid.

101. John Lennon, quoted by Greil Marcus, "The Beatles," in *The Rolling Stone Illustrated History of Rock & Roll*, ed. Jim Miller (New York: Random House, 1980), p. 177.

5

Folk Music and Its Uses

The real art of politics is to make what appears to be impossible, possible.
Pete Seeger[1]

In the 1930s the social and economic agonies of the Great Depression produced a complex process of stock taking and reevaluation of American culture in which may be discerned diverse radical, liberal, and conservative impulses. Among many, but especially radicals predisposed already to the social critiques of the Marxist left, and from those in or close to the Communist party, there was "a profound loss of faith in the American Dream and an effort by intellectuals to discover some new value system that might fill the void."[2] For many, that new value system was sought in what was naively thought to be the Soviet Union's spectacular successes in rebuilding a nation after the disasters of World War I, a civil war, and associated economic chaos. The Soviets were seen as addressing successfully a host of problems similar to those faced by the United States. These American problems, some thought, could be traced directly to an economic system based on profit. Edmund Wilson declared in 1932, "Karl Marx's predictions are in the process of coming true. . . . The money-making period of American history has definitely come to an end. Capitalism has run its course, and we shall have to look for other ideals than the ones capitalism has encouraged."[3] The United States could provide some answers, but these were to be essentially details of a postcapitalist model based on "the people."

Part of the search for a new value system involved a search for the sources and roots of a new American culture in precapitalist and anticapitalist sources. As a consequence there arose, Richard Pells notes in *Radical Visions, American*

Dreams, "an extraordinary interest in folk cultures, agrarian communities, and peasant life."[4] This search among radicals, but also among conservatives who sought reaffirmation of traditional individualistic ideals, involved intellectual pilgrimages to villages in Mexico and an emergent romantic organicism celebrating the apparent cohesive and fulfilling life of an idealized small, "folk" community, which seemed to offer something profoundly settled compared to the alienation and individualism endemic to an American society, from much contemporary evidence, disintegrating in the Great Depression. It was also a time of renewed seeking for that America that poet Walt Whitman had years before characterized as a condition to be sought, a relationship that must be endlessly lost and renewed.[5] These internal searches for the real America produced a huge literature of self-examination, most of it now forgotten. But the period especially saw the rise of an effort to "document" American life, evident in works such as James Agee and Walker Evans' *Let Us Now Praise Famous Men*, perhaps the single most effective work of this period, first commissioned in 1936.[6]

It is important to recognize the incredible complexity of motives involved in this 1930s effort to document the nation and its character that would carry over into the World War II period and a conservative reaffirmation of democracy, individualism, apple pie, and related values.[7] The New Deal policies of the Roosevelt administration and several crucial advisors to FDR encouraged and sponsored the documentary impulse to provide supporting testimony concerning the needs for administration policies. Against this background the emerging concern of intellectuals with the *music* of "the folk" should be understood. In particular among liberal and leftist political activists of the 1930s was a concern to identify and *use* the music of "the people" for progressive causes. In Joe Klein's biographical social history, *Woody Guthrie: A Life*, is a lucid account of the ideas on the political left in the 1930s concerning finding the "real" folk music, at least as it came from what many liked to talk about as "the working class." Ironically, and amusingly, when presented with the music of a representative of the real thing in the person of Aunt Molly Jackson, a genuine member of the proletariat from Kentucky who had been involved in union organizing and driven out of the state in the labor wars, and who composed and sang "I'm a Union Woman," the leftist composers who were members of the American Communist party–sponsored Pierre Degeyter Club (named after the composer of the radical anthem "La Internationale") couldn't agree that what Jackson was singing was "folk" music. Most wondered whether it had any connection with their idealized proletariat. Indeed, the ideal of a proletarian folk music was easier to stomach than the pinched and nasal tones of real worker-singers. At this early 1930s juncture, before the party sought a closer collaboration of all "progressives" as part of the Popular Front, rather ponderous choral exhortations in the style of the German leftist composer Hans Eisler were in vogue as the most appropriate and genuinely proletarian sort of music.[8]

The incident is an instructive illustration of the struggle for the definition of the meaning of the term *folk music*. The past half century has seen a continuing contest over defining folk music and control of that definition among political activists, academics, performers, and just plain "folks." In a 1950s concert recording with Pete Seeger, the bluesman Big Bill Broonzy, then in the "folk" phase of his long career, said that "all the songs I ever heard were folk songs—I never heard horses sing 'em!"[9] There may be more wisdom in that definition than might seem immediately apparent.

With the modern era has come an increasing almost romantic interest in what historian Peter Laslett called (in reference to English working-class culture) "the world we have lost." Traditional musical forms are part of that lost world, and a longing for them is a utopian impulse that is part of the psychological "quest for community."[10] Such traditional music was transmitted within a "continuous musical culture," a process that operated in its purest sense without writing or recording.[11] In this sense it may be considered a kind of natural music because it was not acquired through the same kind of formal study today undertaken with private teachers or in various schools or colleges. Thus a young singer in a traditional setting might learn a ballad in a manner similar to learning a language—through hearing it repeatedly. A young person might acquire knowledge of instrumental performance through imitation of elders without formal instruction, though as such works as David Evans' *Big Road Blues* indicate, there was a process through which such oral musical tradition was imparted.[12]

With the advent of radio as a mass entertainment medium in the 1920s, the accelerating process of erosion of oral musical traditions is usually supposed to have begun. Instead of listening to Grandma or Uncle Henry on the back porch singing the "old songs" such as "Barbara Allen,"[13] the whole family listened to Bing Crosby on the radio. But they also listened to the Grand Ol' Opry, to some degree a reflection of and directed toward the needs of a particular audience for a program based on the musical culture of rural America. Some cultural observers saw little of negative consequence in these developments because, as viewed by social psychologists Hadley Cantril and Gordon Allport, radio in 1935 provided "an imaginative sense of participation in a common activity."[14] The same people had listened to records for a generation before the radio. And their ancestors in the British Isles had before them bought "broadside" songs (cheap printed songs on single sheets of paper) from the 1600s on. By one account, an English broadside on the execution of a murderer sold 2.5 *million* copies.[15] Was this "popular" or "folk" music? Much of what has passed for folk music in North America is nothing other than the popular music of the past imported from the British Isles two centuries or more before.

The supposed erosion of regional culture in the early twentieth century was a much more complex process than normally supposed, given that phonograph records in the South were sold to meet preexisting demands of regional cultures that wanted to hear their own kinds of music.[16] Record companies found as early as 1923 that loyalty to local musical preferences led to unacceptably low levels of record sales. As a consequence, talent scouts combed the region for outstanding local musicians, who were recorded and then sold to both black and white populations in those same areas and diffused to other areas as well.

In the blues tradition are accounts, for example, of how such ostensibly "primitive" and "black" artists as the terrifying Howlin' Wolf (Chester Burnett) developed their sound. Howlin' Wolf, who came to Chicago about 1950 after becoming known for his work out of Memphis in the late 1940s, developed his distinctive, high-pitched falsetto moan not wholly as a result of the complex socialization processes attendant to transmission of "oral culture" in the Mississippi Delta region, where he was born in 1910. The processes *did* exert considerable influence on him through bluesman Charley Patton.[17] But Wolf claimed that he developed his style through his attempts at emulating the "blue yodel" he heard *on records* of the white singer Jimmie Rodgers, "the singing brakeman."[18]

This Jimmie Rodgers, not to be confused with the later Chicago bluesman Jimmy Rodgers of the 1950s Muddy Waters bands, was one of the most popular "hillbilly" recording artists of the 1920s and 1930s.[19] Indeed, he started what is today called country music. From 1927 through 1933, when he died of tuberculosis, Jimmie Rodgers dominated the music industry. He virtually created a national style of country music. His particular contribution, Norm Cohen notes in *Long Steel Rail*, consisted in "welding together the images of cowboy and railroad wanderer, the risqué classic blues lines and the sentimental ballads of Tin Pan Alley." Rodgers was also the first major country performer to use in the studio unidentified sidemen such as Louis Armstrong, thus establishing a pattern standard in popular music: He was the "star"; they were anonymous accompaniment. Rodgers was also especially significant as an ethnic cross-influence because he popularized a form of white blues music.[20] Largely through his recordings, but also through personal acquaintance, he had a host of black bluesmen among his admirers who remember him as a *blues* singer.[21] Black bluesman John Jackson corrected one interviewer who, when speaking of Rodgers, said, "You mean the 'hillbilly' singer?" Jackson responded, saying emphatically, "Jimmie Rodgers sang *blues!*"

Certainly Rodgers' career shows the incredibly complex processes of the mediation of allegedly natural and folk forms and provides but one example of ethnic cross-influence and interaction, all based on a process of essentially oral transmission, but one mediated through phonograph records and radio in addition to personal appearances.

Robert Palmer, in *Deep Blues*, and others[22] provide insight into how the once shadowy Mississippi figure of the 1930s, Robert Johnson—the "King of the Delta Blues Singers" according to his Columbia reissue albums[23]—perfected his style. Johnson, who was so influential on later Chicago bluesmen and white rockers, perfected his style through listening at length to phonograph records and incorporating elements of the styles of the likes of bottleneck wizard Kokomo Arnold and another guitarist, Scrapper Blackwell, as well as the "Devil's Son-in-Law" Peetie Wheatstraw, who were all popular recorded black artists of the

1930s whose records all far outsold those of Johnson at the time of their original issue.[24] The folk blues was a highly mediated phenomenon as soon as the phonograph developed, its transmission being not simply oral but also aural.

What, then, constitutes *authentic folk*, or country people's, or traditional regional, or "grass roots," music? What are the differences between it and what is termed popular music? Musicologist Charles Hamm defines *popular song* as something very different from folk music, the latter coming out of oral tradition.[25] The term *popular song* is applied to a piece of music that is

written for, and most often performed by, a single voice or a small group of singers, accompanied by either a single chord-playing instrument or some sort of band, ensemble or small orchestra; usually first performed and popularized in some form of secular stage entertainment, and afterward consumed (performed or listened to) in the home; composed and marketed with the goal of financial gain; designed to be performed by and listened to by persons of limited musical training and ability; and produced and disseminated in physical form—as sheet music in its early history, and in various forms of mechanical reproduction in the twentieth century.[26]

By contrast, folk music has usually been seen as something *natural*, an expressive product that records the daily life of a simpler, preindustrial, largely rural folk community. Its essential nature seems, according to all authorities, to derive from this process of oral transmission. According to one of many professional definitions adopted by the International Folk Music Conference in 1954, "Folk music is the product of a musical tradition that has been evolved through the process of oral transmission. The factors that shape the tradition are: (i) continuity which links the present . . . [to] the past; (ii) variation which springs from the creative individual or the group; and (iii) selection by the community, which determines the form or forms in which the music survives."[27]

Such distinctions probably overstate the degree of separation between folk and popular song. Tony Russell, in his engaging exploration of black-white cross-influences in the blues, *Blacks, Whites and Blues*, raised significant questions concerning the degree to which folk music grew wholly from daily existence, noting examples of use of popular ditties by supposed "folk" artists before the origination of the phonograph and the incorporation of material on record when it became available.[28] In *The Folk Songs of North America*, Alan Lomax points out, for one example of the process, how through oral circulation a composed blues such as "Trouble in Mind," written by Richard M. Jones in 1926, became part of the repertory of numerous southern folk blues singers.[29] The significant point is that the material on records was issued to be sold to a market—a preexisting demand of a "folk" community that was already there, but that demanded "nonfolk"-created cultural commodities.

Even folk music itself, as it is known today, must be considered a highly mediated phenomenon. It is affected by live performances, recordings, and radio and television broadcasts of composed so-called popular music as well as by art and sophisticated music, that is, the "higher" forms of composed, so-called classical musical culture associated with names such as Charles Ives, Aaron Copland, and Roy Harris among Americans and Beethoven, Antonin Dvořák, or Bela Bartók and Anton Kodály among Europeans, who all composed pieces ostensibly based on the folk music of their countries. Today folk music as most have heard it is performed by highly skilled, usually formally trained artists and is often written out, with regular meter and key signature. If not heard live or on live/taped radio broadcasts on public radio, folk music is heard as captured on recordings from all parts of the earth collected by professional folklorists over a period of nearly 70 years. Its collection has been governed by and is subject to a variety of theoretical and collection biases that are probably inevitable for any human phenomenon but pose problems for assessing a cultural form or product that is presented as real, genuine, natural, and an authentic product of "the people."

SOUTHERN REALITY AND THE FOLK MYTH

Common understandings of folk music derive from rural people's music of the rural Southeast of the United States (roughly the area from Virginia and Kentucky south to Alabama and west to Texas). It is often argued that this region was, for much of the twentieth century, and certainly in the century before, the closest to what might be termed a textbook conception of folk culture.[30] Folk culture reflects a situation in which culture is "relatively homogeneous and customs are shared across class and ethnic lines."[31] Although such a conception might for nostalgic reasons exercise a certain mythic appeal, it is important to be sensitive to the historical distortions it fosters.

Moreover, the emotional weight that Americans attach to conceptions of the rural folk community suggests that there are layers of meaning here that tell more about collective *emotional needs* than provide a description of any preexisting social reality. It is important to emphasize the degree to which common understandings of the rural folk community, at least as it exists in ordinary discourse, reflects the power of *myth*. It is always almost subconsciously "there" and nonproblematic. It seems almost natural, "a way of thinking so deeply embedded in our consciousness that it is invisible."[32] Perhaps there exists a need to think there was such a place or condition to remind people that they might have been other than they are. (That is also an important function of the popular image of the Native American in our culture).[33] There are, as well, potential hegemonic functions of this myth in perpetuating and legitimating the long-standing rule by white economic elites throughout the South, a rule achieved through selective application of repressive violence and widespread legal restrictions such as the poll tax.[34]

This Southeast of the mythic folk culture is a vast area of the nation, which has historically included not only big planters and ranchers but also independent small-size and medium-size farmers, and an ever-increasing percentage of sharecroppers both white and black. It is significant that this Southeast was the center of the slave system and reflects its legacy. Profound inequalities in distribution of wealth and land existed in the region before the Civil War and grew more pronounced in each decade following it. One example of the extreme inequalities, which raise questions concerning commonly expressed notions of a homogeneous folk culture, lies in the relations of agricultural production and economic status of millions of poor white and black farmers. *Both* white and black farmers experienced a rapid decline into debt peonage in the decades after the Civil War up to the eve of the Great Depression.[35] In the former Confederate states plus Kentucky the rate of tenancy grew from 37 percent in 1880 to 39.1 percent in 1890. By 1900 it reached 47.2 percent, growing to 48.6 percent in 1910. The rate of increase was even more rapid in the Deep South states of the Carolinas, Georgia, Alabama, Tennessee, Mississippi, Arkansas, Louisiana, and Texas, where tenancy rates reached 52.9 percent in 1900 and 55.1 percent in 1910.

In succeeding decades, of course, as with all of U.S. agriculture, there was a massive flight from the land. Historically, migration reaches its high points when so-called push factors are reinforced by pull factors, such as the high-paying industrial jobs available during and after World Wars I and II. As shown earlier in Table 4.1, U.S. Census figures reveal a net loss of population from the South through migration through the first half of the twentieth century.[36]

Over the period of a century the United States became the first nation in history with more college students than farmers. By the 1980s farmers even ceased to be a separate category in the U.S. Census. It is to such developments as these one must look to understand the origins of successive waves of the appeal of folk, and perhaps even more significantly, country music in the United States.

Far from an idyllic folk culture, the South was and remains an area of tremendous racial and economic conflict. In the latter part of the nineteenth century, as Lawrence Goodwyn described in *Democratic Promise: The Populist Moment in America*, these conflicts produced a powerfully stated and well-organized critique of the existing economic system and, indeed, a coherent if ill-fated pragmatic challenge to the existing structures of the U.S. party and financial system.[37] All this is evident in the statements and actions of an organization of southern origin, the National Farmers Alliance and Industrial Union. It provided the foot soldiers and organizational basis of what would later be known as populism.[38] Its organizers created major political organizations in each of the states of the Old Confederacy and in many others by the time of its first major convention in Ocala, Florida, in 1890. A product of profound social conflict, it was much more than what one observer termed "a backward look toward the Jeffersonian ethos."

The populist moment produced a profound *movement culture*. It was one, Goodwyn suggests, that demonstrated "how people of a society containing a number of democratic forms could labor in pursuit of freedom, of how people could generate their own culture of democratic aspiration in order to challenge the received culture of democratic hierarchy." Especially significant for the present study, this agrarian revolt "demonstrated how intimidated people could create for themselves the *psychological space* to dare to aspire grandly—and to dare to be autonomous in the presence of powerful new institutions of economic concentration and cultural regimentation."[39]

The great achievement of this failed episode took place in the face of a rural existence that after the demise of the movement grew increasingly tenuous in economic and social terms as rural poverty, disease, and tenancy grew not just in the South but also in the Midwest. Thus by 1935, for example, "some 49 percent of Iowa farms were tenant-operated . . . and the land so organized amounted to 60 percent of the farm acreage in the state."[40]

The achievement of populism was to articulate a profoundly simple idea: "The Populists believed they could work together to be free individually. In their institutions of self-help, Populists developed and acted upon a crucial democratic insight: to be encouraged to surmount rigid cultural inheritances and to act with autonomy and self-confidence, individual people need the psychological support of other people. The people need to 'see themselves' experimenting in new democratic forms."[41]

If there was a folk culture here, it existed in terms of an evocation of the democratic possibilities of a world forever lost before the wrenching transformations of an agricultural economy in capitalist development.[42] Indeed, the findings of modern social historians who have focused on rural life make clear that "variations in rural America make it unlikely there was *ever* anything approaching a single rural ethos or social structure."[43] Whether there was ever anywhere even a unified *regional* ethos or folk culture is open to considerable question. If, as Stuart Hall argues, culture is the struggle over meaning, then understanding the regional folk culture of the South or any area requires adequate historical understanding of what that struggle involves—the fundamental bases of conflict and the contending social forces. To them one must look for examples of musical culture. In the interest of historical accuracy and achieving an adequate understanding of the real roots of folk and country music, it is important to recognize the ultimate deceptions of a romantic metaphysics of a rural folk culture, even if grown out of nostalgic self-deception or more significant utopian longings for an alternative past that provides some relief to the pressures of the present.

The notion of the South as a folk culture also plays into the century-old hegemonic conception imposed by a coalition of southern whites that allowed the continued domination of whites over blacks and legitimized the failure of Reconstruction to alter in any positive way the situation of former slaves and crushed the populist challenge.[44] In his massive *Huey Long* T. Harry Williams pointed out that "every southern state had a tradition of government by an elite" of "planters and merchants and professional politicians" that dominated each of the states of the South between 1870 and 1900.[45] In the twentieth century new power contenders have been admitted from time to time, but profound inequalities remain.

In its music were unique aspects of this southeastern part of the United States that led to its heavy documentation on records even though the population center of the nation had shifted appreciably to the Midwest. From 1923 onward record companies began to comb the area for talent to record. Further, from 1928 under Robert Winslow Gordon, but especially from 1933 on under John and Alan Lomax, the Folk Song Archive of the Library of Congress created an additional source of documentation of the rich folk life of the area. A third factor had to do with the waves of strikes that seemingly spontaneously swept the region between 1929 and 1933. Outside reporters, leftist intellectuals, and organizers, all of whom had been attracted by the numerous labor uprisings and celebrated trials as early as the 1925 Scopes trial in Tennessee and later the Scottsboro Boys case and trials in Alabama of 1931 and 1935–37, discovered the music of the region.[46] Progressive labor organizers who went into the South or Border States in the 1930s discovered in West Virginia and in Harlan County, Kentucky, where they sought to aid in organizing the coal miners, and in the textile mills of Marion or Gastonia, North Carolina, where they sought to aid the "linthead" textile workers, a rich and vital local musical culture. Amazed by the vitality and power of local musicians and musical traditions, many sought ways of fusing the powerful local music with progressive causes. They brought back to the North stories of heroism and brutality, and examples of songs such as those of Florence Reese, composer of one of the most stirring of the great labor hymns, "Which Side Are You On?" Soon, northern Progressives found themselves hearing in person singers like Aunt Molly Jackson and Sara Ogun Gunning who had been driven out in the labor wars and established themselves in New York City and would infuse their musical culture and experience of undeniable brutalities accompanying "class struggle" in the coal fields into the life of the new radical political movements of the day.

A new music began out of this process. The cultural flowering that emerged from the fusion of radical, more formal ideology from the North with the realities of class conflict and the rural ballad-making tradition from the South produced "a group of topical songs using old melodies to set off intensely stark and militant texts. In a sense, Piedmont mill villages and Cumberland mine camps became meeting grounds for the ideologies [as diverse as those] of Andrew Jackson and Karl Marx, Abraham Lincoln and Mikhail Bakunin."[47] This curious amalgam of ideologies became evident in the new folk music that would spread across the nation, becoming a mass popular phenomenon a quarter of a century later in the 1960s (though whether its practitioners had much understanding of its roots is open to question).[48]

That there is general agreement that folk music is a product of an oral tradition has far-reaching implications for common understandings of music. A good deal of the roots of black folk expression in the area of spirituals and the blues was developed in preceding chapters. The whole tradition of black music has been conceptualized as largely oral, as opposed to literate, in its cultural origin.[49] The *immediate* nature of oral communication as opposed to the perceptual orientation of literate culture (based on print media) associated with the industrial era societies of Western Europe and North America is significant. The person from the oral culture "has a unique approach to the phenomenon of time in general" and is "forced to behave in a spontaneous manner, to act and react (instantaneous feedback) simultaneously."[50] The message itself is essentially the medium here (paraphrasing McLuhan's famous formulation).

The perceptual orientation of the oral person tends to produce an *emotional involvement* through communication acts, rather than the intellectual detachment associated with the orientation of the literate culture. The possibilities for this involvement are obviously of great significance in the creation of forms of popular culture that speak to the needs of masses of people. From the perspective of political activists who seek to "move" people to action, the music should really touch people and appear as somehow more "genuine" and "authentic." From the point of view of record companies, this quality can produce recordings that function as desirable cultural commodities to be sold in the market.

American society is and has been for several decades in transition from one kind of orality, through the stage of literacy and print media, to a society of what has been termed secondary orality.[51] During the folk music revival of the 1960s the folklorist B. A. Botkin described the transition that was occurring in folk music as one from orality to "aurality" based on the media of radio and recordings: "It is a burgeoning made possible by the mass media, and by the substitution for 'oral' transmission of the 'aural' transmission of the phonograph, radio and television."[52] This media effect, as is generally recognized, both (1) increased the size of the audience and (2) accelerated the rate of diffusion of all songs. Moreover, Botkin observed two additional significant effects on "the folksong process": first, "the tendency to substitute for the folk exchange of songs in a social situation, rote learning of songs from records, radio and television (imitations of imitations or imitations in style and text)"; second, "the compensatory desire of the singer to make a song his own by changing it to suit his taste or whim, and often for no other reason than to make it his own."[53] Often, this change was done to secure copyright and its attendant economic rewards.

In this transformation of the traditional "collective and cumulative creative folk process" there is often a confusion of conscious and unconscious alteration of material that approaches caricature of the traditional process of transformation through oral transmission. There was as well an associated acceleration in the process of creation, diffusion, and transformation of the "topical ballad." Indeed, as noted already concerning the blues, and as will be pointed out concerning rock music, it was this quality of individuality in song composition and the eventual infusion of individual authenticity into one's own compositions that became a central standard of critics of folk-rock and rock music from the late 1960s to the present.

It is the quality of emotional involvement that may explain the recurrent fascination that preindustrial, agrarian, rural or "folk" culture has generated, first for intellectuals, especially those around the Communist party seeking the "real" and "proletarian" America in music, but later for virtually anyone writing advertising copy. For several generations they have seen it as somehow more genuine, real, authentic, than the mundane, detached, even alienated existence that characterizes life in contemporary urban society. Of course, this fascination may be largely illusory when the harsh realities of existence in the idealized folk community are studied more closely as for example in Oscar Lewis' reexamination of Redfield's idealized "little community."[54] However, this probably makes little difference because the notion of the folk community has a tremendous *emotional* appeal.[55] Many Americans seem to associate the idea of the small community with a special and perhaps increasingly elusive quality of human relationship. This unfulfilled longing exerts a kind of romantic magnetism that functions in a utopian way—a kind of conservative romantic longing that harks back to an earlier and allegedly simpler and somehow better time. Although illusory, it embodies an ideal and a hope for alternative modes of existence to the alienation and atomization experienced in a society subject to increasingly rapid transformation. Positive response to imagery in country and folk music might be a subconscious response of people experiencing oppressive and unfulfilling lives while simultaneously undergoing psychological stress from the extreme rapidity of change. As such, it has important political dimensions as romantic protest and unfocused longing for alternative modes of existence.

If the good old days were not as good as they are portrayed in song, representations of them nonetheless provide at crucial times in the history of our popular culture an infusion of what passes for down-home authenticity—the real music of real people (who, of course, don't exist anymore and perhaps never did)—such as the romanticized images in TV toothpaste ads showing the corner drug store with marble countertops and the druggist who really cares about the absence of cavities in little Jimmie's teeth or the grandparents on the farm porch drinking an artificially flavored and colored lemonade mix that evokes "country" and a past "time" in its brand name. But these romantic ideals are important, for they represent a recurrent source of material used in our popular culture. Such romanticism is far from an irrationally conservative impulse. It is a theme that television advertising returns to constantly because it responds to some very basic human longings. And that is where the appeal of folk and country music enters.

The Farm Aid concerts of the 1980s continue the increasingly tenuous connection between music and the land. Yet there is a certain irony here as performers of country music increasingly find there are fewer and fewer people actually working on the land. It is almost as if the performers find there is no "country" there anymore on which to draw from for their country music, and they are desperately concerned to salvage the remnants of a way of life vanishing before corporate agriculture. Country music, for example, has become a music of truck drivers on interstate highways and has been taken up by a generation of "urban cowboys," who respond to nostalgic constructed images of an idealized world.

ORAL TRADITIONS AND FOLK MUSIC REVIVALS

While the oral tradition is usually regarded as coming out of essentially rural, preindustrial, "folk" communities, at various points over the past 100 years the tradition and the communities have mixed or impinged upon one another in two major waves of folk music revivals. The first wave began in the 1930s, though there were earlier scholarly pursuits of song and ballad hunters such as John Lomax and John Jacob Niles, and even much earlier song collectors in the nineteenth century.[56] The systematic effort to collect songs and find singers in the 1930s and continuing into the 1940s is closely associated with the efforts of "progressive" or leftist intellectuals to study working-class and rural people's music. There was a substantial movement of serious scholarship, field research involving collecting and recording, and concurrently the creation of a whole new genre of composition of union and social commentary songs that could be performed before very receptive union and leftist intellectual audiences. It was a period when the Lomaxes discovered in a Louisiana prison in 1932 that striking figure, "Leadbelly" (Huddie Ledbetter), a black songster with an incredible repertory. Arranging a pardon and securing his release in 1934, they brought him to New York to sing in striped convict clothes—for "exhibition purposes," as John Lomax liked to put it. At the same time, John Hammond, Sr., fortunately free of Depression era financial worries due to inherited wealth, was active in jazz and blues, traveling through the South and producing the Spirituals to Swing concerts in New York.[57]

Several "traditional" black artists who had moved to New York in addition to Leadbelly, such as Brownie McGee and Sonny Terry, Josh White and Big Bill Broonzy, would perform for white audiences, many of whom seem to have held a somewhat patronizing and romantic ideal of blackness that appreciated muscular black male bodies glistening with sweat almost as if they were statuary. (This was a trend that would reappear in the 1960s black reaffirmation, of which there were some excruciatingly awful examples such as the Muddy Waters album cover with a close-up photo of the performer's face and shirtless upper body covered with oil, and his holding a toad!). This kind of idealization began in the 1920s with sophisticated whites who patronized Harlem night spots like the Cotton Club, where only black artists performed and only whites could come in the front door.[58]

The black "folk" artists, along with such whites as Woody Guthrie and Cisco Houston would perform in well-enunciated tones (so the words could be heard) to sophisticated and largely left-wing audiences who were interested mainly in the lyrical content and social significance of their music. Audiences in this first period of interest in folk music were often mainly responsive to the real or imagined "ideological stance" of a singer than the quality of presentation. In one case, Leadbelly, presented by Earl Robinson at a leftist summer camp, in his first set offended some in the audience with his songs of women, drink, and knife murders but redeemed himself after Robinson explained the audience to him at the break, winning the folks over with a rousing version of "Bourgeois Blues."[59]

WOODY GUTHRIE: "SHAKESPEARE IN OVERALLS"

In the early 1940s the arrival in New York City of Woody Guthrie, a "Shakespeare in overalls" from the dust bowl of Oklahoma, amazed many progressive intellectuals searching for the authentic anticapitalist voice of the real America, who found his native populist radicalism almost too good to be true. One Communist writer, Mike Gold, had previously discoursed at length on folk and popular song, expressing the need for a "Communist Joe Hill" in his column in *The Daily Worker*.[60]

Joe Hill (born Joseph Hillstrom in Sweden in 1879) had been an itinerant laborer and an organizer for the old Industrial Workers of the World (IWW), known as "the Wobblies."[61] He wrote over 25 songs in wide use in the pre–World War I period of radical labor activism in which the IWW played the central role before succumbing to massive government and "patriotic" citizen vigilante repression during the war.[62] Hill's songs, collected in a small booklet designed to fit into a worker's pocket and popularly known as *The Little Red Songbook*, were in wide circulation.[63] Tens of thousands were printed and each new IWW member got a copy with the membership card. Guthrie had acquired a copy in his travels in the early 1930s as he became acquainted with older radicals, particularly among the hoboes and itinerant workers, who had been one of the significant social bases of IWW support.[64]

Joe Hill's career,[65] while fascinating, was secondary to the role he subsequently played as a character in novels and plays and film from the 1930s on as the preeminent labor folk hero and martyr, assuming the status of myth-hero in the radical pop culture of the 1960s. Arrested on a robbery-murder charge in Salt Lake City in 1914, Hill was tried and convicted on very questionable (largely circumstantial) evidence.[66] A major campaign to have a new trial or at least a stay of execution failed to have any impact on the Utah authorities.

Joe Hill was executed by firing squad by his own command to fire on November 19, 1915, in the face of massive international protests. Hill's exuberance and humor as a writer of popular and widely used labor songs,[67] which now sound rather quaint and very dated in their rigid class-consciousness and especially in their utopian optimism concerning the future, as do many of Guthrie's songs from 30 years later, was perhaps exceeded by the skillful manner in which he directed his own performance as a martyr. Hill was a master of melodramatic eloquence, never bending in his public statements. He is perhaps best remembered for his final words in a telegram to IWW leader Big Bill Haywood urging him not to waste time mourning but to "organize!"

Hill's canonization and elevation to mythic status, beyond the narrow subculture of old-time socialists and labor radicals who knew his story well, was aided by his appearance as a character in John Dos Passos' 1932 novel *Nineteen*

Nineteen and the wide circulation of the 1938 Alfred Hayes and Earl Robinson song "Joe Hill" with its famous line saying the singer dreamed he saw Joe Hill last night.[68] Pete Seeger has sung the song in his performances for almost half a century. Probably the song's greatest exposure came with Joan Baez's performance before half a million people at Woodstock in 1969 and subsequent recordings, establishing a link between the counterculture of the 1960s and an earlier generation of radicalism. A 1971 Swedish film directed by Bo Widerberg, though limited in circulation to art houses and campuses, effectively portrayed an accurate version of what is known of Hill's life, though it was not the pop culture artifact that the movie life of Woody Guthrie became a few years later.

Symbolizing the incredible, often naive revolutionary zeal of the anarcho-syndicalist IWW with its almost mystical faith in the innate creative ability of workers to build a new world "within the shell of the old," Joe Hill became the first and greatest radical culture hero, largely through the way he seems to have masterminded the symbolism around his own death. He became the man who "never dies" in leftist political culture because virtually all the public has ever known about him originated in his songs and the heroic myth he was able to create from his cell with the aid of thousands of leftist supporters across the country and in Europe. Sending out telegrams and letters with lines like "I have lived like an artist, and I shall die like an artist" and "I'm going to get a new trial or die trying," Hill became a figure still well known in leftist political culture around the world. Indeed, U.S. students, who know little of his life, report being asked about him in places as far away as Finland. The Hill legend has apparently become a part of worldwide leftist political cultural images concerning the suppression of native radicalism in the United States. This is understandable in terms of the theoretical functions of such images, as noted earlier.[69] Like the Mexican revolutionary Emiliano Zapata, lured into a carefully planned assassination four years after Hill's death, Hill represents an idealized, even utopian, wish-image of the kind of clear-eyed and fearless radical who never sold out his convictions or his cause, a model needed both by individual radicals and movements in struggle against the often seemingly insurmountable power of existing authorities. Because Hill's image so effectively represents and contains the hopes and anxieties of rebels against the American "Eden," he truly will be the man who "never died." Musical references have played the most significant role in the maintenance of his image.

The Arrival of Woody Guthrie

Though it took perhaps four decades for its significance to be fully evident, the arrival of Woodrow Wilson Guthrie in New York in 1940 was possibly the single most significant moment in the history of folk music and one of the pivotal moments in the growth of an oppositional popular political culture in the United States.[70] Woody Guthrie was just one of the many great individuals who collectively make up any movement of popular culture. The details of his life have become familiar to folk music buffs and scholars interested in popular folk music, or "people's music," but assumed mythic proportions in the 1960s with Bob Dylan and other singers acknowledging him as their hero, becoming a celluloid fantasy in the 1970s with Hal Ashby's 1976 film *Bound for Glory* released by United Artists and starring David Carradine as Guthrie. Loosely based on Guthrie's own autobiography of the same title, the film contained some beautiful photography but failed to say anything concerning Guthrie's Communist organizational commitments, further obscuring the popular myth and further (a more serious omission) contributing to the denial of the significance of the party in U.S. life that has become an element of the dominant political cultural consensus.

Born in Okemah, Oklahoma, on July 14, 1912, of an essentially downwardly mobile family, an itinerant ramblin' man, hobo, songwriter, and country singer in the Depression years, Woodrow Wilson Guthrie roamed across the nation absorbing the sounds and soul of a rural America economically disintegrating in the "hard times" and experiencing a massive flight of population off the land. But Woody Guthrie encountered another side of Depression-era America, one demonstrating the tough and gritty resilience of hundreds of thousands of displaced "Okies" and other poor ordinary people who fought for and maintained a measure of dignity whether on the road, in migrant workers' camps, or as new arrivals in a number of major cities—a comforting finding, affirming important elements of U.S. culture and institutions that led many to a more conservative view of what the country needed.[71] Guthrie early on, while thoroughly "American" in cultural origins, had apparently concluded traditional two-party, "free enterprise" politics did not provide the answers to the problems he had seen and lived in his journeys across the country. No more authentically native American leftist has ever existed. But his story has had to be rescued from a continuing process of mythologizing. Anyone with more than a passing interest in the social history or popular music of the United States should read Joe Klein's *Woody Guthrie: A Life*, which deals with this period with acute sensitivity and sympathy and does more than any work this writer has encountered to recapture the essence of a time whose memories have been suppressed by over four decades of cold war denial. Klein's book is, for anyone interested in popular music or oppositional political culture, quite simply one of the most instructive and informative works on twentieth-century America—a biography and a social history of an era.[72]

The United States had a vitally significant left political subculture in the 1930s and 1940s that exercised a very significant influence in popular culture, not through some sort of insidious "infiltration," as hysterical government Communist hunters and congressional investigators of the 1950s might have imagined, but because it was grounded in some of the economic and social realities that the nation has often seen fit to forget, deny, or censor. Only recently, with commercial films such as Warren Beatty's *Reds* (1981) and documentary films such as Julia Reichert's *Seeing Red* (1983) has an effort been made to begin to counteract the decades of suppression and denial of this part of our history.

It would be grossly inaccurate to identify the leftist counterculture of the half century of United States political history preceding the conformist and paranoid 1950s exclusively with the experience of those who were members of the American Communist party; nonetheless that group, Joseph Starobin pointed out in his appraisal of the party's declining years, involved "several hundred thousand Americans who gave the attempt to build a revolutionary community in a non-revolutionary situation their best years, their immense energies, and highest hopes."[73] The music of Woody Guthrie should be understood in the context of the experience of a community of men and women who in Starobin's terms by "trying to fuse the experience of a rich past and confront the urgent issues of their times, . . . built what was by far the most powerful and pervasive radical movement in American life and then helped to shatter it."[74] Their community was, Starobin suggested, a political party

which they tried to make into a fraternity of comrades, animated by the great ideal of human brotherhood and the aim of making the whole society conform to such brotherhood. It was a community that went beyond national boundaries and differences of race and creed: it was driven by the certainty that man's sojourn on earth could be happier if only . . . social relations were transformed from competition to cooperation. These Americans were sure that a universal strategy for creating a new society had been found in the experience of Russia and China.[75]

That virtually all political persuasions from left to right now recognize how shortsighted and wrong their strategy was for the United States does not detract from the fact that their hopes and immense energies powered many movements for change in the twentieth century and that many of the individuals within or close to the Communist party made important and enduring contributions to our popular culture. Woody Guthrie himself always denied any formal membership in the party and authorities are conflicting in the evidence concerning the fact, but much of his work was done for the community of people centered around that organization.[76]

Guthrie's Significance

So much has been written and said and sung about Guthrie, and so many individuals have tried to emulate what they thought his lifestyle was, that his life has become something of a myth beyond explication. Yet given the distortions of his film biography, and the naive efforts to gloss over the complexities of the history of communism in the United States, there are several things that must be reemphasized concerning his contribution to popular culture and music in the country.

Guthrie's significance, musically speaking, is that he virtually *reinvented* a traditional form, the folk ballad, transforming it into a powerful instrument of political cultural commentary. In the over 1,000 songs he wrote, he chronicled an era. Indeed, through some of those songs, such as "So Long, It's Been Good to Know Ya,'' ''Pastures of Plenty,'' and ''This Land Is Your Land'' (the latter sometimes mentioned as a new national anthem), he transcended time and place to originate new and subsequently enduring elements of a national popular political culture.

His music fuses some of the best raw materials of traditional grass roots regional musical culture with an insight and human concern for the ordinary person, the underdog, and the dispossessed that was utterly unique at the time and remains so. Such composer-singers as Bob Dylan in his 1963 album *The Times They Are A-Changin'* and Bruce Springsteen in his 1982 album *Nebraska* and in both earlier and later songs such as ''The River'' (1979) and ''Seeds'' (1985), among many, have tried to emulate Guthrie's thematic concern with the lives of ordinary people and the spirit of his identification with the nation. However, because the precise historical circumstances of disintegration of a widely shared rural life experience that provided Guthrie with his opportunities will not be repeated, the character of their contributions remains of a different kind, though still significant.

If Woody Guthrie had a kind of genius that included a devastatingly critical eye combined with a wry wit and humor that only rarely appears, he was also a product of a rural regional subculture that he clearly tried to escape but that somehow also must have engendered and nurtured these very qualities. His vivid figures of speech and turns of phrase remind me of some of the sparkling similes I heard from former in-laws during journeys through rural Missouri, a corner of Oklahoma, and Kentucky over a quarter century ago (one example of an expression that sticks in my mind: ''He was as fat as a town dog!''). Guthrie was unique, and although clearly a leftist intellectual in spite of his efforts to create a folksy identity, he assumed at times (such as his month of writing songs about the Columbia River region[77]) an almost Whitmanesque quality—he *was* grass roots America. His native folk radicalism is typified by his definition of folk music in a letter to Alan Lomax:

I think real folk stuff scares most of the boys around Washington. A folk song is what's wrong and how to fix it, or it could be whose hungry and where their mouth is, or whose out of work and where the job is or whose broke and where the money is or whose carrying a gun and where the peace is—that's folk lore and folks made it up because they seen that the politicians could find nothing to fix or nobody to feed or give a job of work. We don't aim to hurt you or scare you when we get to feeling sorta folksy and make up some folk lore, we're doing all we can to make it easy on you. I can sing all day and all night sixty days and sixty nights but of course I aint got enough wind to be in office.[78]

That Woody Guthrie and his songs continue to inspire the admiration of some of the greatest popular artists would by itself constitute sufficient judgment of his importance. From Bob Dylan, whose unique self-creation was modeled after Guthrie (and also ''Ramblin Jack'' Elliott, who himself affected an almost uncanny vocal resemblance to Guthrie over a decade before Dylan), Phil Ochs, and Tom Paxton through Bruce Springsteen (who sang "This Land Is Your Land" consistently during his 1980–81 and 1984–85 tours, introducing it as "the greatest song ever written about America"), there has been a consistently recurring recognition of Guthrie's qualities. Descriptions like "artless," "simple," "direct," and "eloquent" are frequently applied to his songs and style.[79] Woody Guthrie clearly remains a "culture hero."[80]

An additional dimension exists that might help explain the Guthrie appeal. In the images that come down to the present of his detached, rambling existence, he touches deeper sources of romantic individual longings to break free and "hit the road." His lifestyle provides a model of freedom, an alternative model of existence when the chains of civilization and the daily grind begin to chafe. Lee Hays found, working at a resort in the Adirondacks, that young people had a tremendous interest in Guthrie. One expressed what seems to be the persisting appeal: "Most kids reach a point where they really want their freedom. You had school, your parents—anything that stands in the way. All you can think about is getting *out*. You want to hitch a ride, hop a freight, go wherever you want. Woody, I guess, represents that kind of freedom for me."[81]

This myth of radical, authentic self-creation resonates within many Americans. It is a central element in the promise of American life, to the American Dream, that *here* one can become whatever one wants to be. If most find themselves eventually trapped on webs of their own devising, that prevent them from getting away, the Guthrie myth may embody that escape. Elements are evident (with a greater sense of the ambiguities and ultimate deception in the promise), in the work of Springsteen in such songs as "Born to Run" and "Thunder Road," and especially from the songs of *Darkness on the Edge of Town* (1978) onward through the album *Nebraska* (clearly inspired by Guthrie) to the powerful social criticism of "Seeds."

This first period of folk revival contained little of the microscopic examination among fans of style and technique that would emerge in the second stage of the 1950s and 1960s. Indeed, during this first stage some urban folk proponents tended to regard integral aspects of traditional style such as vocal timbre, phrasing, diction, and metrical "irregularities" as mere "embarrassing mistakes" caused by poor education.[82] That, of course, was not the case with most of those around Guthrie—professionals such as Alan Lomax, and especially Pete Seeger.

PETE SEEGER: THE FATHER OF THE FOLK REVIVAL

Of the several important talents in addition to Woody Guthrie who emerged in this period, none was more important than Pete Seeger. In many ways Seeger with his discipline and commitment to causes has been the truest and most effective facilitator of the amalgam of traditional rural culture and progressive, often Communist-associated, politics that lay at the heart of both folk revivals. A graduate of Harvard and the son of the prominent musicologist Charles Seeger, Pete represented the other side of the folk music character. He was organized and disciplined where Guthrie was often wildly and irresponsibly out of control. But in his missionary zeal in both politics and music Pete Seeger was always a person truly transformed by the music and culture in which he was immersed. In this sense he might be seen as a prefiguration of the 1960s "flower child," but one with a powerful and disciplined radical and populist consciousness. That was evident as early as 1940. In 1940 Seeger spent much of the year studying the five-string banjo. He went to Washington, D.C., to the Library of Congress, listened to recordings of the handful of players in their collection, and then sought those very individuals in the countryside of Florida, Alabama, and Tennessee, spending days on the front porches of little houses in out-of-the-way locales to learn their styles. By December of 1940 he was a rather good performer on the banjo and subsequently has probably done more than any other single individual to popularize the instrument in the folk community.[83] He also was instrumental in spreading a diversity of styles on 6- and 12-string guitar.

Seeger was the driving force behind the Almanac Singers in the 1940s. With several others he was a founder of the People's Songs organization and magazine in New York in 1946. He played a major role in the singing group the Weavers, apparently leaving when pressures of the blacklist concerning his past Communist connections threatened their growing popular success. (In the face of such pressures, the group itself disbanded in the early 1950s, reassembling in 1955 with Seeger, who left in 1958 to go solo.) Seeger persisted in his commitment to a wide range of folk music in spite of being hauled before congressional committees and threatened with prison during the anti-red paranoia of the time and repeatedly being denied bookings because of his political views and the prevailing blacklist (which, in Seeger's case it seems, persisted into the 1960s, keeping him off the popular television folk music program *Hootenanny*). In the late 1950s, through the efforts of John Hammond, Sr., he was given a contract by Columbia Records and helped fuel the folk revival of the 1960s with his numerous albums for Columbia and Folkways, writing songs such as "If I Had a Hammer" that were sung throughout the 1960s, even appearing in Spanish versions as far away as Chile, where this writer heard them sung during visits there in 1967 and 1969.

One of Seeger's most significant political acts was in helping to develop with Zilphia Horton of the Highlander Folk School in Tennessee the song "We Shall Overcome," from an old hymn brought to a 1946 strikers' meeting by two unidentified members of the tobacco workers' union. Although he has often sung the song, he has taken no composer's credit for his role in fashioning one of the most influential political anthems in history. It was in 1960 that Guy Carawan introduced the song to black students in a civil rights–organizing workshop at the Highlander School.[84]

The Highlander Folk Center in Tennessee was founded by Myles Horton before World War II and designed then as a training school for labor organizers. It was modeled after adult education and training schools developed in Denmark earlier in the century. The school's program emphasized carefully developed intensive workshops designed to train selected individuals in community-organizing techniques. It grew to focus on early civil rights workers throughout the South and served as the model for a number of Citizenship Schools first established in 1957 in Georgia through the efforts of Hosea Williams and spread throughout the South after 1960 under the coordination of Andrew Young. The song ''We Shall Overcome'' was part of the ritual and symbolism of these schools, playing an important part in sustaining the emotional commitment of those in training. As such, it grew to become the anthem of the civil rights movement. The song would not have been the song it was without, at least in part, the earlier contribution of Pete Seeger.[85]

Seeger, like the Highlander School, is one of the often hidden yet highly influential resources of American oppositional political culture. He has persistently been near the center of labor organizing in the early 1940s, in opposition to the anti-red witch hunts of the 1950s, an early civil rights activist, present in major anti–Vietnam War rallies in the 1960s and 1970s, an active environmentalist—especially involved in efforts to clean up the Hudson River valley, and an outstanding proponent of peace and antinuclear power and weapons causes up to the present.

Similarly, most people are not aware that civil rights activist Rosa Parks, who is usually understood as some sort of individualistic heroine who refused to go to the back of the bus in Montgomery, Alabama, on December 1, 1955, thus starting that city's influential bus boycott (over two years after the Baton Rouge boycott, which began in June, 1953), was a veteran movement activist who had recently undertaken training at the Highlander Folk School.[86]

Following the onset of Woody Guthrie's long-term illness and tragic physical deterioration due to the effects of a rare, genetically transmitted disease called Huntington's chorea and his hospitalization in the 1950s, up to Guthrie's death in 1967, and ever since then, Pete Seeger has been perhaps the most ardent proponent of Guthrie's music and its humane populistic political themes. Seeger has maintained throughout his career such a consistently broad kind of popular front leftism that seems absolutely open in its appeals, utterly populist and all-American, yet internationalist in its message, that one can find no trace of any kind of sectarianism some might associate with images of a long-time member of the Communist party. Seeger appeared in Julia Reichert's documentary film *Seeing Red* in 1983, openly discussing his long years as a member of the party.[87]

For over four decades Peter Seeger has followed active campus concertizing, partially because the blacklist kept him out of network radio and television. There he consistently urged students to play and sing and write their own songs about whatever was bothering them and to sing them from their hearts.

In the period since Woody Guthrie's death he has traveled, performed, and recorded with Arlo Guthrie, the only genuinely successful ''folk singer'' among the large number of children that Woody left behind.[88]

Seeger, more than perhaps any other figure in the left-leaning political folk music movement, has perfected his musical and psychological skills such that he has always seemed able to fuse art and politics in a manner that could really move an audience emotionally, whether with labor songs such as "Which Side Are You On?" or anti-Vietnam parables such as "Waist Deep in the Big Muddy" or the civil rights anthem to which he made an important contribution, "We Shall Overcome." Half a century after first hitting the road with Woody Guthrie, Pete Seeger, more than any other figure, remains consistently active and the most important folk voice embodying a vision of the possibilities of a truly political music that entertains, is emotionally uplifting, and moves people to action. His ability to use the great contribution of the critical force of the topical ballad was evident during the many years he sang during antiwar rallies in the 1960s and 1970s. Heard by this writer in an impromptu outdoor recital on the campus of Washington University in St. Louis in 1971 (he was there for one of the first Earth Day celebrations), Seeger could seemingly grab the souls of the audience with a few songs that resonated with utter conviction. There was not a trace of cynicism or manipulation in his manner, though it was clearly his intention to tell an important story, raise concern, and urge people to take action. Through a few songs pulled out of his head on the spot from a repertory of a lifetime and addressed to the environmental activists and curious onlookers standing around him, Seeger seemed able to convey the feeling that "we're all in this together, so let's get moving!" Nothing could do it like music. Nobody could make the music speak to people better than Pete Seeger. After three songs there were streams of tears running down my face. Twenty years after the event I can feel as an emotional prod each plucked note of his banjo and the power of electric inspiration that radiated from the man. More than Guthrie and more than Dylan, it has been this image of Pete Seeger that has remained an empowering presence over half a century of folk music politics.

THE SECOND STAGE OF THE FOLKSONG REVIVAL

The 1950s was a time of cultural alienation in the United States, especially among the educated.[89] It was also a time of "conformity," a concern evident in and captured by such films as *Invasion of the Body Snatchers* (1956).[90] It was, too, a time of paranoia over alleged Communist subversion. The blacklist was in effect, keeping people like Pete Seeger off television. These phenomena were all products of world and national conflicts and transformations many ordinary people did not understand (to a significant degree because of conscious government manipulation of the content of mass media[91]), conflicts and transformations that were evident only in the erosion of traditional certainties of family, politics, economics, and religion. Neither were they permitted to understand, at least through the mass media, because of a cold war "consensus" carefully nurtured by the president, Congress, and the CIA. In his influential *White Collar* (1951), C. Wright Mills spoke of a "usurpation of both freedom and rationality" by the emergent giant bureaucracies of business and government. Most educated middle-class individuals saw no plan of life, "no culture to lean upon except the contents of a mass society that . . . shaped'' and sought to manipulate them, in Mills' terms, ''to its alien ends.''[92]

Against this cultural background, with its widespread desire among a stratum of the educated (a new mass-produced college-educated intelligentsia) to withdraw from the blandishments of urban consumer culture, the second stage of the folk revival began. In the late 1950s many sought a way of expressing their dissatisfaction with the conformity and materialism of their cultural surroundings. Commercial music of the time presented the likes of Eddie Fisher and Perry Como and Doris Day as its finest expression. But things were changing. Viewers of television's *Hit Parade* were treated to the amusing struggles of the very straight singers to cover some of the emerging rock 'n' roll hits of the day. While the first wave of rock 'n' roll was generating a tremendous appeal among youth— an appeal which terrified their parents—intellectuals remained distant, not considering rock 'n' roll an art until the mid 1960s when elite music and social science intellectuals began comparing the songs of the Beatles to those of Schubert or became themselves entranced by elements of the counterculture, sometimes arriving at professional conventions in beads, bellbottoms, and peasant shirts to indicate they had ''dropped out'' of ''straight'' society. Music, of course, was an important part of their transformation. It had begun in the 1950s.

THE APPEAL AND LIMITATIONS OF JAZZ

Jazz in the 1930s and early 1940s, in the various permutations of swing, was America's popular music. But by the 1950s it had become an art form, with its panoply of mythic saints like Charlie ''Bird'' Parker embodying a tremendous mystique for significant minorities of the educated and initiated.[93] After Parker's death in 1955 ''Bird Lives!'' appeared on coffee house walls across the country. Jazz presented through clubs and recordings the possibilities of a kind of passive bohemian consumption by the alienated ''hipster''—the ''white Negro'' of Norman Mailer's memorable phrase.[94] As Mailer described hipsters as a cultural phenomenon, they represented ''a new breed of adventurers, urban adventurers who drifted out at night looking for action with a black man's code to fit their facts.'' The hipster had, Mailer suggested, ''absorbed the existentialist synapses of the Negro,'' for all practical purposes virtually becoming a ''white Negro.''[95]

But jazz could not become a vehicle through which a new educated stratum could actually participate in expressing their alienation. The major problem with jazz as a mode of self-expression for the white intelligentsia was, and remains, that although at its best it is the most intelligent and complex music there is, it is too difficult to play. Years of study are required before one can play jazz well enough to use it effectively, to develop the ''chops'' to improvise well enough to genuinely ''tell a story,'' to find one's own unique voice. The fulfillment provided by listening to jazz is not unlike that provided by watching a group of professional athletes. One watches and appreciates their genius, but from a distance. Indeed, jazz became an art form, and a difficult one to enter. Those who actually experienced it then through participation (as now) constitute an exclusive, elite group—almost a sect. The hipsters and other alienated but appreciative jazz-loving intellectuals who consumed the music couldn't play it. They were part of a reemerging avant-garde cultism that appeared on, but did not sweep, campuses; this tendency was summed up by and ran parallel to the Beat Generation poets in San Francisco and New York and a few pockets in between. It was all too intellectual, complex, and cultish, however, to achieve a mass following beyond widespread affectation of black turtlenecks, bongo drums, and a taste for espresso.

Such a path was not adequate to meet the needs of most of the emerging new intelligentsia, an often alienated, if outwardly conformist, generation of educated whites, unfamiliar with poverty in the postwar affluence, who sought something beyond the blandishments of consumer culture, something both more "genuine" and "real," something that could serve as an easy and accessible means of self-expression.[96] For many, folk music provided it. Anybody could buy an acoustic steel string guitar, learn a few chords, and begin to sing. Writing songs and fitting them to a few chords was not far beyond that. It was especially acceptable to the college-educated, if only for the romantic and nostalgic reasons already noted. Whatever the appeal, it hit the campuses, as one observer put it, "like a chinook wind coming down off the mountains."[97]

The reasons for this mass acceptance are not difficult to understand. Folk music had several things to offer: a "fresh" enthusiasm in place of a burned-out professionalism; "honest" expression of individual feelings and social issues in place of phony show-biz theatrics; and an eloquent simplicity as opposed to the complex, elegant, and intellectually demanding rigors of jazz or the shallow, if sometimes elegant, gimickry of show business. Most significantly, folk music was relatively easy to understand and to play, and it embodied highly romanticized associations of a more honest and more personable, if mythical and utopian, rural folk culture.[98]

Folk music thus provided just what significant numbers of alienated white educated youth needed at a time where there was no center, no controlling ethos, when, as Allen Ginsberg put it in "Howl," "the best minds of a generation" and many others felt that they were being destroyed as individuals—were becoming like the zombie-like aliens of *Invasion of the Body Snatchers*.[99] It would soon become a mass phenomenon, both as folk music and as transmitted into other genres through folk-rock.[100]

Through relatively apolitical, well-groomed, crew-cut groups in the late 1950s and early 1960s such as the Kingston Trio, the Limelighters, the Chad Mitchell Trio, the Tarriers, the New Christy Minstrels, the Rooftop Singers, Peter, Paul and Mary, Joan Baez (who was highly political from her teens[101]), and many others, it became clear there was a substantial market for the style. Multimillion sales of the Kingston Trio's version of "Tom Dooley" broke the market wide open for white folk in 1958, though the Weavers had reached the charts in the early 1950s with "Good Night, Irene" and Josh White, Sr., had one of the first black million-selling records, essentially a folk novelty song, with "One Meat Ball" several years earlier. Numerous folk singles and albums achieved major chart success over the next few years.

These developments, beginning in the late 1950s, created at least the possibility for millions of Americans to be indirectly linked to a radical folk-protest tradition identified with and nurtured by a minority of Communists and associated activists. Whether and to what degree they appreciated the intentions of its originators is much more difficult to gauge, though the appeal of Woody Guthrie's music and personal myth was strong on campuses across the nation. There is no doubt that in the person of one individual, Robert Zimmerman of Hibbing, Minnesota, who became the pop culture hero "Bob Dylan," the most important American popular musical figure of the 1960s, this radical tradition seemed for a time to be carried on, fused with elements of the black country blues tradition and elements of virtually every other kind of American music, first in traditional acoustic folk forms, then in a fusion of these folk forms with emerging forms featuring electric instrumentation that produced the transitional folk-rock, and then shattered and discarded it with the emergence of a new mass cultural phenomenon—rock.

Dylan's significance, his blurring of all musical genres, was overwhelming and form shattering throughout the 1960s. By 1964 his influence was so pervasive that almost single-handedly he nearly destroyed both the topical song and folk music revivals as mass popular cultural phenomena when he began to move from them with his controversial electric instrument backed appearance at the Newport Folk Festival.[102] Dylan's manager Albert Grossman and Alan Lomax, dean of progressive folk music scholars, actually got into a fistfight over it. With the initiation of this, his folk-rock period, in the albums *Another Side of Bob Dylan* (1964) and *Bringing It All Back Home* (1965) Dylan validated the trend already initiated through the striking electric adaptations of his songs by the Byrds and the smash-hit electric adaptation of such material as "House of the Rising Sun" by Eric Burdon and the Animals, which reached number 1 on British and U.S. charts in 1964. Dylan's masterpieces *Highway 61 Revisited* and *Blonde on Blonde* were the most influential U.S.-generated, full-blown "rock" albums of the 1960s, paradigmatic examples of the new form of music. (Dylan's later political significance is discussed in Chapter 9.)

The folk-rock period was of limited duration. This hybrid form in its fusion of folk song and electric instrumentation between about 1963 and 1968 (peaking about 1965) served as a transitory junction through which passed virtually every American popular musical style. In a sense folk-rock was the meeting place for a generation of young white musicians who appreciated the older styles of Guthrie and Seeger, Jimmie Rodgers, the Carter Family, Hank Williams, the Appalachian musical traditions, Doc Boggs, Doc Watson, and Bill Monroe, as well as the black country acoustic blues tradition evident in the widely active artists of the ongoing "blues revival." Older acoustic black blues artists such as Mississippi John Hurt, Son House, Furry Lewis, Elizabeth Cotten, Bukka White, and the Reverend Gary Davis were concertizing regularly, as were the younger but equally influential Chicago blues artists such as Muddy Waters, who in the early 1950s had already pioneered the more powerful urban fusion of Delta blues forms and electric instruments which would come back to the United States through the Rolling Stones. Some acoustic blues guitar masters such as Gary Davis literally gave lessons. Davis in fact taught a number of younger white artists his amazingly fleet ragtime finger-picking styles, and many young New York–area artists such as Dave Van Ronk were influenced by him. Bob Dylan and Mike Bloomfield hung around Mississippi Delta nine-string guitarist Big Joe Williams. Members of the group Canned Heat followed and performed with Mississippi Delta legend Son House; indeed, they were instrumental in his re-discovery and restarting a performing career. Guitarist John Fahey found the powerful 1930s bluesman Bukka White by sending a postcard to his old home-town of Aberdeen, Mississippi. Thus on it went as Dave Ray, Spider John Koerner, Ramblin Jack Elliott, Mike Seeger, the New Lost City Ramblers all started out modeling the styles of older black and white artists. Bob Dylan's first album, *Bob Dylan*, which was released in 1962, is evidence of a variety of debts to Woody Guthrie, Big Joe Williams, Bukka White, and the recordings of Blind Lemon Jefferson and Robert Johnson.

Besides Dylan, the groups significant in this folk-rock phase included the Byrds, who produced the greatest number of best-selling recordings, themselves a fusion of Dylan and the Beatles; the Lovin' Spoonful; the Mamas and the Papas; Donovan; Simon and Garfunkel; and the Buffalo Springfield. In addition, some of the more interesting groups included the Holy Modal Rounders, the Jim Kweskin Jug Band, and Richard and Mimi Fariña (the latter folk-singer Joan Baez's younger sister).

The early example of Guthrie and the model of Dylan, but also the example of Chuck Berry—who was one of the first to *write* his own immensely popular songs filled with subtle social commentary[103]—opened the way for numerous politically concerned topical-song writers who moved from acoustic to electrical instrumentation, thus establishing a tradition of critical commentary and personal reflection in song writing that aimed at widespread popularity. These impulses would become the central qualitative standards of rock. Some, like Phil Ochs, tried and failed to achieve commercial success. Others, such as members of Buffalo Springfield (Neil Young, Steve Stills) and Graham Nash of the Hollies, would become rock superstars in later years. Whether folk or folk-rock, Tom Paxton, Buffy St. Marie, Eric Andersen, Tim Hardin, Janis Ian, Leonard Cohen, Joni Mitchell, and others would emerge at this moment of the early and mid–1960s.

The fusion of folk forms and instruments in bands such as Buffalo Springfield, the Byrds, the Turtles, and Lovin' Spoonful paved the way for the various San Francisco bands, especially the Jefferson Airplane; the Band, formerly Dylan's electric back-up group, the Hawks; the Eagles, major stars in the 1970s; and many more. The sounds, especially the all-pervasive influence of Dylan, and the focus on powerful and thoughtful original lyrics echo a quarter century later in the 1988 explosion of urban neo-folk artists such as Tracy Chapman, Suzanne Vega, and Michelle Shocked and groups such as They Might Be Giants, the Cowboy Junkies, and Edie Brickell and the New Bohemians.

THE POLITICAL INFLUENCES IN THE SECOND FOLK REVIVAL (1958–65)

There is an exoteric and esoteric dimension to the folk revival. The songs composed and cultural organizational efforts started by Communists and other "progressives" responded to continuing desires of Americans to express needs not taken up by the two major parties. The role of Communist party intellectuals who sought to influence the direction and use of folk music in the 1940s is important, but the party was not the only leftist force. Indeed, after 1946 the party was thrown out of most unions, although unions still used songs in organizing. Organizations such as People's Songs lasted through the ill-fated 1948 Progressive party campaign of Henry Wallace, even publishing a *Wallace for President Songbook* and leaving the influential *People's Song Book* for the 1960s generation.[104] Later in the 1950s some of the same people were involved in creating the journal *Sing Out!*, which provided an outlet for their expression and an important link to the movement of the 1960s. People's Songs failed in the overwhelming cultural counterattack launched overtly by government agencies and covertly through the massive blacklisting of leftists, both designed to destroy the internal left linked to the Communist party and any other manifestation of oppositional thought. However, in creating numerous topical ballads and giving them and other songs currency, it created models for the protest songs of the 1960s, which themselves proved to be further models that endure through the present.[105]

As Jerome Rodnitzky pointed out in *Minstrels of the Dawn*,

People's Songs symbolized the faith that solidarity and communication through music could generate social action. That optimism is still the most striking difference between the earlier protest writers and today's more cynical younger artists. The close connection to the unions probably oversimplified the struggle for the older writers. Their solution was always to join ranks, sing, and bring about reform by the growing weight of numbers.[106]

At the end of the 1960s, Pete Seeger would reaffirm the optimism he and Guthrie and so many others had infused into this stream of American music. But Seeger went beyond the often-cited statements by the likes of Speaker Sam Rayburn and President Lyndon B. Johnson that politics was "the art of the possible." Rather, Seeger insisted that "the real art of politics is to make what appears to be impossible, possible."[107] Music provided the vehicle, then, to try to do just that, far more than it had in previous eras, and as it continues to do into the present.

NOTES

1. *Sing Out!* 19 (December-January 1969), p. 39. Cited by Jerome Rodnitzsky, *Minstrels of the Dawn* (Chicago: Nelson-Hall, 1976), p. 11.

2. Richard Pells, *Radical Visions and American Dreams: Culture and Social Thought in the Depression Years* (New York: Harper Torch Books, 1974), pp. 99–101.

3. Edmund Wilson, cited by William Stott, *Documentary Expression and Thirties America* (New York: Oxford University Press, 1973), p. 239.

4. Pells, *Radical Visions*, p. 101.

5. Stott, *Documentary Expression*, p. 241.

6. Pells, *Radical Visions*, pp. 246–51. Stott, *Documentary Expression*, contains an excellent analysis of the text and photographs of the Agee and Evans work, pp. 261–314.

7. See Stott's perceptive overview of "conservative" documentary reportage, *Documentary Expression*, pp. 238–57.

8. Joe Klein, *Woody Guthrie: A Life* (New York: Ballantine Books, 1982), pp. 141–50.

9. Verve/Folkways album FVS 9008, *Big Bill Broonzy and Pete Seeger in Concert*. Broonzy moved from an urbane, ragtime-influenced style in the 1920s through a small-band jazz style in the late 1930s and early 1940s with "Big Bill and His Chicago Five" featuring Memphis Slim on piano and New Orleans trumpet legend Punch Miller, among others. See Biograph album BLP-C15, *Big Bill Broonzy: 1930s Blues*.

10. My account here is heavily in debt to Larry Sandberg and Dick Weissman, authors and editors of *The Folk Music Sourcebook* (New York: Alfred A. Knopf, 1976), pp. 99–103. This is a comprehensive guide to all aspects of folk music: history, styles, recordings, and performance.

11. Sandberg and Weissman, *The Folk Music Sourcebook*, p. 99.

12. David Evans, *Big Road Blues: Tradition and Creativity in the Folk Blues* (Berkeley: University of California Press, 1982).

13. Nick Toshes in *Country* (New York: Scribners, 1985), p. 5, reports references to "Barbara Allen" in 1666. Toshes' whole book is filled with references to origins of country songs dating as far back as pre-Christian Greece. He provides other examples showing how what is commonly thought to be folk music of the South was first pop music of the British Isles a century or two before.

14. Pells, *Radical Visions*, p. 265.

15. Leslie Shepard, *The Broadside Ballad: A Study in Origins and Meaning* (London: Herbert Jenkins, 1962), cited by Norm Cohen, *Long Steel Rail: The Railroad in American Folksong* (Chicago and Urbana: University of Illinois Press, 1981), p. 36.

16. See Tony Russell, *Blacks, Whites and Blues* (London: Studio Vista, 1970), pp. 25–26; Jon Pankake, Notes to New World Records NW245 "*Oh My Little Darling*,"—*Folk Song Types*.

17. See Evans, *Big Road Blues*, and Robert Palmer, *Deep Blues* (New York: Penguin Books, 1982).

18. On Howlin' Wolf's emulation of Jimmie Rodgers see accounts in Peter Guralnick, *Feel Like Goin' Home* (New York: E. P. Dutton, 1971), p. 131; Russell, *Blacks, Whites and Blues*, p. 69. But there is no mention of this in David Evans, *Big Road Blues*. See Evans, pp. 274–76 on Wolf's falsetto.

19. For an excellent discussion of sales of recorded race and country music in the 1920s and 1930s see Cohen, *Long Steel Rail*, pp. 21–38. His Chapter 2, "America's Music: Written and Recorded," is the best discussion I have found on the recording industry in its first decades.

20. Cohen, *Long Steel Rail*, p. 30. *There is an excellent chapter on Jimmie Rodgers in Bill C. Monroe*, Country Music, U.S.A. (Austin: University of Texas Press, 1985), p. 77–92. Also see the perceptive analysis in Tony Russell, *Blacks, Whites and Blues*.

21. John Jackson, in Bruce Cook, *Listen to the Blues* (New York: Scribners, 1973), p. 63.

22. Palmer, *Deep Blues* (New York: Penguin Books, 1982), pp. 110–131; Peter Guralnick, "Searching for Robert Johnson," *Living Blues* 53 (Summer-Autumn 1982), pp. 27–41; Greil Marcus, "When You Walk into the Room—Robert Johnson: The Sound and the Fury," *Village Voice*, December 9, 1986, pp. 63–66.

23. *Robert Johnson: King of the Delta Blues Singers*, Columbia CL 1654, and *Robert Johnson: King of the Delta Blues Singers*, vol. 2, Columbia C 30034.

24. Yazoo Records has assembled an album of some of these sources Johnson utilized in fashioning his style.

25. Charles Hamm, *Yesterdays: Popular Song in America* (New York: W. W. Norton, 1983), p. xvi.

26. Hamm, *Yesterdays*, p. xvii.

27. Cited by Jon Lovell in *Black Song: The Forge and the Flame*, (New York: Paragon Books, 1986), p. 12.

28. Russell, *Blacks, Whites, and Blues*, pp. 25–26.

29. Alan Lomax, *The Folk Songs of North America* (Garden City, N.Y.: Doubleday, 1960), p. 589.

30. The notion of the South as folk culture is expressed most forcefully in Bill C. Malone's *Country Music, U.S.A.* (Austin: University of Texas Press, 1985), pp. 1–29 and 417–28. But this idealized concept, an old one in social science dating from Robert Redfield's anthropological studies of the Yucatan in the 1920s, was subjected to a telling critique in succeeding generations beginning with Oscar Lewis' *Life in a Mexican Village* (Urbana: University of Illinois Press, 1951). See especially "Critique of Redfield's Concept of Folk-Urban Continuum," pp. 432–48. To speak of a "folk" culture leaves out the other half of the continuum. More significantly, the concept carries implications of characteristics of life, "the good 'ol days," that simply did not exist in rural areas, or also existed in urban environments. In short, the qualities identified with rural life reflect an *idealized image* projected upon a region and an era rather than the realities of existence. Also see George M. Foster's classic critique, "What Is Folk Culture?" *American Anthropologist* 55 (1953): 158–71.

31. Jon Pankake, Notes to New World Records NW245, *"Oh My Little Darling"—Folk Song Types*.

32. Neil Postman, *Amusing Ourselves to Death: Public Discourse in the Age of Television* (New York: Penguin Books, 1986), p. 79.

33. I am reminded of the series of public service television spots of a sad-looking Native American (Iron Eyes Cody) shedding a tear at smoggy freeways or polluted streams.

34. On the poll tax and its effects see J. Morgan Kousser, *The Shaping of Southern Politics: The Suffrage Restriction and the Establishment of the One-Party South, 1880–1910* (New Haven: Yale University Press, 1974). On the role of repression in one locale

see Lawrence C. Goodwyn, "Populist Dreams and Negro Rights: East Texas as a Case Study," *American Historical Review* 76 (1971):1435–56. Repression of the Populists in East Texas was not unlike the repressive activities of "death squads" in Central America in the 1980s.

35. See Bruce Palmer, *"Man over Money": The Southern Populist Critique of American Capitalism* (Chapel Hill: University of North Carolina Press, 1980), p. xiv; Theodore Saloutos, *Farmer Movements in the South, 1865–1933* (Berkeley: University of California Press, 1960), p. 237.

36. U.S. Census data presented in Mike Rowe, *Chicago Breakdown* (New York, Drake Publications, 1975), p. 26.

37. Lawrence Goodwyn, *Democratic Promise: The Populist Moment in America* (New York: Oxford University Press, 1926).

38. Ibid., p. xviii.

39. Ibid., p. 542.

40. Ibid., p. 544.

41. Ibid., p. 542.

42. See the essays in Steven Hahn and Jonathan Prude, eds., *The Countryside in the Age of Capitalist Transformation* (Chapel Hill: University of North Carolina Press, 1985).

43. Ibid., "Introduction," p. 9.

44. See C. Vann Woodward, *Reunion and Reaction* (New York: Doubleday Anchor Books, 1956).

45. T. Harry Williams, *Huey Long* (New York: Alfred Knopf, 1969), pp. 182, 185.

46. See, for example, John Hammond, Sr.'s, description of traveling to the Scottsboro trial with a car full of progressives and reporters in John Hammond (with Irving Townsend), *John Hammond on Record* (New York: Ridge Press/Summit Books, 1977).

47. Archie Green, Notes to Sarah Ogun Gunning, *Girl of Constant Sorrow*, Folk-Legacy Records FSA–26. Cited by Monroe, *Country Music, U.S.A.*, p. 129. Monroe's discussion of the meeting of North and South in the labor struggles of this period was particularly helpful in formulating my ideas. The intensity of the conflicts would seem to contradict his broad contention that the region constituted a homogeneous rural folk culture.

48. Archie Green in *Only a Miner: Studies in Recorded Coal-Mining Songs* (Urbana: University of Illinois Press, 1972), pp. 195–238, notes the evolution, for example, of "Buddy Won't You Roll on down the Line" from a ballad of economic protest by Uncle Dave Macon through several transformations until it appeared on a Kingston Trio album with no contextual information, explanatory notes, or spoken introduction.

49. Ben Sidran, *Black Talk* (New York: DaCapo Press, 1981).

50. Ibid., p. 3.

51. See the discussion of the transition from primary to secondary orality in Meyrowitz, *No Sense of Place: The Impact of Electronic Media on Social Behavior* (New York: Oxford University Press, 1985), pp. 17ff.

52. B. A. Botkin, "The Folksong Revival: Cult or Culture?" in *The American Folk Scene: Dimensions of the Folksong Revival*, ed. D. A. DeTurk and A. Poulin, Jr. (New York: Dell Publishing, Laurel Editions, 1967), p. 96.

53. Ibid.

54. Oscar Lewis, *Life in a Mexican Village* (Urbana: University of Illinois, 1951). One of the best discussions of the controversy in historical context is Chapter 2 of Thomas Bender, *Community and Social Change in America* (New Brunswick, N.J.: Rutgers

University Press, 1978). An excellent overview of the issues is also provided in Horace Miner's article on "community-science continua" in D. Sills, ed., *The International Encyclopedia of the Social Sciences*, vol. 3 (New York: The Macmillan Company and the Free Press, 1968), pp. 174–180.

55. See Bender's acute insight into this emotional appeal in *Community and Social Change in America*, p. 6: "Americans seem to have something else in mind when they wistfully recall or assume a past made up of small-town communities. This social memory has a geographic referent, the town, but it is clear from the many layers of emotional meaning attached to the word *community* that the concept means more than a place or local activity. There is an expectation of a special quality of human relationship."

56. The concern with folk music goes back many centuries and is linked with the pastoral ideal. See Ralph Rinzler, "Roots of the Folk Revival," in *The Folk Music Sourcebook*, ed. L. Sandberg and D. Weissman, pp. 114–16.

57. See Hammond's fascinating memoir of the period, *John Hammond On Record*.

58. Chris Albertson, *Bessie* (New York: Stein & Day, 1974), pp. 138ff, presents an interesting account of Carl Van Vecten's fascination with blacks and black artists.

59. Klein, *Woody Guthrie: A Life*, pp. 148–49.

60. See ibid., p. 145, on Mike Gold; more generally, see Richard A. Reuss, "The Roots of American Left-Wing Interest in Folksong," *Labor History* 17 (1971):259–79.

61. The major historical treatment of the IWW is Melvyn Dubovsky, *We Shall Be All: A History of the Industrial Workers of the World* (Chicago: Quadrangle Books, 1969).

62. On the repression against the IWW see the good brief account in Wayne Hampton's *Guerilla Minstrels*, (Knoxville: University of Tennessee Press, 1986), pp. 83–85. Also, Dubovsky, *We Shall Be All*. More generally concerning repression of radicalism as a recurrent phenomenon see Alan Wolfe's provocative work, *The Seamy Side of Democracy: Repression in America*, 2nd ed. (New York and London: Longman, 1978).

63. Richard Brazier, "The Story of the IWW's 'Little Red Songbook,' " *Labor History* 9 (Winter 1968):91–105.

64. See the account of Hill's influence on Guthrie in Klein, *Woody Guthrie*, pp. 82–85.

65. Hill's career is profiled briefly and concisely in Hampton, *Guerilla Minstrels*, pp. 60–92, under the chapter title "Joe Hill: The Man Who Never Died."

66. A good overview of the evidence in the case was presented by historian Philip S. Foner, *The Case of Joe Hill* (New York: International Publishers, 1965). Novelist Wallace Stegner, who wrote a novel on Hill, *The Preacher and the Slave* (Boston: Houghton Mifflin, 1950), was convinced of his guilt. See Wallace Stegner, "Joe Hill: The Wobblies' Troubadour," *New Republic*, January 5, 1948, pp. 20–24, and the reply by IWW veteran Fred Thompson in a *New Republic* letter of February 9, 1948. A longer IWW view was in the November 15, 1948, *New Republic*.

67. Two good albums of "Joe Hill" and other IWW songs are Utah Phillips, *We Have Fed You All a Thousand Years*, Philo Records 1076 (distributed by Rounder Records), and Joe Glazer, *Songs of the Wobblies*, Collector Records 1927 (P.O. Box 1143, Columbia, MD 21044).

68. Complete lyrics and music to "Joe Hill" appeared in *The People's Song Book* (New York: Oak Publications, 1948; and many subsequent editions).

69. Especially in Fredric Jameson, "Reification and Utopia in Mass Culture," *Social Text*, I, 1979.

70. There is no better introduction to the spirit of the time than Klein's chapter "American Spirit" in *Woody Guthrie*.

71. See the numerous essentially conservative, affirmative reactions discussed by Stott, *Documentary Expression*, pp. 238–57.

72. Klein's *Woody Guthrie* was discussed repeatedly by Bruce Springsteen during his 1980–81 tour as part of his introduction to singing "This Land Is Your Land." Hear the introduction to the performance on *Bruce Springsteen and the E-Street Band Live, 1975–85*, Columbia Records.

73. Joseph Starobin, *American Communism in Crisis, 1943–1957* (Cambridge, Mass.: Harvard University Press, 1972), p. ix.

74. Ibid.

75. Ibid.

76. On Guthrie's associations with the party see Klein, *Woody Guthrie*, pp. 156–57; Hampton, *Guerilla Minstrels*, p. 95, cites as evidence of formal membership a *Broadside* magazine statement of Gordon Friesen, who knew Guthrie well: "When I knew him he was a full-fledged member of the village branch of the Communist Cultural Section, and proud of it."

77. Klein, *Woody Guthrie*, p. 195.

78. Cited by ibid., p. 168–69.

79. See the extensive list of bibliographical material in Hampton's *Guerilla Minstrels* and the bibliographical notes in Klein, *Woody Guthrie*, pp. 451–57.

80. Much of his recorded work has been reissued in compact disc format, and a new celebration of his and Leadbelly's songs, *A Vision Shared*, was issued by CBS in 1988 featuring contributions by Dylan, Springsteen, U2, Taj Mahal, Arlo Guthrie, and others.

Two interesting works on folk-protest music utilize the concept of culture hero: Jerome L. Rodnitzky, *Minstrels of the Dawn* (Chicago: Nelson-Hall, 1976), and Hampton, *Guerilla Minstrels*. Hampton's work is the more substantial of the two in terms of the depth of inquiry into similar subject matter and individuals (Joe Hill, Woody Guthrie, Bob Dylan, John Lennon) but, curiously, fails even to mention the Rodnitzsky work, which is certainly worth examination and would seem to be the source of the conception.

81. Klein, *Woody Guthrie*, p. 421.

82. Sandberg and Weissman, *The Folk Music Source Book*, p. 100.

83. Klein, *Woody Guthrie*, pp. 183–87.

84. On the origins of "We Shall Overcome," see Frank Adams, *Unearthing Seeds of Fire: The Idea of Highlander* (Winston-Salem, N.C.: John F. Blair, 1975), pp. 75–76, 154–55.

85. This perhaps explains some of the gripping, indeed overwhelmingly moving qualities of Seeger's performance of the song on his Columbia *Town Hall Concert* album and on *Pete Seeger's Greatest Hits*, available on Columbia records and compact discs.

86. See Aldon Morris, *The Origins of the Civil Rights Movement* (New York: The Free Press, 1984) on Rosa Parks, the Highlander Folk School, and other movement halfway houses. See also C. Alvin Hughes, "A New Agenda for the South: The Role and Influence of the Highlander Folk School, 1953–1961," *Phylon* vol. 46, no. 3 (September 1985):242–50; Frank Adams (with Myles Horton), *Unearthing Seeds of Fire: The Idea of Highlander* (Winston-Salem, N.C.: John F. Blair, 1975); John M. Glen, "The Highlander Folk School: Fostering Individual Growth and Social Change," *Chronicle of Higher Education*. June 15, 1988, p. B5; John M. Glen, *Highlander: No Ordinary School* (Lexington: University Press of Kentucky, 1988).

87. David King Dunaway has written the major biography of Seeger, *How Can I Keep from Singing: Pete Seeger* (New York: McGraw-Hill, 1981).

88. Pete Seeger and Arlo Guthrie, *Pete Seeger and Arlo Guthrie: Together in Concert* (1975), Warner Bros. Reprise Records 1198, and *Precious Friend* (1982), Warner Bros. 2BSK 3644. Arlo's younger brother Joady recorded an album in 1985 produced by Country Joe MacDonald entitled *Spys on Wall Street*, Rag Baby Records 1027 (P.O. Box 3316, San Francisco, CA 94119).

89. One of the best accounts of the emergence of 1960s sensibility from the "cold war blues" of the 1950s is Morris Dickstein, *Gates of Eden: American Culture in the 60's* (New York: Basic Books, 1977), pp. 3–88. Also especially relevant is Kenneth Kenniston, *The Uncommitted* (New York: Harcourt Brace, 1960; reprinted in expanded version by Dell, 1970).

90. See Stuart Samuels' revelatory essay on *Invasion of the Body Snatchers*, "The Age of Conspiracy and Conformity," in *American History/American Film: Interpreting the Hollywood Image*, ed. J. O'Connor and M. A. Jackson (New York: Frederick Ungar, 1980), pp. 203–218.

91. The 1989 PBS series *Secret Government* on the CIA's role in American foreign and domestic policies revealed once again the extent of systematic U.S. government manipulation of public images of Italy in 1948, Iran, Guatemala, Cuba, and other areas, through the Reagan-Bush administration construction of false images of the Sandinistas and contras in Nicaragua in the 1980s.

92. C. Wright Mills, *White Collar* (New York: Oxford University Press, 1951), p. xvi.

93. On Parker's life and times see Ross Russell's *Bird Lives!* (London: Quartet Books, 1976). It is one of the best jazz biographies and a fine social history of jazz from 1935 through Parker's death in 1955.

94. Norman Mailer, "The White Negro: Superficial Reflections on the Hipster,"[1957] in *Advertisements for Myself* (New York: G. P. Putnam's Sons, 1959).

95. Ibid.

96. Sandberg and Weissman, *The Folk Music Source Book*, p. 101.

97. Ibid.

98. Ibid.

99. Samuels, "Age of Conspiracy and Conformity."

100. A good brief, though occasionally snide, survey of the folk-rock movement can be found in Paul Nelson's "Folk Rock," in *Rolling Stone Illustrated History of Rock 'n' Roll*, ed. J. Miller (New York: Random House, 1980), pp. 231–34.

101. See her revealing autobiography *And a Voice to Sing With* (New York: Dell Books, 1988).

102. Nelson, "Folk Rock," p. 233.

103. See Keith Richards' and Eric Clapton's insights into Berry's genius in the 1987 film *Chuck Berry: Hail, Hail, Rock 'n' Roll*.

104. Rodnitzky, *Minstrels of the Dawn*, p. 9.

105. Ibid., p. 11.

106. *Sing Out!* 19 (December–January 1969), p. 39, cited by Rodnitzky, *Minstrels of the Dawn*, p. 11.

107. Rodnitzky, *Minstrels of the Dawn*, p. 11.

6

Rock 'n' Roll: Sexuality and Expressive Rebellion

In a society fueled by imposed discipline, pleasure is subversive.

Stanley Aronowitz[1]

Although the United States of the 1950s was in many ways a repressive and conformist society, a good deal more was going on beneath the surface. National bewilderment at a world of increasingly rapid change that began immediately after World War II led to a national tendency to reaffirm old but eroding verities and see external enemies as the cause of change. This national consensus was not exactly a natural development, however. A genial, golf-playing old general presided as president over a nation involved in what was actually a highly manipulated and carefully contrived political cultural consensus on the part of national elites at the highest levels of government. Termed by critical sociologist C. Wright Mills in 1955 "the American Celebration,"[2] this false consensus masked a number of social conflicts.

Significant criticism of and certainly more organized movements to alter this "consensus" were viewed with fear or grave suspicion on the part of monitoring elites in government and allied private organizations that contrived an elaborate blacklist affecting the employment possibilities of tens of thousands of individuals. The blacklist functioned in several areas of popular culture. Foreign relations were dominated by the repressive measures of the cold war era and the Truman Doctrine (actually beginning in 1947). Domestically, Senator Joseph McCarthy and a legion of other Communist-hunters, including Representative (later Senator) Richard M. Nixon and others, pursued and pilloried a generation of those who had earlier, in the Depression years, associated with leftist organizations now far outside the emerging and carefully prepared hegemony of the cold war.

Socially, this consensus masked multiple layers of repression. When Betty Freidan published the *Feminine Mystique* in 1963, she peeled back a scab to reveal the psychological prison life had been for women of preceding decades. Victims of "the problem that has no name," women sought something more than a shine on the floor; they got instead tranquilizers, the adult drug of choice for the 1950s.[3] Women had no real voice beyond their newly reinforced containment as housewives after the brief moment of nationally encouraged World War II labor-force participation.[4] Where were women's voices in the 1950s?

Literary culture experienced the Beat Generation. Allen Ginsberg's poem "Howl" (1956) expressed the rage of an alternative America, a visionary intelligentsia with a sense that its best minds were being destroyed.[5] In addition, the music world saw careers come to an untimely end in the deaths of revolutionary musical geniuses such as jazzmen Charlie "Yardbird" Parker at 35 (in 1955) and Parker's idol, Lester Young, at 49 (in 1959) and Billie Holiday, the quintessential jazz vocalist and perhaps the single most significant woman in formulating a jazz discourse, who passed on at 44 (in 1959). Each performer had shown another side of life in what I. F. Stone called the "Haunted Fifties."[6] Together they represented its underside, the black bohemian world of life after dark. Although each was heavily involved in drugs or alcohol, all have remained for decades models of cultural opposition celebrated in later popular films— Holiday in the 1972 *Lady Sings the Blues*, Young in the 1986 *'Round Midnight*, and Parker in Clint Eastwood's *Bird* (1988).

While it is true that comfort and conformity in all its forms were, at one level, celebrated during the 1950s, it was also a decade of an immense amount of social analysis and criticism. Sociologists particularly produced classic works such as David Reisman's *The Lonely Crowd*, William F. Whyte's *The Organization Man*, and C. Wright Mills' *White Collar*. These helped contribute elements of a counterportrait of American life—a smug, often stultifying social conformity and a national and corporate-bureaucratic ethos that fundamentally repressed classical liberalism's allegedly central value of individualism. Such studies contributed to the realization among a minority of social observers that the underlying value system in the United States in many ways attempted to exercise control as effectively total as the "totalitarian systems" located "behind the iron curtain," though the means used were more subtle.

In reality an immense amount of criticism and conflict existed underneath the celebratory exterior. In domestic politics there had already emerged a civil rights movement that showed how the black minority could pursue a disciplined march against segregation—through the courts, eventually to achieve the 1954 *Brown v. Board of Education* victory that began the desegregation of public schools, and at the same time through organized demonstrations such as the Baton Rouge bus boycott of 1953 and the Montgomery bus boycott, which Aldon Morris described as the "watershed of the modern civil rights movement."[7] Although the Montgomery boycott started when Rosa Parks refused to give up her seat to a white passenger as segregation regulations required, Mrs. Parks' action was actually well-planned in advance. It had grown out of her membership in the National Association for the Advancement of Colored People (NAACP) and her experience at the Highlander Folk School in Tennessee.[8] As noted earlier, well before the Supreme Court's decision in *Brown v. Board of Education* the Highlander School launched a series of workshops designed for both black and white community leaders and students centering on desegregation of public schools and eventually growing to deal with the full range of community integration. The point being that this is one of several areas in which the upheavals of the 1960s actually began in the allegedly conformist 1950s or out of movements that had existed in the 1940s. The same pattern existed in music, as will become clear.

At the level of mass popular culture, however, perhaps because of puzzling social transformations and external threats inadequately explained to the mass public, perhaps because of the accumulating residue of psychic numbing produced by the nuclear balance of terror, an underlying fear, even paranoia, seemed to lurk in the minds of Americans. It was evident particularly in popular film culture,* where a variety of extraterrestrial or otherwise alien creatures haunted the screen from *The Thing* and *The Day the Earth Stood Still* (1951), to *Invaders from Mars* and *It Came from Outer Space* (1953), to perhaps the best of the genre, *Invasion of the Body Snatchers* (1956).

The latter film presented a striking portrait of a small California town in which people are taken over by identical replicas of themselves hatched from gigantic pods. The most terrifying and persistently arresting quality of the film is perhaps the manner in which it effectively plays simultaneously into the anti-Communist hysteria of the time and the growing cultural recognition of the nature and effects of the oppressive social conformity characterizing the era. Traditional values become grotesquely perverted, nothing is as it seems, and the central character, a small-town physician, Dr. Miles Bennell (played by Kevin McCarthy), survives only through desperate efforts to affirm his individuality and sanity (in contrast to the remake 20 years later in which the audience is left with no hope at all).[9] If, as the official story would have it, the national psyche justifiably feared the changes to the American way of life posed by the "threat of communism" externally and internally, and by "juvenile delinquency" domestically, what was widely extolled was a comfortable conformity on the order of that preferred by 1940s radio stars Ozzie and Harriet, who began a family situation TV show in the 1950s that would last until 1966. Even the Nelsons would find their quiet,

---

*Popular films have always to some degree been significant sources of data on popular perceptions, both as reflective of astute market sensibilities of the film industry (reinforced in later years by sophisticated audience preference and market research) and as exercising an influence on consciousness by providing substitute imagery reinforcing images and stereotypes. Before television became universal films were widely viewed; they thus constitute indicators of images widely held by the public.

complacent suburban existence interrupted by a strange invader—rock 'n' roll. Their son Ricky (1940–85), who joined his parents on their TV show in 1952, would discover the music and try singing when a girlfriend told him she was in love with Elvis Presley. In 1957 he appeared on the TV show, soon becoming Rick Nelson, teenage heartthrob, with a major chart success, a (number 2 in the *Billboard* charts) cover of Fats Domino's "I'm Walkin." What happened? How did an apparently brainwashed, conformist surburban kid end up singing a song by a black man from Louisiana?

What happened in American popular culture appeared to be a virtual revolution in popular music, though it was less that and more a shift in the music's social basis. It was probably synergistic with and reflecting far-reaching transformations in a society in which it had become increasingly difficult to contain some of the basic impulses previously seen as requiring repression (as Freud had argued) for civilization to survive, particularly the overt expression of sexual needs.

Perhaps in part a product of the wave of post–World War II births, part a result of the increasing communication revolution, some major transformations were underway in an era that national elites had dedicated to "containment." Particularly significant was the emergence in popular films of themes of cultural rebellion and the phenomenon of youth resistance, popularly known as juvenile delinquency.

In popular films nobody (at least in retrospect) can ignore *The Wild One* (1954) with Marlon Brando as the quintessential biker-hood. *The Blackboard Jungle* (1955) featured Bill Haley and the Comets' "Rock around the Clock" played over the opening credits to a storyline that contained the powerful image of teenage students breaking a teacher's copies of 78 rpm records from the 1920s and 1930s by Bix Biederbecke and others. Nicholas Ray's *Rebel without a Cause* (1955), starring the ill-fated trio of James Dean, Natalie Wood, and Sal Mineo, was a third film that helped raise the question of youth rebellion to the level of public discourse. With this development emerged the possibility of identifying with the alienated and/or rebellious youth who found themselves in a world they did not make nor in any way approve.

Each of these films in different ways overtly spoke to the adult fear of the juvenile delinquency of the time (often mild by end-of-the-1980s standards of gun-packing teenage junkies and crack gangs). Their characters, which the producers must have seen as repugnant or at best ambiguous, became culture heroes, even pop icons, to portions of the audience.* Here was one of the first indications

---

*Brando had appeared in Elia Kazan's 1952 film *Viva Zapata!* The film was a life of the martyred Mexican revolutionary leader designed as a vehicle to present a cold war and anti-Stalinist view of a reluctant revolutionary to a conservative U.S. society and at the same time provide a "responsible" correction to leftist tendencies in Hollywood films seen by Washington witchhunters. The irony is that the film and the image of the rebel Zapata, while not quite catching on in the early 1950s, would become a cult classic in revival houses and on television during the 1960s, giving a new generation a portrait of an incorruptible revolutionary with which to identify. The film prefigured, though the public response did not, the process of identification at work with the three films on

of the modern phenomenon of popular culture as contested terrain. The "meaning" of the films became what audiences *made* of them.

The producers of these films anticipated by years the enormous wave of theorizing about youth culture of the late 1960s. They sought to play off adult fears of loss of control over their children, portraying for an "adult" audience the emergence of a stratum of rebellious youth (this was before that youth stratum became the predominant consumers of film as popular culture). But the effect was much more complicated. Although in the films there was even some effort to suggest there might be better ways of dealing with or responding to the "problems" of youth, the most significant function of such films was, ironically, to provide youth an enduring cultural model of alienation and personal anguish of the sensitive "outsider" in Dean, whose immortality as pop icon was assured by his death in a high-speed car accident just before the film's release. Brando, perhaps because of his greater age (29) and posture of more overt, even nihilistic rebellion (when asked in *The Wild One* what he was rebelling against, he shrugged and said, "What have you got?"), was more difficult for large numbers to identify with. Nonetheless, his and Dean's characters provided the raw materials to fashion a new youth subculture of resistance to existing authorities.

This mass response to youth subjects was only one kind of movement, although culturally highly significant, given the greater sensitivity and responsivity of the film industry to shifting cultural tastes compared to the stodgy attitudes of ASCAP and the major record companies (or the attitudes of national power elites generally!).[10]

The other movement was in popular music. The story of the emergence of rock 'n' roll has often been told, many times and in many ways.[11] But its rootedness in and direct connection to black rhythm and blues is unquestionable.[12] And it *was* an important series of events, though which ones are most crucial is not clear, and probably best understood as a complex matter of multicausality and polygenesis. But its meanings, effects, and uses are perhaps more significant to consider than the causes because they may tell more concerning the underlying social and psychological demands to which the music responded, providing a "negotiated" kind of response—high energy music with some erotic power— to a more fundamental hunger for social transformation.[13]

Although Elvis Presley and the Sun Records synthesis of country and rhythm and blues is usually seen as something radically new, a virtual "reinvention" of form, with white artists translating black music to the white youth audience, earlier crossovers had actually been accomplished by black artists years before. The first great crossover artists were the powerfully propulsive "boogie-woogie" pianists such as Albert Ammons, Meade "Lux" Lewis, and Pete Johnson with his partner, blues shouter Big Joe Turner, all of whom provided an energizing

youth that followed *Viva Zapata!* See Paul J. Underwood, "An American Cold Warrior: *Viva Zapata!* (1952)," in *American History/American Film*, ed. J. E. O'Connor and M. A. Jackson (New York: Frederick Ungar, 1979), pp. 183–202.

music of compelling vitality linked to the blues. All became widely heard by white audiences in the boogie-woogie craze that swept the nation in the period 1938–42. They began appearing to tremendous acclaim in New York in 1938, first at Carnegie Hall concerts produced by John Hammond and later at such clubs as Cafe Society and the Famous Door.

Boogie-woogie, basically a fast blues, eight beats to the measure, may have originated as a bass-range guitar derivative.[14] It began in the earliest years of the century, according to the testimony of such musicians as songster and folk-bluesman Huddie "Leadbelly" Ledbetter (d.1949) and jazz pianist-composer Ferdinand "Jelly Roll" Morton (1885–1941), who liked to claim, "I invented jazz." Texas bluesman Aaron "T-Bone" Walker (1909–75) said, "The first time I ever heard a boogie-woogie piano was the first time I went to church. That was the Holy Ghost Church in Dallas. That boogie-woogie was a kind of blues."[15]

The form incubated and developed in various versions through the first three decades of the century, making its way onto records in the 1920s with such exponents as the ill-fated pianist Clarence "Pinetop" Smith, who met an early demise from a stray bullet fired in a barroom brawl.[16] A few generations of other pianists contributed to related piano blues styles before boogie-woogie burst on the scene on the eve of World War II.[17]

Throughout the swing era of the 1930s and 1940s those aware of trends in the music were aware of the tremendous energies the great all-black orchestras could generate for dancers in such places as Harlem's Savoy Ballroom and even earlier for the white audiences at the Cotton Club in Harlem (the arrangements of such orchestras as Duke Ellington's were so exciting that members of white bands would arrive armed with music paper to try to copy them). The power of dance music to release repressed frustrations had long been a part of one segment of black culture (as Albert Murray so eloquently extolled in *Stomping the Blues*). Of course, as has been discussed in Chapter 4, from well before the turn of the century another segment of black society had viewed any kind of dance music, as well as the blues, as "the devil's music."[18] The jitterbug craze of the 1930s and 1940s involved large numbers of the white population in a form of expressive activity, suffused with the basic eroticism of existence.

Whatever reemerged among white performers in the 1950s was more a re-discovery of the repressed than anything radically new. Black groups such as Louis Jordan's Tympany Five and numerous other scaled-down "swing blues" or "jump"-styled rhythm and blues bands were active from the late 1930s on doing essentially what in the 1950s whites would call rock 'n' roll.

The first white rock 'n' roll* group to hit big and become highly popular was Bill Haley and the Comets. During 1955 and 1956 the Haley group was the most popular rock 'n' roll group in the world. Haley (1925–81) began his career in

---

*The term *rock 'n' roll*, incidently, originated as a euphemism for sexual intercourse. It tended to become *rock and roll* after about 1958, and simple *rock* in the mid–1960s.

country-and-western music. As a record librarian at radio station WPWA in Chester, Pennsylvania, he heard the music of black rhythm and blues master Louis Jordan and the Tympany Five and was impressed by their high energy level, wondering whether a country group could do rhythm and blues.

Jordan was probably the biggest-selling black artist to cross over to the white market. A singer–alto saxophonist, with the shuffle-boogie-styled Tympany Five, he produced several million-selling or top ten disks such as "Is You Is or Is You Ain't My Baby?" (1944), "Choo Choo Ch-boogie" (1946), and "Saturday Night Fish Fry" (1949). He is unquestionably the most significant figure, although the least celebrated, in the development of rock 'n' roll.[19]

Bill Haley simply sought to copy Louis Jordan. Initially billing himself as the Wandering Yodeler, Haley had a succession of groups until a successful cover of Jackie Brenston's 1951 rhythm and blues hit "Rocket 88" that sold over 10,000 copies convinced him to drop the cowboy image and settle on "Bill Haley and the Comets" in 1952. Another rhythm and blues cover, "Rock the Joint," sold 75,000 copies. The group was the very first to hit the *Billboard* pop charts with a rock 'n' roll record, "Crazy Man Crazy," in 1953. A contract with Decca followed. Milt Gabler, who had produced Louis Jordan and the Tympany Five for Decca, produced Haley and the Comets' "Rock around the Clock" in 1954. It sold well at first on its own; but after being featured in the film *Blackboard Jungle* in 1955, it shot to number 1 in the *Billboard* charts. Between 1955 and 1956 Bill Haley and the Comets had 12 top 40 hits in the United States, exceeded only by Elvis Presley.

Their sound was based on replacing the Jordan horn voicing with guitars and retaining the tenor sax in a supplementary but essential "honking" role, a style pioneered in the early 1940s by Illinois Jacquet and Arnett Cobb in the Lionel Hampton bands. It was a sound that came from a tradition of black rhythm and blues that stretched 15 years back to Jordan's first recordings for Decca in 1938. As Jordan put it to Arnold Shaw, "When Bill Haley came along in '53, he was doing the same shuffle boogie I was. Only he was going faster than I was."[20] Contrary to the conventional wisdom, perhaps most significantly spread by Greil Marcus' illuminating essay on Presley in *Mystery Train* that suggests rock virtually began with Elvis and his Sun recordings for Sam Phillips,[21] the Louis Jordan–Bill Haley–Milt Gabler association (detailed best by Shaw in *Honkers and Shouters*) clearly must have equal or preemptive status. This is not to deny Presley's overarching achievement, his talent, his transcendently unique and enduring powers as a performer, and his exceptionally broad appeal across age groups and social classes.

One might suggest that *both* Presley and Haley represented versions of the response to the "invitation" provided by a black musical form—rhythm and blues—that was not "reinvented" (a favorite word in the lexicon of *Rolling Stone* writers over the years). It was instead taken up and invested with white energies and then translated to the newly available, mobilized white audience. And the audience found in it those same affectively empowering qualities that had served black America's expressive needs for over half a century. It started with the blues and boogie-woogie, becoming a fast swing blues or "jump" blues in the late 1930s and 1940s performed by such bands as Lionel Hampton, Tiny Bradshaw, Earl Bostic, Lucky Millinder, Cootie Williams, and Roosevelt Sykes and his Honeydrippers, in addition to Louis Jordan. But the roots also go back to the "riff"-based improvisation that incubated in Kansas City and the southwestern United States during the 1930s.[22]

In the 1950s the music virtually invaded white popular culture. Two predominant kinds of response came from white society. One had a resistance that involved either completely shutting out rock 'n' roll (see the 1978 Paramount film *American Hot Wax* for a dramatized version of such conspiratorial opposition to the spread of rock 'n' roll). A related impulse was the attempt to redirect and contain rock 'n' roll's energies with softened "cover" versions. Paradigmatic examples are the Pat Boone versions of Little Richard originals.

The prevalent alternative, of course, was enthusiastic acceptance and a working through the form that invested it with the kind of energy that could lead the uninitiated to believe that here was an utterly new, radically emergent cultural phenomenon. Its most extreme white manifestation was "rockabilly," the early sound of Sun Records in Memphis in the mid–1950s, described by Marcus as the white "lust to beat the black man at his own game."[23] Elvis Presley is the best known exponent, although there were several others, notably Jerry Lee Lewis, Roy Orbison, and Carl Perkins. There were also rockabilly women, such as Rose Maddox, who recorded and performed but never got access or promotion to communication networks that so furthered the career of Presley. Marcus termed rockabilly "the only style of early rock 'n' roll that proved white boys could do it all—that they could be as strange, as exciting, as scary, and as free as the black men who were suddenly walking America's airwaves as if they owned them."[24] Thus the so-called Memphis synthesis was both less and more than it appeared. It was a tremendous reinvestment (this time by white artists and audiences) in forms that were a product of the great river of black cultural resistance in the United States that had begun with the importation of the first slaves from Africa.

The attention directed to Elvis Presley as the "King of Rock and Roll" grew out of the fact that mass communication made Presley seem so significant. Incredible though it might seem, probably more people saw Presley perform via his three appearances on Ed Sullivan's television show in 1956 and 1957 than had seen all the significant black blues and rhythm and blues performers in person in the preceding half century! This was indeed a radically new phenomenon. Presley entered a vast new kind of public arena, the electronic community established by mass television communication, which really was something that had never before existed in the history of the world. His appearances on the Ed Sullivan Show were according to some accounts watched by the highest percentages of the television audience (82.6 percent) to watch any event in the history of the medium.[25] As subsequent developments in succeeding decades have borne out, particularly the rise of MTV and music video programs, television sells records.[26]

Marcus' "Presliad" in *Mystery Train* and his devastating dissections of Albert Goldman's biography *Elvis* have contributed to and reflected a view among rock "intellectuals" and other pop music writers concerning the uniqueness of the Presley phenomenon.[27] For all his talent, Elvis also happened to be the right person in the right place at the right time. Certainly Presley was an incredible performer, but he was one whose persona was carefully created and nurtured until he developed an appeal unique in its cross-age, cross-class nature.[28] Probably no individual will ever be able to equal it. Presley achieved mythic status partly because of his appearance before a mass television audience; and yet he had something to offer that audience—the musical expression of human sexuality in a particularly physically overt manner. This kind of expression of sexuality and eroticism was especially significant because it represented the first mass musical appeal to a white audience to be founded on this most basic and elemental human impulse as expressed orginally in black musical culture. Presley rode the crest of a wave of an accumulation of repressed eroticism, youth rebellion, a communication revolution, and an overdue mass white recognition of the power of black cultural forms to become the first and greatest "king" of rock and roll.

PLEASURE AND EXPRESSIVE REBELLION THROUGH MUSIC

Understanding the tremendous white attraction to rock 'n' roll in the 1950s is easier if one recalls Freud's view that civilization begins with the renunciation of integral satisfaction of human needs for pleasure, that history is nothing less than the history of human repression. This triumph of the "reality principle" over the "pleasure principle," provisional though it might be, is seen as the beginning and necessary foundation of productive society. Such a quest for pleasure may be seen, in its simplest senses, as subversive of the productivist view of society emphasizing delayed gratification—the view that was dominant in the United States throughout World War II. Of course, in advanced industrial society matters are rather more complicated, and the quest for pleasure is tied to commodified satisfaction of desires stimulated by a complex network of cultural industries. But rock 'n' roll could be effectively utilized by those industries.

In the years after the war a continuing era of prosperity produced a stratum of youth who had not experienced economic privation and for whom the ideology of repression of instincts and delaying gratification became increasingly incredible, though it was upheld in most popular cultural artifacts of the period until the birth of rock 'n' roll.

Thus in films such as Howard Hawks' *Red River* (1948), revived and celebrated by Peter Bogdanovich in his 1972 film *Last Picture Show* in a clip of the film's famous sequence of the beginning of a cattle drive, one could see the emerging conflicts within prevailing capitalist social ideology fighting it out in the persons of John Wayne as Tom Dunson, the cattle rancher who represented the old ways of predatory internal imperialism and authoritarian and hierarchical management styles, versus the younger Matthew Garth, played by Montgomery Clift, representing an alternative: an emerging, more human version of masculinity and a more consenual and participatory management style.[29]

In the 1956 original *Invasion of the Body Snatchers* one saw a residue of this ideology of delayed gratification when the two main chracters, Dr. Miles Bennell (played by Kevin McCarthy) and his friend Becky, both divorced, find themselves drawn to each other at the end of one evening. Miles makes a remark that could be interpreted as suggesting it might be nice *not* to say goodnight, but Becky (played by Dana Wynter) admonishes Miles, "That way lies madness." Though 15 years later it would seem unusual for two such mature, independent people not to spend the night together, at that time mass beliefs still upheld a sex-within-marriage ideology and Hollywood censors would never have approved of an illicit liaison.

ROCK 'N' ROLL AS EXPRESSIVE REBELLION

The emergence of rock 'n' roll in the 1950s was not, however, simply the unleashing of generations of repressed sexuality. Indeed, teenage subculture was *already* permeated with sexuality by the time of the emergence of Little Richard, Elvis Presley, and Chuck Berry.[30] Certainly the music helped to *order* that sexuality in particular ways (as will be discussed in the next chapter); but in a more basic sense, the tremendous initial white response to the music might be read as an expression of what Herbert Marcuse at the time in *Eros and Civilization* (1955) described as the basic force of life itself, *eros*, against the complex social reality of emergent centralized politicoeconomic and mass communication systems. Marcuse somberly suggested in this work, which remained 35 years after its writing one of the most radically revelatory modern reinterpretations of Freud, that the emergence of these systems all but eliminated the possibilities for free development of the individual personality. Perhaps, then, a major part of the appeal of rock 'n' roll lay less in its explicit sexuality than in its broader possibilities as a form through which millions could engage in an expressive revolt that was affectively empowering in a largely unconscious struggle against such centralization and conformity. Rock 'n' roll offered a musical way out, a structured means, with its male performers and a mass of male and female consumers, to invest the incredible psychic energies of an emerging generation—a kind of negotiated cultural free space.[31] Rock 'n' roll thus anticipated, or prefigured, the more systematic countercultural critiques of the 1960s.[32]

NOTES

1. Stanley Aronowitz, reviewing books on the 1960s, *Zeta Magazine*, January, 1988.
2. C. Wright Mills, "On Knowledge and Power (1955)," in *Power, Politics and*

People: The Collected Essays of C. Wright Mills, ed. Irving Louis Horowitz (New York: Ballantine Books, 1963), pp. 602–603.

3. Betty Freidan. *The Feminine Mystique* (New York: Dell Books, 1963).

4. On the postwar containment of women's aspirations see Elaine Tyler May, *Homeward Bound* (New York: Basic Books, 1988).

5. On this period see Morris Dickstein, *Gates of Eden* (New York: Basic Books, 1977), pp. 1–88.

6. I. F. Stone, *The Haunted Fifties* (New York: Random House, 1963).

7. Aldon Morris, *The Origins of the Civil Rights Movement* (New York: The Free Press, 1984), p. 51.

8. On the role of the Highlander School see sources in note 87, Chapter 5.

9. See Stuart Samuels' revelatory essay, "The Age of Conspiracy and Conformity: *Invasion of the Body Snatchers* (1956)," in *American History/American Film*, ed. John E. O'Connor and Martin A. Jackson (New York: Frederick Ungar, 1979), pp. 203–218.

10. See Charlie Gillette, *Sound of the City*, rev. and expanded ed. (New York: Pantheon, 1983), p. 19.

11. Perhaps most notably by Gillette in *Sound of the City*.

12. Arnold Shaw, *Honkers and Shouters: The Golden Years of Rhythm & Blues* (New York: Collier Books, 1978); Arnold Shaw, *Black Popular Music in America* (New York: Schirmer Books, 1986).

13. The notion of negotiated response was discussed earlier in Chapter 2.

14. Shaw, *Honkers and Shouters*, p. 52.

15. Ibid.

16. MCA LP *Piano in Style*, MCA–1332, provides examples of the best of Pinetop Smith.

17. James Lincoln Collier, *The Making of Jazz: A Comprehensive History* (New York: Delta Books, 1978), pp. 207–208.

18. Giles Oakley, *The Devil's Music: A History of the Blues* (London: BBC, 1979).

19. See Shaw, *Honkers and Shouters*, and Gillette, *Sound of the City*, for more detail on Jordan's career. Nearly all his recordings have been reissued in the 1980s.

20. Shaw, *Honkers and Shouters*, p. 74.

21. Greil Marcus, *Mystery Train: Images of America in Rock 'n' Roll Music*, new ed., rev. and expanded (New York: E. P. Dutton, 1982).

22. On the Kansas City style and its influence see Ross Russell, *Jazz Style in Kansas City and the Southwest* (Berkeley: University of California Press, 1973).

23. Marcus, *Mystery Train*, p. 169.

24. Ibid.

25. Ibid., p. 276.

26. See R. Serge Denisoff's discussion of the effects of MTV on sales in *Tarnished Gold* (New Brunswick, N.J.: Transaction Books, 1986).

27. Greil Marcus, "Lies about Elvis, Lies about Us," *Village Voice*, November 18, 1981 (*Village Voice Literary Supplement*, December 1981, pp. 16–17), is the most succinct and devastating critique of the Goldman version of Elvis. More of the Goldman brush technique would be evident in the controversy over his John Lennon biography of 1988.

28. On Elvis' appeal, see Linda Ray Pratt, "Elvis, Or the Ironies of a Southern Identity," in *Elvis: Images and Fantasies*, ed. J. L. Tharpe (Jackson: University Press of Mississippi, 1979), pp. 40–51.

29. For an illuminating examination of the themes of this film see Robert Sklar, "Empire to the West: *Red River* (1948)" in *American History/American Film*, ed. Connor and Jackson, pp. 167–182.

30. This point is well expressed in Simon Frith, *Sound Effects: Youth, Leisure, and the Politics of Rock & Roll* (New York: Pantheon, 1982), p. 238.

31. On the notion of free spaces see Sara M. Evans and Harry C. Boyte, *Free Spaces* (New York: Harper & Row, 1986). My use of the term in a cultural sense is a fusion of elements of the approach of Evans and Boyte and the notion of public arena created by communication networks as discussed by Joshua Meyrowitz in *No Sense of Place: The Impact of Electronic Media on Social Behavior* (New York: Oxford University Press, 1985).

32. See Dickstein's comments on the impact of Marcuse's work in *Gates of Eden*, pp. 68–74.

7

Women's Voices, Images, and Silences

The silences I speak of here are unnatural; the unnatural thwarting of what struggles to come into being, but cannot. In the old, the obvious parallels: when the seed strikes stone; the soil will not sustain; the spring is false; the time is drought or blight or infestation; the frost comes premature.

Tillie Olsen,
Silences[1]

Ways of thinking about gender and sexuality structure broader conceptions of what is possible and what is not. That seems especially evident in popular music.[2] There is a significance that transcends sexuality and sex roles here as one considers the role of music as a "voice"—as a means of expressing *personal* politics as well as as a means of effecting change in society more generally. In the United States since the mid–1960s the wider political uses of popular music have been limited by the fact that expressive functions of that music have been profoundly skewed toward the needs of men.

Women began the second great wave of feminism at the end of the 1960s. Much of the impetus toward action grew out of their frustrations and indignation at their experience in other progressive movements for social change in the immediately preceding years. Sara Evans has chronicled the personal journey of many politically active women in this way in *Personal Politics*.[3] For many more married women, the transformations grew out of the generalized malaise and feelings of alienation, the "problem that has no name," described so effectively by Betty Freidan in *The Feminine Mystique* (1963). This eventually involved them in a fundamental critique of inequalities in the then-prevailing model of the institution of marriage. Prior to the 1960s, if there was a usual popular cultural linkage of sexuality to marriage, it was especially seen as a desirable status for women. A clear cultural double standard existed: Consider the relative status of images of "old maid" and "bachelor." In popular culture these trends are evident in movies of the 1930s through the 1950s, though there seems to have been a significant cold war reemphasis on marriage and the family in the 1950s as a bulwark against communism as Elaine Tyler May demonstrates in *Homeward Bound.*[4] Marriage rates increased, altering a trend of decreasing marriages through previous decades. Birth rates increased as well. The baby boom was the result. The frequency with which marriage seems to be mentioned in dialogue in movies in the years before the 1960s is striking for what it demonstrates of the significant changes in consciousness that have subsequently emerged in spite of the concerted efforts of the cold war era to contain the aspirations of women beyond the home.[5] In the 1970 census 13.7 percent of women aged 18 to 44 were single and never married. By 1986 this rose to 18.3 percent.[6] A comparable figure for males was 18.9 percent in 1970, rising to 25.3 percent in 1986. Nonetheless, the overwhelming fact that emerges from these data is that nearly all men and women at some point in their lives *do* marry, in spite of a growing preference for single status. Nearly 81 percent of women who marry have a child (80 percent of white women, 88.5 percent of black women).

In the late 1960s and early 1970s criticism of conventional family structure and sex roles became evident in popular culture, but it was expressed far better in widely seen films than in the popular music of the era. The content of the music contained a significant number of one-sided male appeals to women to accede to the men's sexual desires. The film industry, in contrast, seems to have been particularly attentive to changing audience composition and tastes.

The late 1960s version of the popular cultural criticism of marriage began imperfectly in such film caricatures as Paul Mazursky's *Bob and Carol, Ted and Alice* (1969) and the widely seen *Diary of a Mad Housewife* (1970). In *Desperate Characters* (1971) Shirley MacLaine moved as though drugged (psychically numbed?) through a bleak, neorealist nightmare of the terrifying boredom marriage can be. Peter Bogdanovich's acclaimed *The Last Picture Show* (1971) portrayed Cloris Leachman as the neglected coach's wife in the impoverished sort of marriage millions knew, while in the same film Ellen Burstyn's character expressed only cynicism and realism through pointed dialogue explicitly making the way of the world clear to her daughter, played by then cover girl Cybill Shepherd. The same year saw Glenda Jackson's strong performance as the New Woman in John Schlesinger's *Sunday Bloody Sunday*. Marjorie Rosen in *Popcorn Venus* saw it as "the most gloriously intelligent" film on issues of gender and sexuality of the era.[7] Here one sees Jackson involved in another, rather less appealing strategy of survival, differing from that of socially marginal blacks who did so much with music from the blues to rap. As Rosen put it, "Even if it means more loneliness, perhaps permanent loneliness, Jackson is embodying not a mythic vision of courage, but the kind of small but hurting bravery today's divorced, widowed, or single women must face in day-to-day living."[8] By the 1980s, however, fewer younger, educated single women would put up with such a design for living, which held neither promise of fun nor real happiness. Their impatience would be evident in the popular music of the time in such figures as Madonna and Cyndi Lauper.

The early 1970s were filled with conflicting images. The period also saw a number of highly popular and critically acclaimed films depicting brutalizations and rapes of women. *A Clockwork Orange* (1971), *Straw Dogs* (1971), and *Klute* (1971) all involve extended brutal treatment of women, often coupled with the suggestion that women could not solve problems without the aid of a man. *Straw Dogs* and, a bit later, *Last Tango in Paris* involve forcible rape, but with a twist—eventually the woman is portrayed as becoming sexually aroused and enjoying it.

Yet all these films might still be seen as both reflecting and facilitating the social identifications of those on various sides of the extracinematic social conflicts and transformations underway in sex role expectations. The reaction against liberation of women from traditional gender roles and family structures would crest in the 1980s, becoming part of the massive reaffirmation of traditional family values in the Reagan era evident in *Ordinary People, Kramer vs. Kramer, On Golden Pond,* and *Terms of Endearment*[9] and culminating in the box-office and home-video smash success of *Fatal Attraction* in 1987–88.

Undermining of the old ideology of unequal marriages and male dominance proceeded in the early 1970s to the point that in succeeding years, at least for a stratum of feminist radicals, such words as "home" and "family" could (from this writer's experience) be hurled by women as epithets, redolent with the most biting sarcasm and negativity, as these institutions came to be understood in a generational subculture familiar with a growing body of powerful feminist theoretical analyses as the sites of unspoken terror, psychological and physical violence, or for a minority of greater numbers a longer-term slow, numbing psychic death. But this particular perspective would not emerge in mass popular culture until the middle of the 1980s with such TV productions as *The Burning Bed* (1984), itself a pop culture phenomenon. It gained in two showings one of the largest audiences captured by a TV movie production and featured a stunning and committed performance by former pin-up and star of the *Charlie's Angels* TV series, Farrah Fawcett. Popular music lagged far behind with the first major popular song on violence against women not emerging until Tracy Chapman's "Behind the Wall" in 1988.

Critical themes would infrequently appear in popular music, aside from the initial emergence of several nonfeminist folk singers in the early 1960s such as Joan Baez, whose first album reached number 3 on the album charts, or early protofeminist works such as Lesley Gore's striking early 1960s "You Don't Own Me" and the uniquely revelatory reworkings of male material by Aretha Franklin. Indeed, Franklin's brilliant 1967 transformation of "Respect" is a striking example of a functionally feminist deconstruction and revisioning of the macho Otis Redding original, which she followed with similar work such as "Think." When critical themes did appear, they often sold very well. The early 1970s period produced some searing dissections of relationships in recorded songs by Dory Previn and Joni Mitchell. Carole King's number 1 ranked "It's Too Late" from the 1971 megaplatinum *Tapestry* album of her own compositions, which sold some 13 million units over the next few years, with its open recognition of a relationship that couldn't be saved, or "Will You Still Love Me Tomorrow" (though it first appeared as a number 1 hit in 1961 by the Shirelles), which illuminated once again the way women's expressive sexuality was used by men, this time in the alleged openness of the late 1960s and early 1970s counterculture, are intelligent examples in the era's mass popular music. Similarly, Helen Reddy's "I Am Woman" reached number 1 status in 1972–73, and she was nominated for a Grammy. King's and Reddy's tremendous market appeal functioned as positive role models for women in music generally. In spite of sales success, however, they remained overall rarities in a culture governed at the personal level by the search for what Christopher Lasch termed the "haven in a heartless world"—the ideal marriage or relationship.[10]

Critical comments on the institution or the frustrations and duplicities in sexual relations generated by it appeared in productions not in the pop mainstream, or they appeared in so-called women's music in the 1970s and 1980s. There, too, visions of the good or "equal" relationship—whether conventionally heterosexual or homosexual/lesbian—seemed to lie as a utopian hope beneath the surface. Overt critiques of inequality and violence in relations between the sexes never appeared in mainstream musical product, even at the end of the 1980s, until Chapman's "Behind the Wall," the first song on any popular album, let alone a number 1 album, that deals with violence against women.[11] Similarly, songs exulting in women's independence or the joys of freely chosen sexuality, aside from the blues and rhythm and blues idioms, were, with the exception of Janis Joplin's statements, quite rare until the mid–1980s.

LIMITS OF THE 1960s COUNTERCULTURE

If in the late 1960s figures such as Janis Joplin and Grace Slick provided the appearance of strong role models for women, they were highly problematical images, given the realities of the time. Slick, of the San Francisco–based Jefferson Airplane, provided searing vocal lines and an almost menacing image of beauty and controlling strength, but she provided little lyrical or ideological critique of male-female relationships beyond a persona that seemed to convey that she would always be in charge of herself and perhaps her partner, too. Slick's potent image was softened somewhat when integrated with the overall counterculture posture of the Airplane (later, Jefferson Starship, or just Starship).

In retrospect the counterculture was exceptionally one-sided in the sexual liberation promised and promoted. Ellen Willis, one of the few women who have had status among the largely male fraternity of rock intellectuals, put it thus in her essay on the tragic figure of Janis Joplin: "The male-dominated counterculture defined freedom for women almost exclusively in sexual terms. As a result, women endowed the ideal of sexual liberation with immense symbolic importance; it became charged with all the secret energy of as yet suppressed larger rebellion. Yet to express one's rebellion in that limited way was a painfully literal form of submission."[12] There was, from all appearances, a lot of submission. The dimensions of the inequality are striking.

In the *Rolling Stone Illustrated History of Rock & Roll* (1980), which focuses largely on the period from 1950 through 1980, there are 82 articles of which just 3 are exclusively on women (the "Girl Groups," "Janis Joplin," "Aretha Franklin") and perhaps 5 others include a substantial amount of material on women.[13] This 10 percent is a fair representation of the significance of women in this variety of music so overwhelmingly present in recent cultural history. Numerous other studies document the relative absence or minority percentage of women performers in recorded music for half a century until the emergence of a number of strong female performers in the 1980s.

Peter Hesbacher and associates studied artists who had reached the number 1 position on *Billboard* singles charts. They found that between 1940 and 1974 only 12 percent of those reaching the top position were solo female artists, 5 percent were female groups, and 7 percent mixed male-female groups.[14] In a 1980 study of careers of male and female artists, Peter Hesbacher and Bruce Anderson developed three "epochs" ranging from 1940 to 1978. Women's careers showed slightly less longevity than men's in each of the three periods when measured by period between first and last number 1 chart appearance.[15]

Although such chart success is not the only indicator of success or influence in popular music, it is easier to measure and a sure indicator of visibility. One must remember, of course, that though a useful indicator in a capitalist music market, chart success certainly provides no measure of quality nor enduring cultural influence. Annual singles ranking based on the top 50 annual songs provides a more comprehensive view of the industry than the number 1 rankings noted above, but by the end of the 1980s, the singles category became less and less relevant as an indicator. In a study of women in popular music from 1955 to 1984 based on the top 50 ranking, Alan Wells found women often exceeded the 12 percent figures in the previous studies, registering an even 18 percent in the 1980s.[16] A weighted score by position on charts put women with 20 percent or more of total points in 1955, 1962–66, 1973, 1977, 1979, and 1981. In spite of the intervening wave of feminism at the end of the 1960s and into the early 1970s, no consistent pattern of greater representation over time was evident. Women held a similar approximate 20 percent of the top 100 albums in the *Rolling Stone* annual charts in the period 1979–84.[17] A glance at the charts in any recent issue of *Billboard* or *Rolling Stone* demonstrates that the situation continues, for usually something less than 20 percent of the entries are by women.

In the 1980s, studies of videos on music television reveal a similar bias. Jane D. Brown and Kenneth C. Campbell found videos with white males taking up

83 percent of MTV time. Those with women as central figures made up 11 percent of a 24-hour period, with blacks in even smaller percentages. Even in the limited opportunities for representations of women to be shown, there was considerable bias toward male definition of roles. In their characterization "white women are often shown in passive and solitary activity or are shown trying to gain the attention of a man who ignores them."[18] Although other interpretations, which will presently be considered, suggest alternative feminist readings of the minority of female images in popular music, the sheer weight of numbers raises important questions.

WHOSE MUSIC IS IT?

To whom has this sexually expressive popular music spoken over the nearly four decades of its existence? Much popular music analysis has emphasized the manner in which black forms have been appropriated or "ripped off" in a society dominated by whites. It is ironic, then, that the liberatory theoretical perspectives applied, usually by male observers, to analysis of the role of blacks in American music have rarely been directed to the way the music and music business have dealt with women.[19]

Where were the women? What were they doing? Why were they silent (or underpresented) musically? Steven Chapple and Reebee Garofalo in *Rock 'n' Roll Is Here to Pay* (perhaps the best discussion to date on the problem) place the blame on the overwhelmingly male character of the industry (as do other writers).[20] The problem is probably even more profound and basic, however. There are interrelated explanations: Women, of course, simply were not involved in music or any area of the workforce outside the home in the same numbers as men, though their representation in popular music has not appreciably changed with their increased presence in the workforce over the past two decades. In addition, within popular music they might have been less "popular," even if involved, though that may reflect less aggressive company signing and development of female artists as well as underemphasized promotion and marketing of them. The latter pattern is evident from a survey of recording artists based on biographies distributed by companies undertaken by R. Serge Denisoff and John Bridges. It had a sample of 522 males to 58 females, with a rock music subsample of 266 males to 10 females.[21] Clearly a more fundamental yet very complex process of bias and exclusion was at work.

THE SEXUAL LINE OF FAULT

A profound disjuncture exists between the ways popular music has been thought about and discussed—as sociologist Dorothy Smith put it in another context, in the "symbols, images, vocabularies, concepts, frames of reference, institutionalized structures of relevance"[22]—and the way life is actually lived for over half the population, that is, for women. What does it mean that virtually the entire popular music business, especially rock, from its inception is and has been run, controlled, commented on, and written about almost exclusively by men?

In one of the few significant early essays in the sparse literature on rock music, gender, and sexuality, Simon Frith and Angela McRobbie suggested rock operates simultaneously as a form of "sexual expression" and a "form of sexual control."[23] If the initial flowering of rock 'n' roll to a white audience in the 1950s was to significant degrees based on release of repressed sexuality, it was one importantly biased as far as *performance* toward a particular kind of male expression. The alleged liberatory quality of the 1960s rock that followed did little for women. That there were significant and powerful female figures throughout the period since the 1960s has not produced a position for women as performers in popular music in any way approaching their representation in the population at large. Women's participation in popular music since the 1950s has been much more through *consumption*—in buying pop cultural musical "product" responsive to their psychological needs and fantasies.[24] The effects of the so-called rock revolution on social roles was not very great. As Frith put it in another context, rock "works with conventions of masculinity and femininity that situate both performers and audiences along clear gender lines—males as active participants, females as passive consumers."[25]

The last quarter century has not, however, been without some positive roles for women, nor of movements which critiqued and sought fundamentally to alter or broaden roles of men and women in popular music. Two of them were punk rock in Britain and the United States and the Women's Music movement in the United States (discussed later in the chapter).

Certainly the often savage social critiques of the punk movement in Britain and the United States during the late 1970s, persisting in "hard core" punk through the 1980s and in more subtle and elegant statements from the numerous postpunk "new wave" bands such as Blondie and the Talking Heads (the latter the most thematically searching, culturally critical, and artistically creative group to arise in the period), all opened up possibilities for a greater and more egalitarian status for women in bands and a somewhat wider range of sexual orientation and "gender bending" in the 1980s. At first this occurred through sheer obliteration of previous "cock-rock" styles and a frontal assault on all social convention. Part of the significance of punk for girls and women is based on its outright rejections of "conventions of traditional sexuality."[26] Both the "hippy ideal of free 'permissive' love *and* the straighter conventions of love, such as romance and engagement rings, were attacked, undermined, and repudiated outright. In every way punk sexuality was angry and aggressive, implicitly feminist."[27] With British punk rocker Tom Robinson opening the way with "Glad to Be Gay" in 1978, which received significant air play in U.S. cities, over the succeeding decade several explicitly homosexual male rock groups arose in Britain, though their images were softened or blurred beyond recognition by U.S. promoters.[28]

Yet these developments did not significantly improve the career opportunities of women in spite of the emergence in the 1970s of such radically contrasting models as Patti Smith or Debbie Harry out of the New York punk/new wave scene. After attaining significant attention they both practically vanished from the popular music arena. Smith reappeared in 1988 (after having children) with the powerful and critically acclaimed *Dream of Life*. Harry struggled to make it in a major way as an independent artist after achieving widespread pin-up status at the end of the 1970s; she again attained some success by the end of 1989. These are problematical examples. Perhaps part of the problem is generational, for there is a process of aging which is separate from the phenomenon of "ageism," though the two are intertwined. It is simply easier for record-consuming youth to relate to singers closer to their age. Thus Madonna and Cyndi Lauper supplanted Debbie Harry.

There is, overall, another important, and deeper, pattern. Since the 1950s the development of popular music in the United States, especially the most commercially successful product, rock, reveals the continued operation of a sexual "mobilization of bias," that is, a set of "predominant values, beliefs, rituals and institutional procedures that operate systematically and consistently to the benefit of certain persons and groups at the expense of others."[29] In the music business it mirrors and reinforces sex bias in the larger economy and society, often presenting the most extreme caricatures of sex role models, as a few hours of watching MTV or other television music-video programs demonstrates.

Because of the prevalence of male performers, existing popular music might better be labeled the "male-stream" of music. No equivalent channel has existed for women, who have had to fight for representation as performers and to assert any authorship of their commercial products. As consumers women, especially feminists, must search long and diligently for positive models. They must often engage in "against the grain" reinterpretation of images presented to them. As Frith and McRobbie argued, "Any analysis of the sexuality of rock must begin with the brute social fact that in terms of control and production, rock is a male form."[30] The dimensions of male domination are overwhelming. Most popular musicians, and even more writers, creators, technicians, engineers, and producers, are men. The roles of women in creative roles are limited and "mediated through male notions of female ability." Among the women musicians who "make it," nearly all are singers. Usually it is in areas of publicity that women in the business are found, pushing a largely male defined product. The female image is made by males. Indeed, in general, the "images, values, and sentiments" of popular music are male products. The situation is so profoundly biased that male images as well as female are constructed, though a perhaps greater variety of "male sexual poses" are presented, but "most often expressed in terms of stereotypes."[31]

Yet the relationship is not as unidirectional as once it appeared. There is always a dialogic aspect to the popular music process. At the basic level of consumption women are aggressively attentive actors as fans. As Sue Steward and Sheryl Garratt argue in *Signed, Sealed, and Delivered,* the whole structure of popular music "rests on the backs of these 'silly screaming girls.' They bought the records in millions and made a massive contribution to the early success of Elvis, the Beatles, the Stones, . . . Michael Jackson and many of the others who have since been accepted by the grown-ups and become monuments, reference points in the rock hierarchy."[32] Importantly for both males and females, the music either in performance or consumption meets or responds to needs, providing a way for making some sort of "sense" of one's own gender role and sexuality. Although this orienting of roles often takes place in structured, illusory, sterotypical, and highly alienated ways, nonetheless people still utilize popular music and its imagery "to understand what it means to have desires, to be desirable."[33]

There remains the profound disjuncture between women's experience and the availability of forms through which that experience can be socially expressed. Nowhere is that more evident than in rock, the most widely heard musical form. In some other genres of music, notably country and some black gospel, among the limited number of women active in the blues, and among jazz vocalists, that is much less the case. As a general rule, however, women in popular music have until very recently found themselves speaking in voices created by others, in a musical vocabulary and tradition of discourse established by men. What are the consequences?

At one level the very fact of *any* kind of participation of women may have certain liberating consequences and provide role models that might further stimulate other women to consider doing more than clutching at the ankles of posturing males on the stage or buying their records. Whatever the sexism in the predominant content of popular musical product in recent decades, the creative free space provided by the music does open powerfully expressive possibilities. In spite of the sexist content, there is some emancipatory potential in the free spaces provided by the liberating structure—the opportunities for individual improvisation and development of a unique style, voice, and persona. But to examine the overwhelming body of popular musical product is to discover crucial biases in the materials that have been produced through the 1980s.

If popular music is correctly seen as a medium of mass communication, unique aspects of most women's life experiences have *not* been effectively communicated. There are important differences in the way women and men live their lives, in the degree of autonomy permitted each by the realities of social life. Both physiologically and culturally, through myriad forms of social determination of gender, the kinds of experiences they undergo, and the socially structured pattern of sex role expectations, the lives of women and the ways they see the world are profoundly different from those of men. If functional biological differences between the sexes are no longer credible bases for role determination, gender remains one of the most significant deciding differences in determination of work roles in the society. This division of labor is a product of cultural role expectations that significantly influence conscious choice by the majority of employed women who find jobs within 20 of 420 classifications developed by the U.S. Department of Labor.[34]

There are real differences between the sexes in cultural meanings given to physical differences, and in the reality of life experiences. Women discover early that they menstruate, men do not. Women get pregnant, and of the 82 percent who marry, 80 percent bear children; men experience this only indirectly through their partners if they are close enough to notice and, of course, through the legal expectation that they will pay their share of child support (an expectation often not fulfilled on their part or frequently rejected by the mothers who, for a variety of reasons, do not seek further connection with the child's father). Even among single women never married (18.3 percent of the total population in 1986), increasing percentages of women 18 to 44 report having a child (14.3 percent in 1970, 6.5 percent of whites, 47.8 percent of blacks; by 1986, 18.1 percent of all single, never-married women, 8.5 percent of whites, and 44.7 percent of black single, never-married women had given birth to one or more children).[35]

Women, far more frequently than men, are subjected to personal and sexual abuse, incest, rape, battering, unwanted pregnancy, and the financial and psychological costs of raising alone children they did not plan nor want and for which they are inadequately compensated through lack of effective enforcement of child-support laws. Women are more frequently impoverished, falling into poverty at such increasing rates relative to males that the "feminization of poverty" became a significant object of social analysis in the mid–1980s. Women in the mid–1980s earned about 65 cents to every dollar earned by men. They are less likely to be covered by medical insurance. Women are victimized, moreover, by double standards concerning sexual behavior and appearance. Ageism is rampant in popular culture, but women suffer more. Many male film stars, for example, have endured across generations to play opposite an ever-revolving cast of younger women. Women are much more likely to be used and "used up." When discarded in divorce, their economic status is almost always substantially lower that it was prior to divorce. Profound inequalities in pay scales and salaries between women and men persist, so that in spite of token integration of most job classifications, most working women still remain in such "women's" jobs as secretary, waitress, nurse, domestic, or elementary educator. How many of these phenomena, which are social issues involving the situations of tens of millions of women and their children or the greater numbers of single women who do not have children and seek fulfillment through a career, all widely studied and written about, ever make it into popular music?

These life experiences have produced distinctive ways of thinking and looking at the world, ways the male-dominated social science disciplines began to discover only when feminist critiques pointed out that most social science models were based *almost wholly* on studies of men. Carol Gilligan's *In a Different Voice* (1982) and the multiauthored *Women's Ways of Knowing* (1988) signaled the emergence among a new wave of feminist social scientists of recognition of women as beings distinctively different from men in their modes of thinking, moral reasoning, and orientation toward the world.[36]

Musically, these differences exist masked within modes of critical and theoretical discourse largely practiced by men and constructed, as political theorist Carole Pateman put it, "from within a division between the public (the social, the political, history) and the private (the personal, the domestic, the familial), which is also a division between the sexes."[37] Pateman and a broad range of feminist thinkers have argued that theorizing about social phenomena generally, as well as the standards that evaluate such theorizing, proceeds within a largely masculine, public world, a "universal" sort of world in which "the private world of particularity, natural subjection, inequality, emotion, love, partiality—and women and femininity" is repressed.[38] Generally the sociological fact of the patriarchical separation of the two spheres and its influence on the ways virtually anything is discussed in popular culture, and certainly popular music, has until the last decade rarely been considered. While rock and other popular music critics might be generally politically "liberal" or "progressive," they are almost always men. What does this mean? What are its implications?

Much of popular music has been the domain of musical discourses of heroic *male* individuals seeking an authenticity of expression and existence that take for granted a conception of individuality based on a sexually particular character of the individual. This "individual" is distinctly masculine, but he appears or is made to appear somehow as universal. If there has been bias in the nature of the system of popular music, then the counterview might be expressed by a well-intentioned (and usually male) consciousness; the remedy should be simply to incorporate the excluded individuals. This would, however, leave intact "the sexually particular characterization of the public world, the individual and *his* capacities."[39] This public world as presently known has largely been a male world.

According women a position of genuine equality in popular music becomes inevitably a demand for the social autonomy of women generally. And that will require significant changes in the overall structure of priorities in the larger society. If it is no longer credible that the capacities of women as performers/creators necessitate their exclusion, it does not suffice simply to assert that there are no differences between the situations of women and men, nor that existing differences are irrelevant.

The history of art and popular culture is full of "silences."[40] Those of women relate significantly to powerful cultural stereotypes concerning gender-"appropriate" public postures and role models, prescribing demeanor in relating to men in relationships and in the workplace, but also to the private world of marriage, maternity, family, and childcare and to general cultural expectations that because women must bear children, they must assume primary responsibility for caring for and raising them. This does not deny that increasing numbers of women consciously choose to forgo having children and choose to live alone (18.3 percent of the total population); however, these remain the minority of women.

Whatever their status and whatever the proliferation of role models, there remains the persisting social effects of a long-standing and continuing overwhelming social bias toward women not only giving birth to children but also assuming virtually total responsibility for child rearing and care. This bias persists in spite of 1970s and 1980s yuppie images of the child-toting ''new father.'' This factor alone may be the most significant in accounting for extended gaps in the careers of women in any creative area. It has still not been adequately considered in the public consciousness, being dealt with only occasionally on film and television and rarely if ever in mainstream popular music.

It is difficult to find a male equivalence to the enforced absence from career imposed upon woman by child rearing. Perhaps Elvis' stint in the army or perhaps John Lennon's alleged period of preoccupation with caring for his child and his relative absence from public musical life for several years are situations in which the equivalent effects of this bias have been dramatized to men.[41] Other examples might be the jail terms that cut short careers for many male artists, whether for drug possession or other crimes. What are the implications for women in imposed child-caring roles of such imposed male silences? Why is not such experience unique to women reflected in popular music in proportion to their position in the general population? These women are not a minority. They constitute well over 50 percent of the adult population of the United States. Yet, their existence at all social class levels and as part of all ethnic and racial groups has inhibited, or at least segmented, the development of a particularly feminist kind of mass musical ''culture of resistance'' that developed historically in the black musical tradition. Nonetheless feminist or distinctive women's perspectives have entered ordinary discourse over the past two decades, at least in terms of rhetorical invocations of women's equality made by male politicians and efforts to reduce sexism in language. A distinctive feminist culture is evident in art, poetry, literature, and film. If this may be said to exist in music, it is in a particularly underrepresented, distorted, and attenuated form.

A WOMEN'S MUSICAL DISCOURSE?

When Kate Millett in *Sexual Politics* and, earlier, Betty Freidan in *The Feminine Mystique* began to unveil the essentially ideological nature of all that had previously been taken for granted as the role of women, the relations between the sexes, and especially the lived experience of the daily life of women, they opened up the possibility of thinking about that experience and expressing it in musical discourse in ways different from those in which it had been previously expressed. But what forms could it take up? Which would be open enough to permit the investment of energy and content in ways that would be effectively empowering and satisfying to listeners?

Sociologist Dorothy E. Smith has described her early experience as a student in literature and her personal conflicts growing out of her reaction to aspects of the work of D. H. Lawrence, who was presented to her as ''a genius.'' She recognized that his ''ultimate idealization of sexual relations between women and men was one where woman's consciousness, her sensation, was so totally annulled before the man's that she should forego even orgasm and accept essentially the annihilation of her own consciousness in the sexual act."[42] Smith *felt* this but saw, at that time, that she had no vocabulary, no effective tradition of discourse, in which to express her criticism without being typed, among several possible deprecating characterizations, as "unwilling to accept her femininity"—a model of femininity defined by others. There was a gap between her experience and the established, sanctioned, social forms of expression, which were located in the middle of a male-dominated system of relations of power between men and women.

In music, a similar situation has prevailed in critical work and in virtually every aspect of popular music creation, production, and distribution. Only the late 1980s experienced a significant movement away from this situation, and that may be a matter of market demographics, for those baby boom generation, socially liberal but economically conservative, upscale "yuppie" consumers, who have moved rapidly into compact discs, for example, seem to value women's equality and women artists. That does not obviate the fact that particular musical forms and modes of expression available to women to formulate their experience have, until the late 1980s, generally been made and controlled and evaluated by men. Although there are important exceptions to this pattern, as noted below, the pattern of bias remains.

Whatever area of popular music over the past century one considers, women simply do not appear to men as men do to each other, that is, as persons involved in the common construction of a particular kind of social reality, a cultural product that is itself a kind of ideological construction, a way of understanding the world. As Smith has described sociological discourse, musical discourse, too, has been characterized by "a circle effect—men attend and treat as significant what men say and have said. . . . What men were doing has been relevant to men, was written by men about men for men. Men listened and listen to what one another say. A tradition is formed, traditions form, in a discourse with the past within the present. The themes, problematics, assumptions, metaphors, and images form as the circle of those present draws upon the work of those speaking from the past and builds it up to project into the future."[43] In music women have for most of the twentieth century been virtually shut out of access to certain styles and performance venues, particularly as instrumentalists; and in other areas, where, for example, they were part of "all-girl" orchestras, it was partly in response to the necessities of World War II. Later in the 1970s and 1980s all-woman groups in rock (Fanny, the Go-Gos, the Bangles, Bananarama) represented the smallest portion of the vast amount of male activity, and their participation has often been structured by adherence to male performance practices as in flamboyant guitar acrobatics, tight leather pants, and other staples of hard rock and heavy metal performance. As instrumental performers in virtually all areas and genres of popular music, women have not had appropriate models nor the equivalent opportunities to develop basic technique and distinctive performance styles and voices. At one level this may be simply a matter of time. Women have been encouraged to sing and play the piano since the 1700s.* Where women have developed a tradition of performing on an instrument—such as the piano—there are examples of genuinely "great" individuals, such as the late MaryLou Williams among jazz pianists, who must be counted on anyone's list among the all-time "greats" on that instrument, regardless of sex. But there are very few major figures among all the other instrumentalists in jazz. As an indication, in the 1988 *Downbeat* readers' poll in 35 categories, women were ranked in only 4 not exclusively reserved for women (i.e., "female singer"), 1 as composer, 2 as arranger, 1 on soprano sax.[44] In other types of music— country, folk, rock—there are a small number of excellent female instrumentalists. One thinks of Bonnie Raitt and Rory Block, for example, among blues-oriented rock guitarists with great facility on their instruments, though they are probably far from making anyone's list of the top 20 guitarists. Barbara Mandrell among country performers puts on a virtuosic display of multiinstrumentality in her stage shows. These are exceptions, however. When a woman is admitted, it is usually as a special individual who, as in jazz, "plays like a man" or is judged to be "good" in terms of criteria of quality defined by men. Women in music, as in most areas of activity, must work inside a discourse which they have little part in making but in whose terms they are judged and with which they are often in agreement. Sheila Rowbotham related a number of years ago a graphic illustration of the way women have been conditioned to treat themselves as they are looked at by men in mass popular culture. She describes how a portion of the Beatles' *Magical Mystery Tour* seen on television demonstrated to her "the extent to which I identified with men, used their eyes. . . . Half of me was like a man surveying the passive half of me as a woman-thing."[45] The crucial events involve a group of people, including the Beatles, who go on a bus trip:

There is the atmosphere of excitement, of all being on the bus together and enjoying a treat. . . . Then at one point all the boys in the film are segregated from the girls. You follow the boys in the film, wriggling in your seat in front of the telly, in mounting excitement. It's like going in the Noah's Ark at Blackpool when you're six or listening to very loud rock music when you're thirteen. I got the same tightening down at the bottom of my spine. Well there I was clenching my cunt and where should they go but into a strip-tease. I had caught myself going to watch another woman as if I were a man. I was experiencing the situation of another woman stripping through men's eyes. I was

---

*From the 1700s on "female piano playing and singing were designed as appropriate forms of musical expression for women and incorporated into the bourgeois woman's role in the family." Lisa Lewis, "Form and Authorship in Music Video," *Communication*, 9 (1987): 373. Moreover, "it was important to a man's prestige that his wife could entertain his guests with music and of course a musical eduation for his daughter served as a good investment for an advantageous marriage." Eva Rieger, " 'Dolce Semplice?' On the Changing Role of Women in Music," in *Feminist Aesthetics*, ed. G. Ecker (Boston: Beacon Press, 1986), p. 141.

being asked to desire myself by a film made by men. Catching myself observing myself desiring one of my selves I remained poised for an instant in two halves.[46]

FORMS INVENTED BY WOMEN

Though the means women have had to reflect on themselves musically have been largely a reflection from outside themselves, that does not mean those forms have not provided them with enough structural freedom and space to make some striking statements. Moreover, even if it remains the case that women communicate best musically through forms established by men, in some musical subcultures they have virtually invented forms. In the classic era of black gospel music from the end of World War II to about 1970, transcendentally powerful women singers such as Willie Mae Ford Smith, Mahalia Jackson, and Clara Ward served as models for legions of male imitators as well as women. In jazz Billie Holiday's vocal style itself became the model for virtually any subsequent female vocalist and, more significantly, for male instrumental improvisation and phrasing (cited as influential by such leading figures as trumpeter Miles Davis).[47] Bessie Smith's raw blues vocals and posture of personal autonomy have themselves been models for two generations of succeeding black women singers through Willie Mae "Big Mama" Thornton and ill-fated white rock vocalist Janis Joplin. Such women have, through the sheer overwhelming power of their genius and remarkable application of energies, broken through existing forms, adding something significantly novel to existing modes of musical discourse and serving as role models for succeeding generations. Do these remain exceptions that may prove a more general rule?

In the jazz tradition the "girl singer" with big bands and later female vocalists, too, for the most part rework jazz and Broadway musical "standards" composed almost exclusively by men. But they have done it in ways uniquely theirs, as with Billie Holiday, Ella Fitzgerald, or Sarah Vaughn or Betty Carter. They have created a women's discourse in jazz that has its own conventions, forms, and style not equaled by any males who sing in that genre. Initially fashioned from materials almost exclusively male developed, especially the "standard" songs of Hollywood and Broadway, their songs have been reworked in creating utterly individualized sounds that serve as enduring performance models for women and men.

More recently, several jazz women, including vocalists Abbey Lincoln and Betty Carter, have been writing their own songs. Carter, who is acclaimed by critics as one of the most exceptional improvisational voices in jazz history, has not only written many of her own songs but started and ran her own label for over a decade until selling her catalog to Verve Records in 1988, retaining complete artistic control. Their example has opened new possibilities for women in other areas of jazz, where women were usually welcome only as pianists, as, for example, were Mary Lou Williams and Marian McPartland. Partly due to her syndicated public radio program "Piano Jazz," the latter emerged after four decades of performance as one of the best-known women in jazz. In the 1970s and 1980s numerous other women have emerged as instrumentalists and composers, as, for example, pianist-composer Carla Bley, pianist Joanne Brakeen, guitarist Emily Remler, saxophonist Jane Ira Bloom, and drummer Terri Lynn Carrington. With such positive role models, greater numbers of women distinguish themselves within the jazz idiom, though they still remain a minority.

THE WOMEN'S MUSIC MOVEMENT

In the 1970s a small (in market terms) but distinctive subculture of Women's Music developed in the United States. Holly Near and Chris Williamson have been among the best-known performers in this genre, which has many loyal followers, though they have probably not sold much over a million recordings between them on the Redwood and Olivia labels. Near began as a folk-protest singer active in the anti-Vietnam War movement and moved in the 1970s toward a "woman-identified" posture with a significant number of lesbian songs added to her powerful folk-protest repertory. Williamson's album *Changer and the Changed* (1975) is one of the most widely known and successful artifacts in the Women's Music movement, but Williamson has, in conventional mass market terms, sold "only" something over 250,000 albums on the Berkeley-based Olivia label. Since 1973 this most successful of the Women's Music labels has issued 32 albums that collectively sold over one and one-half million copies.[48] None of the major conglomerates would find such sales figures indicative of the kind of market potential they seek in a business where a single album could potentially sell from 5 to 30 million copies (the latter figure, Michael Jackson's *Thriller*).

Initially seemingly aimed at feminist separatist and lesbian audiences, but with increasing support among feminist heterosexual women, this music might best be characterized as reflecting a distinctive consciousness of *women-identification*. As one proponent described it, "Written by and for women, it speaks to their real lives, providing role models and choices that popular music has rarely offered to them. In contrast to popular music's prevalent degradation of women, Women's Music holds the feminist and humanist ideals of self-affirmation and mutual support."[49]

In practice such ideals may not distinguish this style from other musical forms that provide significant cultural free space for participants, except that the very explicit gender identification of Women's Music probably discourages most male performers and consumers, though a number of apparently gay male musicians seem involved, as are some male singers who specialize in topical songs from a new or "liberated" male perspective. The appeal of the latter seems limited largely to feminist and lesbian women and the rather small numbers of males involved in rethinking male roles.[50] Although not mass popular culture, though neither are jazz and blues, the widest circulating recordings in Women's Music such as Williamson's *Changer and the Changed* may sell something over 200,000 copies. The movement has nurtured a growing body of female artists, technicians, and producers whose work is available on an increasing proliferation of women's labels such as Redwood and Olivia—all run by and for women.

Influence of the products of Women's Music may be greater than sales might indicate. The consumption and utilization patterns of such recordings may, in their effect on consciousness, be different from those of normal pop product. This is so in that those who buy the albums may already have undergone a "conversion" in consciousness, making the purchase serve as a mark of their new identity and using the recordings to help maintain their new consciousness or recruit others to join with them in their newfound community.

Proponents of Women's Music believe it provides a small enclave against popular music's ruling male apparatus. The male apparatus "rules," not in the sense of a secret manipulation from behind the scenes, but through occupying a set of positions in the industry structure that manage, administer, organize, and produce. The people who hold these positions have come to view the world in distinctive ways. These involve conceptions driven largely by what will sell in the largest quantity and are legitimated in terms of economic return—the "bottom line." As a consequence, they construct images of women artists in market-proven, mainstream, stereotypical ways. What is not heard, sought out, recorded, promoted? Who is silent? Who was never heard or recorded? One can with effort begin to picture what the personal documentation and testimony might be from those women who tried but could not stomach the obstacles and abuse. Chapple and Garofalo in *Rock 'n' Roll Is Here to Pay* and especially Steward and Garratt in *Signed, Sealed, and Delivered* provide a number of examples of the experiences of women in all phases of the music business.[51] It is a long, difficult struggle for women to establish themselves in any autonomous way (and these are stories of the women who were there to be interviewed. The experience of those who did not remain active remains to be told).

The increasingly centralized monopoly of sound-product production and distribution enforces an *effective* silence on the part of those not a part of it. Except for the specialty labels and subcultural movements such as Women's Music where women compose, own, and produce and distribute all their own recordings, this silence has been materially organized. It is a product of a system of class bias and corporate media monopoly that is indeed quite centralized.[52] More fundamentally, it is also a product of a particularly sexist hegemony—a total way of looking at the world—that sees women in limited and stereotypical ways.

At the most basic level hegemony is "an historical process in which one picture of the world is preferred over others."[53] The important aspect of the theory of hegemony is that it is *learned*—it is a product of a particular process of socialization into a "received" culture.[54] As Raymond Williams has put it, "Hegemony goes beyond 'culture' . . . in its insistence on relating 'the whole social process' to specific distributions of power and influence."[55] Hegemony is more than "ideology," and its forms of control go beyond what is normally seen as "manipulation" and "indoctrination." Rather, "it is a whole body of practices and expectations, over the whole of living: our senses and assignments of energy, our shaping perceptions of ourselves and our world. It is a lived system of meanings and values—constitutive and constituting—which as they are experienced as practices appear as reciprocally confirming.''[56] People in any society experience hegemony as a ''sense of reality'' that seems absolute and beyond which it appears for most people in most areas of their lives almost impossible to move. It is, in this strongest sense, a ''culture,'' but ''a culture which has also to be seen as the lived dominance and subordination of particular classes.''[57] An important aspect of hegemony is that it must be continually struggled for. It must be won, but then only temporarily. It is never permanently imposed. Absence of coherent alternatives may allow it to persist longer than it otherwise might.

The effect of a particularly *sexist* kind of hegemony in analyzing popular culture is to discourage certain questions from being asked because the situations involving exclusion of women seem somehow natural. (Thus, for example, I did a double take when I saw a female jazz drummer backing trumpeter Clark Terry at a major jazz club; I felt it, perhaps unconsciously, as somehow ''unnatural'' to see a woman playing drums—it certainly is infrequent—especially backing such a celebrated male figure. This could be interpreted as one aspect of sexist hegemony in operation.) Countering it or moving beyond it in understanding wide variations in the presence of men versus women in any area of activity imposes the requirement of exploring why women are *not* present, then following the received and usually accepted explanations to their social origins, and then ''revisioning'' the society and particular area of cultural practice to permit the possibility of women's involvement. This process is underdeveloped in popular music, especially among critics, although it has progressed substantially more in areas of film criticism.[58]

The predominance of sexist hegemony and the male domination of the whole system of music production in the United States are factors so overwhelming by themselves as to suggest that Women's Music as a particular counterhegemonic cultural movement of resistance will never reach a mass audience, though the proliferation of new women in the popular music market in 1988 and 1989 suggests that it is quite possible for women artists to sell their products through the male-dominated system, whatever their political stance, if they follow existing channels in an era when female artists are deemed more marketable than in the past. Michelle Shocked and Tracy Chapman in 1988 clearly presented themselves from the first as political radicals and social critics, though also as heterosexual. The recent emergence of a number of women artists suggests the untapped reservoir of talent that languished in earlier decades. One especially innovative example is the work of Tracy Chapman, who broke onto a music scene to reach the top of the charts in a year in which magazines such as *Musician* could speak of the ''year of the women.''[59] Chapman is a black woman born in Cleveland in 1964, raised by a single mother, college educated in the Boston area at Tufts. Her album *Tracy Chapman* on the Electra label in August 1988 reached the top position in the British album charts and first place in the *Rolling*

Stone top 50 albums in the United States, remaining there for a considerable period through 1989. Chapman herself appeared on the cover of *Rolling Stone* shortly after. These are indications of significant audience-consumer response. Her album is thus an important pop cultural production.

Chapman's voice has a grain, an assertive but subtle stress and tone, that seems to connect in knowing ways with deep reserves of power and carries implications of a kind of subdued threat. Her use of stylistic elements of the folk-protest tradition recalls the powerful voice of Odetta from the 1960s. To a greater degree her sound recalls Joan Armatrading in the 1970s and 1980s (Armatrading, for all her exceptionally well produced albums has projected neither such a thematic breadth, explicitly "serious" social and political messages, nor overtones of the folk-protest tradition in her personally communicative songs that ring with a kind of resentment). If Chapman's "sound" might be in any way classified as derivative, it demonstrates how one mode of delivery can be taken up and radically transformed through infusion of critical and oppositional content.

Of the 11 songs on Chapman's album, each lyrically and thematically reaches beyond much that has been experienced in a popular music album in many years. In their prophetic menace and power they recall Bob Dylan's *The Times They Are A-Changin'* album of 1964. The lyrics of several songs subtly but incisively explore dimensions of the class and racist reality of American life. "Behind the Wall" is the first major popular song on domestic violence. Four songs present a woman's perspective on one-sided love relations; three others, "Why?" "Behind the Wall," and "Talkin' about a Revolution," could well assume the anthemic role for critical and alienated young people and social critics of the 1980s and 1990s generation that Dylan songs did in the 1960s and 1970s. This is innovative work, novel in the context in which it appears and in the sense it provides thematically evocative songs that raise searching questions and criticisms while suggesting also the possibility of some kind of alternative. Most popular songs with any critical themes raise only questions. Whatever the circumstances, no matter how crushing, Chapman affirms there *can* be alternatives.

Nothing is taken at face value in Chapman's work. If her songs convey "menace and power," they do so, she insists, from a hopeful perspective: "Many of the people who've written about me have described me as an angry, young, black protest singer, but I think they're missing some of the things in my music. Yes, I am angry about certain things and, yes, I am young and black, but I'd hate for people to think that's all there is to Tracy Chapman. For me, all is not gloom and doom. The stories in my songs may appear negative on the surface, but the message I'm trying to convey is positive and hopeful."[60] It is a message through which Tracy Chapman with a minority of other committed artists seeks to transcend the tyranny of the present. In September 1988 she joined the Amnesty International Human Rights Now! world tour with Sting, Springsteen, Peter Gabriel, and others. From press accounts, her sets in whatever national context proved to be exceptionally riveting. In these senses, given the context of the time, she is a "revolutionary" artist and her album is highly "innovative" cultural practice.[61] How those who consume the album use it, how it functions on the contested terrain of popular culture, what role it assumes politically, and what effect her role in the Human Rights Now! campaign has on wider popular consciousness remains to be seen. Future observers must determine whether Tracy Chapman truly is engaged in innovative cultural practice in a manner that prefigures or is instrumental toward more radical change. Although Chapman's approach might seem the most radical sort of popular music, in particular to conventional, older leftist intellectuals, it must be considered in contrast to the cultural creations and widely apparent images of such pop icons as Madonna and Cyndi Lauper.

Despite the success of young women artists such as Chapman, no mass, coherent, immediately identifiable alternative women's musical discourse has as yet had the time or material means to develop so that it is evident in *Rolling Stone* or on MTV (though to seek evidence of such discourse there and find it lacking does not, of course, mean it does not exist; indeed, perhaps imputing a degree of transparency and neutrality to those mediums is quite naive, given the values and biases they represent). Because of this, one must often seek evidence of a women's discourse through "against the grain" readings. As Lewis defines the notion of "reading against the grain," it refers to the "interpretative practice of reading 'through' a dominant male discourse to locate a subtextual female one. . . . [I]t assumes the female voice in a text exists as a secondary and embedded texture or quality."[62] At an earlier period this might have involved the analyst in description of the "grain" and inflections of words and phrases, for example, in recorded performances of Billie Holiday. Today, given the broader range of examples, it may be carried out in any context.[63]

What might a distinctive and overt women's musical discourse include? What would constitute its thematic content? Would it be a popular variety of themes of the contemporary Women's Music movement? Or the urban neo-folk style such as that of Chapman, or Michelle Shocked, and Suzanne Vega that emerged at the end of the 1980s?[64] Elements may already be present, embedded in the recent history of the thousands of women artists in the musical culture of recent years who have confronted the materially organized and overwhelmingly dominant alien culture that denied their full humanity and struggled to assert some measure of authorship of their productions, no matter what the intent of those composing their songs or producing their recordings.[65]

Elements of such a discourse are especially evident in the postmodern aspects of music television, in spite of the apparent overwhelming presence of male performers. Among those few videos involving women frequently cycled on MTV, E. Ann Kaplan points out in *Rocking around the Clock,* the representations of the position of the women toward conventional gender orientations is decidedly ambiguous.[66] Among those noted and studied in detail by Kaplan are Pat Benatar's "Love Is a Battlefield" and "Sex as a Weapon," Donna Summer's "She Works Hard for the Money," and Tina Turner's "Private Dancer." Even this ambiguity has had to be struggled for by the artists. As such, it constitutes a free space, one orientation those involved in construction of a women's discourse in popular music may utilize.

Thus Tina Turner reworked her hit "What's Love Got to Do with It?" As she described it: "The song was this sweet, little thing. Can you imagine me singing like Diana Ross or Barbara Streisand, trying to sound velvety and smooth? I really fought. Eventually, we roughened it out instrumentally and I added some (rock) phrasing, and we changed the song's attitude and got a hit. I have input, not just in song selection but in treatment too. I'll never be a musician, but I know what's right."[67] Although here Turner deprecates her creative role, it is clear her contribution was not simply creative, but a politically empowered creative act.[68] Whether her example prefigures more such statements or a movement based upon similar authorship is not clear.

PROLIFERATION OF MUSICAL GENRES IN THE 1980s

An important and interesting countertrend to the less than promising projections for the Women's Music movement has been the emergence of new musical genres in the 1980s. Whether it be New Age, fusion, jazz, electric "new grass" or acoustic bluegrass, or the classical-improvisational "new music,"[69] it has all been driven by the significant demographics of the baby-boom generation, those born in the 1946–64 period. The roughly 60 million Americans in this group (nearly 30 percent of the population) are, in the view of Will Ackerman, founder of Windham Hill records, mostly 25 to 45 years old, "professionals, predominantly white, upper-middle-class and college educated. . . . These people are appalled by the conformity of radio programming. They are not spoken to eloquently by heavy metal or new wave music."[70]

Seen simply in terms of market demographics, the diverse and sometimes even critical or oppositional consciousness of the baby-boom generation provides new openings for diversity in the music business, as do some of those cultural free spaces already noted as an important aspect of mass popular cultural production under late capitalism (i.e., if it sells, then record it!). Radio programming consultant John Sebastian (not the 1960s folk-rock singer) pointed out, "The point is, the industry is missing the boat in a big, big way by not appealing to the baby boomers, the largest group and the one with the most money. This group is the No. 1 ad agency buy across America—no teens, no 55-plus. All of this audience is in the money demographics."[71]

This social group, which record company research reportedly indicates consumes more records than any other, has opened up new avenues for smaller companies to produce a broader variety of music than that produced by the six megacompanies (CBS-Sony, Warner Communication, RCA-BMG, Capitol-EMI, Polygram, and MCA) that distribute over 80 percent of the recordings sold in the United States. The birth and rapid growth of such alternative labels as Windham Hall, Rounder, Flying Fish, Alligator, Palo Alto Jazz, and many others that have arisen with new technologies such as the compact disc demonstrates some openness—that there is the possibility of creation of new media areas when existing networks fail to deliver the cultural productions for which there is or might be significant demand. The possibilities for the emergence of a significant women's musical discourse on recordings are, then, not entirely closed. The success of Sinead O'Connor, Toni Childs, Michelle Shocked, Tracy Chapman, Suzanne Vega, and others in 1987–89 demonstrated this possibility. But there are limitations as well.

WOMEN'S EMERGENCE IN THE 1980s: DISTORTION AND ILLUSION?

In the late 1980s, despite their minority among the far larger numbers of men, there were legions of "strong" women in rock, with such figures as Chrissie Hynde, Cyndi Lauper, Madonna, the Wilson sisters of Heart, Pat Benatar, Joan Jett, and Tina Turner. And in more broadly pop-oriented categories, Whitney Houston, signed to Arista Records at age 19 in 1984, released two successive multimillion-selling albums. Her debut *Whitney Houston* sold over 8 million in the United States and 14 million worldwide. The tremendous number of ethnic women enjoying multimillion crossover successes such as those of Janet Jackson and Anita Baker, together with the reemergence of such figures as Aretha Franklin, Patti Labelle, the Pointer Sisters, Dionne Warwick, and the numbers of strong white female performers might suggest gender distinctions are declining. Country music and country rock abounds with important women figures— EmmyLou Harris, Dolly Parton, Loretta Lynn, Barbara Mandrell, for example— and there has been perhaps even a greater tendency to support women artists at any stage of their careers. But are these changes merely apparent?

Despite these female cultural models, important aspects of the experience of vast numbers of women remain excluded from mass popular culture so far as popular music is concerned. Among them is the growing phenomenon of the 1980s, the "feminization of poverty." The preponderance of the poor are women and children and that pattern has grown more pronounced.[72] The conventional family of working husband with the wife at home with kids has virtually passed away, constituting the smallest number of household units. Ever greater numbers of children are being raised by a single parent, usually the mother. But the single-mother models on television since "One Day at a Time" in the 1970s have been largely employed middle-class women, a less than accurate representation of the social realities of millions of women. With a film such as *Alice Doesn't Live Here Anymore* (1975), made real by meticulous attention to social and place detail and Ellen Burstyn's Oscar-winning performance, the tenuous situation of single mothers got some exposure. Only with such productions as "The Burning Bed" in 1984 did the bleak and desperate situation of millions of single mothers and married women subject to continual physical abuse make the public agenda. But it happened in film and on television, *not* in popular music. Why? Popular music seems dominated in recent decades by narrow conceptions of public taste, in contrast to the film industry, which has consistently sought to be more responsive to audience tastes and desires. Perhaps the answer lies in the profit potential of the two mediums. More money may be made in film and video in a few days from a major market success than from any recording over many months.

If in the 1980s there was or seemed to be an opening for more women in music, what kind of models did they present? For some of the successful female performers of the 1980s—Cyndi Lauper, Tina Turner, and Madonna, for example—there are extremely complex and even contradictory relationships to conventional notions of femininity and "normal" sex roles.[73] For example, Madonna's brazenly assertive performance in the film *Desperately Seeking Susan* presented a strong young woman (perversely independent or gutsy, depending on one's view) more so than in any of her recordings. Contrast this role to the early 1970s strong career woman portrayed by, say, Glenda Jackson, who endured that "small, hurting bravery" mentioned earlier, a cultural model that promised a measure of personal integrity but almost no fun. Perhaps musical and film models of wild younger women who "just want to have fun" is merely another response to market demographics—there are lots of them and they won't be contained. They, too, in increasing numbers go to movies, buy recordings, rent videos, and especially watch MTV. That might be part of the appeal of the 1987 film *Dirty Dancing* and its two best-selling soundtrack albums, but the major part is more likely the old school-girl fantasy: "My favorite daydream in boring classes at school was of a famous star suddenly walking into the room to take me away, leaving my classmates sighing in regret that they hadn't realized I was so wonderful. I felt that my lover could actually transform me, and many of my friends have confessed to similar cinderella fantasies."[74] There may be more, as Patrick Swayze (the male lead) noted in an ABC television "20/20" interview with Barbara Walters in late 1988: The film has a tremendous cult following of those who have seen it as many as 100 times. They find something in the film—perhaps it resonates so much in their consciousness because it suggests, Swayze reasons, that *each* person has *something* great within himself or herself, if only it can be released.

FATAL DISTORTION

More disturbing popular cultural trends cloud the picture of progress toward greater equality and autonomy for women. The tremendous 1987–88 box-office and number 1 home-video success of the film *Fatal Attraction* suggests a blacklash against this generation's independent women.[75] The director, Adrian Lyne, seemed to have precisely that in mind, constructing in the character of Alex Forrest (played by Glenn Close) an image of one of what he saw as near-psychotic career women "pretending to be men, sort of overcompensating. . . . It's kind of unattractive, however liberated and emancipated it is. It kind of fights the whole wife role, the whole childbearing role. Sure you got your career and your success, but you are not fulfilled as a woman. My wife has never worked. She's the least ambitious person I've ever met. [But] she's a *terrific* wife. . . . I come home and she's there."[76]

My own experience, reviewing and discussing the film with several classes of advanced undergraduates ranging in age from 20 to 40, suggests a common ability among a cross-section of often conservative students to see through and "deconstruct" the incredibly distorted caricature of the independent career woman in the film. The culturally conflicting range of views may produce a widespread ambivalence concerning desirable sex roles. In an economy where for both partners in a relationship there is no choice but to seek employment to pay the bills, the images in *Fatal Attraction*—the highly paid, successful lawyer-husband (Dan Gallager, played by Michael Douglas) and the soft-focused image of the wife (Anne Archer) who does not work outside the home, who is exceptionally beautiful, a stylish dresser, apparently very well educated (but in what?), totally committed to husband, child, and family, may *both* meet utopian wish fulfillment needs for male and female viewers. There have been a puzzling number of nonworking-wife roles in recent films, given the declining number of traditional families (i.e., husband working, wife at home). Perhaps the trend is analogous to the public preference during the years of the Great Depression for films about very rich people living it up in posh hotels and "nite" clubs. Men among the contemporary audience might wish their jobs provided enough income so that wives could choose not to work outside the home. Women who are involved in the daily career rat race or are in unsatisfying dead-end jobs might fantasize about an idealized cozy full-time "home" life.

Discussion of such realities of the actual economic situation may restore a sense of perspective, but the fact that millions responded to the constructed images in *Fatal Attraction* raises more profound questions concerning the unspoken longings of the mass audience. It takes considerable time, discussion, and reading of reviews to transcend the common reaction of both men and women who want Alex, the psychotic "monster" who is the main female character of *Fatal Attraction*, to die, reportedly often shouting "Kill the bitch!" in theaters. The fascination the film provides may derive from a nostalgic longing for a disintegrating world or lifestyle—another "little world" on the way to being "emptied out." It also might represent an underlying desire to return to the certainty of older sex role divisions in society, to escape the ambiguity and terrors of liberation. Others might see some of the response as sheer misogyny.

FEMALE REPRESENTATION AND OPPOSITIONAL IMAGES IN 1980s POP

The impression one got in the late 1980s was that recording companies projected an audience demand for young, beautiful, stylish, darker-skinned, vaguely ethnic (black or hispanic) kinds of women, carefully nurtured by company advertising—neosoul divas. Sade, Lisa Lisa, Gloria Estevan, Whitney Houston, Jody Watley, Anita Baker, and a proliferating legion of others meet that image to some degree, although their very presence constitutes a body of role models. And several, such as Sade and Baker, have immense talent. The two most significant oppositional models for women in the 1980s, however, were probably Cyndi Lauper and Madonna. Their significance does not lie particularly at the level of lyrical content. In fact there isn't much one can find in the lyrics of each that might be interpreted as directly socially critical or oppositional.[77] Most of the empirical literature suggests the majority of the audience is not particularly attentive to the lyrics anyway. The overall image may count for much more. Clearly both Lauper and Madonna have fought to create and maintain such oppositional images, evident in manner, appearance, body language, and a style of dress that has been taken up by millions of young women.

The content of most rock and pop in which women appear would appear to reflect the title of a Cyndi Lauper song from her *She's So Unusual* album, "Girls Just Want to Have Fun" (and be desired, as in Madonna's "Material Girl," flaunting or "parading the desire to be desired"[78]), but there is much more to it than that. The overwhelming proportion of thematic messages seem to deal with relationships and existential dilemmas around them, for that, of course, is where most people live their lives. Moreover, the intimate relations of two individuals as loved and lover have been considered the very core of human freedom, even by the most radical of social critics.[79] It is the commodified use of idealized representations of them that is problematical in much of popular music. In spite of this, such images may, in better moments, function for the audience as substitute imagery, as with some of the recent love songs from a distinctive women's perspective, such as those of Tracy Chapman ("If Not Now . . . ," "For You," "Baby, Can I Hold You") or perhaps those sung by Natalie Merchant of the group 10,000 Maniacs.

The idolization by teenagers of Debbie Harry at the end of the 1970s and of Cyndi Lauper and Madonna in the 1980s should be read in terms of the possibility of oppositional orientation provided by the images. Harry's image was apparently meant initially as a satire on the breathless bimbo persona Marilyn Monroe could brilliantly portray, yet it was apparently not seen as such by the mass audience, and Debbie Harry became during 1979–81 for many the preeminent sex symbol of rock. She lost control of any oppositional or critical direction in the character she created. Identification with Lauper and Madonna, in contrast, may have served to mark a generational critique of parental authority. Madonna, in particular, did seem to play a powerful oppositional role in providing a model for teenagers to question parental authority. Teens who learn to question parents might grow up to question politicians, though, of course, they might simply become cynical. But the associated values seem to accept materialistic consumer culture uncritically and to be concerned with creating that "haven in a heartless world"—the good relationship—within presently existing society, to be able to have the right "someone" with whom to share consumption patterns. In spite of the materialism, these two women as models may have more far-reaching impact in shaping character or in providing independent images within which legions of individual young women could project oppositional orientations.

Tracy Chapman's emergence in 1988 and the reemergence of Patti Smith with *Dream of Life,* with its soaring anthem "People Have the Power," and, perhaps, Pat Benatar's surprising 1988 comeback *Wideawake in Dreamland,* which throughout its socially critical thematic unity clearly reaches for something beyond the present social reality, are more comprehensible to an earlier and older generation. Are these artists, powerful and significant and worthy of note though they may be, perceived by the mass female youth audience as someone to model? From all evidence it appears not at all to the obvious degree Lauper and Madonna were.

Seen in conventional terms, the representations of most contemporary women artists in music present images of heterosexual assertiveness, high sexual energy, and some kind of unique persona—style, clothing, body language. Yet they seem directed at pursuit of essentially individualized solutions within consumer culture. This does not necessarily mean Madonna, for example, should sing songs extolling revolution in El Salvador or opposing funding for CIA "freedom fighters" on the Nicaragua border for her image to serve "political" functions for the audience. She provides an ambiguous image of rebelliousness within the existing system that could become an element of an oppositional orientation.

While the notion of the good relationship as a "haven in a heartless world" is the central longing commonly reaffirmed in popular music by women, there emerges among a few women performers, another focus. Suzanne Vega, for example, represents a somewhat different model. In her *Solitude Standing* (1987) is a kind of longing for peaceful isolation. The implications are potentially, even prefiguratively, rebellious. Vega's posture and her whole persona as an artist have been described as "passively antisocial."[80] If in the last decade of cause-related spectacles there was an effort to recapture the illusive supposed collective elation of Woodstock, Vega's approach represents a model of *individualized autonomy.* This could make her an outcast, but an important one in a cultural context that largely affirms a high-consumption lifestyle, in which even *Mother Jones* contains imported vodka ads, and such empty political rallying cries as "Read-my-lips, no-new-taxes." That the field of popular music is filled with such ambiguities in models for women at least provides possibilities for fashioning alternative oppositional orientations from available materials.

Ironically, although cultural elevation of the family in the 1980s reached almost pathological proportions, one finds not a great deal of discussion of marriage, childbirth, or childrearing in popular music of the period. Most performers, female and male, seem to be presented as free and independent, often aggressively sexual objects, in their videos. By contrast, all the major political figures of the 1988 presidential campaign had wives and families, often larger than average. Apparently those who watch videos, buy records, and attend concerts need to be assured of the continued sexual availability of performers, at least as fantasy sexual objects. With images of presidents there should be symbolic reassurance of stability and a gratification of nostalgic desire for the community of family.

Wider social meaning in music performed by women established often through presentation of stronger but also, probably male-defined, "sexier" role models who might be said to function essentially as aerobicized sex objects. (One thinks, as one example, of the lithe and well-muscled abdominal region of Sheena Easton displayed in her aggressively tough 1989 video, "The Lover in Me.") More appear as self-absorbed sexual subjects with desires to use males for their own pleasure. Reversal of the sexual objectification of preceding decades in such cases should not be read as some sort of revolutionary process, although it might prefigure the possibility of other reversals. Here, in addition to Madonna, examples might be Joan Jett, much of Pat Benatar's early 1980s work, Heart, and even some of Tina Turner's work, and more recently the female heavy metal model of Lita Ford and others. Madonna, Turner, and Benatar having had significant video exposure have also at times presented contrasting ambiguous models, but the possibilities they pose remain to be developed.

With a few exceptions such as Aretha Franklin, until the late 1980s the strongest female role models in the varieties of popular music were presented in the 1920s and 1930s among such classic women blues singers as Bessie Smith and Memphis Minnie, whose influence while small in initial market terms persists in powerful subcultural models of tough "blues mamas" who won't take abuse from anybody, reinvigorated in recent decades by the giant Willie Mae "Big Mama" Thornton (active on records and in live concerts from 1949 through the early 1980s) and white blues-rock shouter Janis Joplin (who, though she died of apparent heroin overdose in 1970, served as a model for several other white blues-influenced women singers). One should not as well the 1980s resurgence of Etta James, a rhythm and blues singer of immense physical proportions with a voice to match, and the vocals of black Chicago blueswoman Koko Taylor, whose reworking of the classic "I'm a Man" into "I'm a Woman" became a minor feminist anthem. (The song was for 30 years identified with Muddy Waters, described by film critic Pauline Kael in reviewing his appearance in the Band's *The Last Waltz* as the quintessence of machismo.) The existence of such highly energetic women models, their retention on recordings and videotapes, creates at least the possibility of drawing upon them as historical raw materials for recharging society with renewed desires for freedom and social autonomy.

One ultimate effect of contemporary representations of women seems to be reinforcement of a competitive ethic of sexual objectification. Only rarely in mass popular culture, for example in such a film as *9 to 5* (1980), in some ways itself an absurd caricature, is there the assertion of an alternative, noncompetitive "women's" ethic and way of adapting to or solving life's problems.

If stronger images of women have appeared in greater numbers, those images do not mean a change in predominant content of the product. But at least the presence of the images provides new possibilities for generation of alternatives. The format of music television provides a few free spaces, a few "windows" in which some exceptionally creative videos portraying women have been presented. These are indeed a minority of the women shown in 11 percent of music videos, yet they are possibly much more memorable shown against the background of the likes of Whitesnake, Billy Idol, Sammy Hagar, Robert Palmer, George Michael, or Guns 'n' Roses.[81]

Is the struggle to overcome gender stereotypes being won by women? Widespread lip service to formal equality of the sexes does not suggest understanding of the more complex realities of women's lives, of their essential inequality and lack of real social autonomy imposed, in one area of life, by underdevelopment of the most elementary and basic public programs of medical, prenatal, and child care and, at another symbolic level, with their functions as objects and fantasized images of male longings for "shelter from the storm." At the level of social power and influence in the controlling bureaucracies of society, only the most modest progress has been evident. If the music business remains a patriarchal structure run almost exclusively by white males, so does the whole society.

Musically, the situation could be characterized as attainment of a partial kind of affirmative action for sexual commodification. Popular music at its worst (the image content of most music videos) usually functions to perpetuate all the old gender stereotypes, with a few spaces for ambiguous (not feminist) alternatives. In some of its better examples, R.E.M.'s "For the One I Love" or several of Tracy Chapman's songs, including the popular "Fast Car," it would seem to seek to go beyond mere equality of sexual objectification and, as with the best popular cultural artifacts, to embody enough ambiguity to permit freely negotiated interpretation and response, "letting us be both subject and object of the singers' needs (regardless of our or their gender)."[82] Beyond that, to demand the revisioning of women's place in popular music is to demand the kinds of fundamental changes in culture and consciousness, as well as programatic transformations of social life, that will permit real social autonomy for all classes and ages of women. Perhaps only then will the construction of more realistic representations of women and men be evident, though that can never be the only function of a people's popular culture, which in its central qualities must also embody frequently conservative, but often futurist, elements of unspoken and utopian longings.

NOTES

1. Tillie Olsen, *Silences* (New York: Delta Books, 1982), p. xiii.

2. Simon Frith and Angela McRobbie, "Rock and Sexuality," *Screen Education* 29, (Winter 1978–79): 3–19.

3. Sara Evans, *Personal Politics: The Roots of Women's Liberation in the Civil Rights Movement and the New Left* (New York: Vintage, 1980).

4. This is demonstrated in Elaine Tyler May, *Homeward Bound: American Families in the Cold War Era* (New York: Basic Books, 1988).

5. Marjorie Rosen, *Popcorn Venus: Women, Movies, and the American Dream* (New York: Coward, McCann & Geoghegan, 1973).

6. Figures from *Statistical Abstract of the United States, 1988.*

7. Rosen, *Popcorn Venus*, p. 361. It is important to reemphasize here that films are important indicators of current thought but obviously should not be taken as wholly indicative of the public consciousness. Films provide significant indications of changing images and suggest trends. Nonetheless, because of the film industry's responsiveness to public sensibilities, films provide an insight into the industry's fairly sophisticated readings, which are based on extensive market research of what the film-viewing audience might find appealing. The huge financial investments involved and the possibilities for huge profits from major box-office attractions increase the corporate need for sensitivity to market preferences. For a perceptive overview of theoretical issues and substantive application to a variety of film genres, see Michael Ryan and Douglas Kellner, *Camera Politica* (Bloomington: University of Indiana Press, 1988).

8. Ibid.

9. See the discussion in Ryan and Kellner, *Camera Politica*, pp. 157–65.

10. Christopher Lasch, *Haven in a Heartless World: The Family Besieged* (New York: Basic Books, 1977).

11. Examples of popular songs dealing with violence against women are scarce. Child abuse themes are evident in Suzanne Vega's "Luka" and Natalie Merchant of 10,000 Maniacs doing "What's the Matter Here?"

12. Ellen Willis, "Janis Joplin," in *The Rolling Stone Illustrated History of Rock & Roll,* ed. Jim Miller (New York: Random House/Rolling Stone Press, 1980), p. 276.

13. Jim Miller, ed., *The Rolling Stone Illustrated History of Rock & Roll* (New York: Random House/Rolling Stone Press, 1980).

14. Peter Hesbacher, Nancy Clasby, H. Gerald Clasby, and David G. Berger, "Solo Female Vocalists: Some Shifts in Stature and Alterations in Song," *Popular Music and Society,* 5 (1977): 1–16.

15. Peter Hesbacher and Bruce Anderson, "Hit Singers since 1940: Have Women Advanced?" *Popular Music and Society,* vol. 7, no. 3 (1980): 132–39.

16. Alan Wells, "Women in Popular Music: Changing Fortunes from 1955 to 1984," *Popular Music and Society,* vol. 10, no. 4 (1986): 73–85.

17. Ibid.

18. Jane D. Brown and Kenneth C. Campbell, "Race and Gender in Music Videos: The Same Beat but a Different Drummer," *Journal of Communication,* vol. 36, no. 1 (Winter 1986): 94–106.

19. In addition to the work of Simon Frith and Angela McRobbie previously mentioned, distinguished exceptions are Steve Chapple and Reebee Garofalo, *Rock 'n' Roll Is Here to Pay: The History and Politics of the Music Industry* (Chicago: Nelson Hall, 1977), especially Chapter 8, "Long Hard Climb: Women in Rock"; and Christine Ferreira, "Like a Virgin: The Men Don't Know, But the Little Girls Understand," *Popular Music and Society,* vol. 11, no. 2 (1987): 5–16.

20. Chapple and Garofalo, "Long Hard Climb," especially pp. 289–96. This remains the definitive treatment of the problem. Just change the names and the situation remains the same. New day, same crap.

21. R. Serge Denisoff and John Bridges, "Popular Music: Who Are the Recording Artists?" *Journal of Communication,* vol. 32, no. 1 (Winter 1982): 132–42.

22. The phrase comes from Dorothy E. Smith's revelatory essay, "A Sociology for Women," in *The Prism of Sex: Essays in the Sociology of Knowledge,* ed. J. A. Sherman and E. T. Beck (Madison: University of Wisconsin Press, 1979), pp. 135–88. Her work

is collected in *The Everyday World as Problematic* (Boston: Northeastern University Press, 1987).

23. Frith and McRobbie, "Rock and Sexuality," p. 5.

24. Simon Frith, in a significant reworking of some of the ideas expressed in the 1978 essay with Angela McRobbie, has pointed to the one-sidedness of the earlier views, rejecting the notion that "sexuality has some sort of autonomous form which is expressed or controlled by cultural practice." See "Confessions of a Rock Critic," *New Statesman*, 23 (August 1985): 23. Reprinted in Simon Frith, *Music for Pleasure* (New York: Routledge, 1988).

25. Frith, "Confessions of a Rock Critic," p. 22.

26. Sue Steward and Cheryl Garratt, *Signed, Sealed, and Delivered* (Boston: South End Press, 1984), pp. 157–58.

27. Ibid.

28. See Frith, "Confessions of a Rock Critic," pp. 21–23.

29. The term "mobilization of bias" derives from political science discourse. It was originated by E. E. Schattsneider; see his *Semi-Sovereign People* (New York, 1960), p. 71. As elaborated by Peter Bachrach and Morton Baratz, the concept represents the tendency of political systems and subsystems to develop "a set of predominant values, beliefs, rituals, and institutional procedures ('rules of the game') that operate systematically and consistently to the benefit of certain persons and groups at the expense of others. Those who benefit are placed in a preferred position to defend and promote their vested interests." Peter Bachrach and Morton Baratz, *Power & Poverty: Theory & Practice* (New York: Oxford University Press, 1970), p. 43.

30. Frith and McRobbie, "Rock and Sexuality," p. 5.

31. Ibid.

32. Steward and Garratt, *Signed, Sealed, and Delivered*, p. 142.

33. Frith, "Confessions of a Rock Critic," p. 23.

34. Bureau of Labor Statistics, *Women in the Workforce*, No. 575, cited in Karin Stallard, Barbara Ehrenreich, and Holly Sklar, *Poverty in the American Dream: Women and Children First* (Boston: South End Press, 1983), p. 19.

35. Data from *Statistical Abstract of the United States, 1987.*

36. Carol Gilligan, *In a Different Voice: Psychological Theory and Women's Development* (Cambridge, Mass.: Harvard University Press, 1982); Mary Field Belenky, et al., *Women's Ways of Knowing: The Development of Self, Voice, and Mind* (New York: Basic Books, 1988).

37. Carole Pateman, "The Theoretical Subversiveness of Feminism," Introduction to *Feminist Challenges*, ed. Carole Pateman and Elizabeth Gross (Boston: Northeastern University Press, 1987), p. 6. On the doctrine of separate spheres see Linda K. Kerber, "Separate Spheres, Female Worlds, Woman's Place: The Rhetoric of Women's History," *Journal of American History*, vol. 75, no. 1 (June, 1988): 9–39.

38. Pateman, "Theoretical Subversiveness," p. 6.

39. Ibid. Emphasis added.

40. On the silences of women artists see Olsen, *Silences,* and the section on silence in Belenky et al., *Women's Ways of Knowing.*

41. For some insights see the chapters of Jon Weiner, *Come Together: John Lennon in His Time* (New York: Random House, 1984), grouped under the heading "Feminist Father," pp. 283–306.

42. Dorothy E. Smith, *The Everyday World as Problematic* (Boston: Beacon Press,

1987), p. 51; also, Dorothy E. Smith, "A Sociology for Women," in *The Prism of Sex: Essays in the Sociology of Knowledge*, ed. Julia A. Sherman and Evelyn Torton Beck (Madison: University of Wisconsin Press, 1979), pp. 136–37.

43. Smith, "A Sociology for Women," p. 137.

44. *Downbeat*, December 1988, pp. 21–23.

45. Sheila Rowbotham, *Woman's Consciousness, Man's World* (New York: Penguin Books, 1973), p. 40.

46. Ibid., pp. 40–41.

47. See Davis' analysis of Holiday's phrasing like a horn in Nat Hentoff, "An Afternoon with Miles Davis," in *Jazz Panorama*, ed. Martin Williams (New York: Collier Books, 1964). Holiday's place in jazz history is assessed in James Lincoln Collier, *The Making of Jazz* (New York: Delta Books, 1979), pp. 303–312.

48. Gina Arnold, "Olivia Records," *Musician*, January 1989, p. 23.

49. Ruth Scovill, "Women's Music," in *Women's Culture: The Women's Renaissance of the Seventies*, ed. G. Kimball (Metuchen, N.J.: The Scarecrow Press, 1981), p. 148.

50. This is not to denigrate the significance of this movement. The substantial success of books by such liberated male proponents as Warren Farrell, *The Liberated Man* (New York: Random House, 1974), and Herb Goldberg, *The Hazards of Being Male* (New York: Signet, 1979) and *The New Male-Female Relationship* (New York: Signet, 1983) suggest there is a considerable interest in such topics. Whether more women than men read their work is unclear.

51. Chapple and Garofalo, "Long Hard Climb"; Steward and Garratt, *Signed, Sealed, and Delivered*.

52. Chapple and Garofalo, *Rock 'n' Roll Is Here to Pay*.

53. Todd Gitlin, *The Whole World Is Watching: The Media in the Making and Unmaking of the New Left* (Berkeley: University of California Press, 1980), p. 257.

54. See the discussion of received culture in Belenky et al., *Women's Ways of Knowing*.

55. Raymond Williams, *Marxism and Literature* (New York: Oxford University Press, 1977), p. 108.

56. Ibid., p. 110.

57. Ibid.

58. Important recent film criticism from women with relevance to popular music includes Annette Kuhn, *Women's Pictures: Feminism and Cinema* (London: Routledge & Kegan Paul, 1982); E. Ann Kaplan, *Women and Film: Both Sides of the Camera* (New York: Methuen, 1983); and E. Ann Kaplan, *Rocking around the Clock: Music Television, Postmodernism & Consumer Culture* (New York: Methuen, 1987). Especially useful is the brief introduction to Mary Gentile, *Film Feminisms* (Westport, Conn.: Greenwood Press, 1985), pp. 3–12.

59. Chapman, *Musician,* June 1988.

60. Ibid., p. 129.

61. On the notion of innovative cultural practice see Henri Lefebvre, *The Sociology of Marx* (New York: Vintage Books, 1969), pp. 25–58, "The Marxian Concept of Praxis."

62. Lisa A. Lewis, "Form and Female Authorship in Music Video," *Communication* 9 (1987): 355–77, quote from footnote, p. 373.

63. See as excellent examples Jackie Byars, "Reading Feminine Discourse: Primetime Television in the U.S.," *Communication* 9 (1987): 289–303, and John Fiske, "*Cag-*

ney and Lacey: Reading Character Structurally and Politically,'' *Communication* 9 (1987): 399–426.

64. See *Musician* 116 (June 1988) for a special report, "The Women's Movement of 1988."

65. In this connection see the comments of Tina Turner cited in Lewis, "Form and Female Authorship."

66. Kaplan, *Rocking around the Clock,* pp. 114–42.

67. Mark Mehler, "Tina Turner's Still Shaking That Thing," *Record,* December 1984, p. 20. Cited by Lewis, "Form and Female Authorship," p. 360.

68. Lewis, "Form and Female Authorship," p. 360.

69. For a comprehensive overview of the hybrid new music see John Schafer, *New Sounds* (New York: Harper & Row, 1987).

70. Will Ackerman, quoted by William Knoedelseder, "Baby Boom Rocks Music Scene Again," *Los Angeles Times,* January 1, 1985, pp. 1, 20–23.

71. Ibid.

72. On the feminization of poverty see Stallard, Ehrenreich, and Sklar, *Poverty in the American Dream.*

73. On the complex and contradictory relation of these women artists to conventional notions of femininity see Frith, "Confessions of a Rock Critic."

74. Steward and Garratt, *Signed, Sealed, and Delivered*, p. 148.

75. Two definitive deconstructions of the film and its transformation from a script that was little short of a feminist parable to a monster movie in which audiences screamed "Kill the bitch!" are Susan Faludi, "Fatal Distortion," *Mother Jones,* February-March, 1988, pp. 27–30, 49–50, and Ellen Willis, "Sins of the Fathers," *Village Voice,* December 15, 1987.

76. Adrian Lyne, director of *Fatal Attraction,* as interviewed by Susan Faludi, "Fatal Distortion," p. 49.

77. Lauper's song "She Bop" deals with masturbation, and her recording the New Orleans classic "Iko Iko" shows her links with the oppositional identifications in that song as explicated in George Lipsitz, "Mardi Gras Indians: Carnival and Counter-narrative in Black New Orleans" presented at the annual meeting of the American Studies Association, Miami, October 27–30, 1988.

78. See Kaplan's revelatory analysis of Madonna's "parading of the desire to be desired" in the video "Material Girl" in *Rocking around the Clock*, p. 115–42.

79. On this point see Russell Jacoby, *Social Amnesia* (Boston: Beacon Press, 1974), p. 114. The case of the Polish-German socialist Rosa Luxemburg's effort to maintain a loving, nurturing relationship is touching. See Elzbieta Ettinger, *Rosa Luxemburg: A Life* (Boston: Beacon Press, 1987). An insightful discussion of this aspect of her personal life was Vivian Gornick's review essay of the Ettinger book, "Woman behind Bars: Rosa Luxemburg's Theory of Revolution," *Village Voice Literary Supplement,* March 1987, pp. 18–19.

80. Barry Walters, "Leave Me Alone," *Village Voice,* July 14, 1987, p. 77.

81. See Kaplan's analysis of a Billy Idol video in *Rocking around the Clock.*

82. Frith, "Confessions of a Rock Critic," p. 23.

8

Springsteen: From the Emptiness of Flight to the Burden of Belonging

> More often than not the triumph of the received culture is so subtle it is not apparent to its victims. Content with what they can see, they have lost the capacity to imagine what they can no longer see.
>
> Lawrence Goodwyn, *Democratic Promise*[1]

> Remember, with nations, just like people, it's easy to let the best of yourself slip away.
>
> Bruce Springsteen, 1985

> I like to think music can shape people's minds and feelings about their own humanity.
>
> Bruce Springsteen, 1988

As Bruce Springsteen repeatedly stood before audiences of as many as 100,000 people, as he did in the concert mentioned earlier in Chapter 1, introducing Woody Guthrie's "This Land is Your Land" as "the greatest song ever written about America," and as a song "about a promise that's eroding every day for a lot of people," he sang in a voice with a grain of raw pain that one would think no one in the audience could ignore.[2] In every performance his voice was choked, and he seemed almost on the edge of tears. Yet every performance began to build, stanza-by-stanza, with a force unlike anything in the folk tradition out of which it came, into a grand anthem for the dispossessed. At the end he often said, with great solemnity, "Remember, nobody wins unless everybody wins!" As he repeated such statements in his shows across the nation and around the world, numerous observers echoed my own question: "What is *going on* here?''[3] One could not recall better versions of any song of protest anywhere, ever. But did the screaming crowds have any recognition of what they had heard? What did Springsteen think he was doing?

If something politically significant was happening there, did the audience know what it was? The Springsteen phenomenon, especially that surrounding his world tours of the 1980s, reflects all the power and contradictions of contemporary popular culture. Interpreting its functions produces significantly variant perspectives. Over a period of several years, becoming aware of Springsteen's work and discussing it with other serious observers of popular music, I rather consistently experienced reactions ranging from "pretentious and boring" from jazz performers to widespread disbelief from academic intellectuals to whom it was suggested that the singer and his songs are an important *political* phenomenon. In contrast to this observer, saturated with enthusiasm, many younger rock, punk, and new wave enthusiasts seemed to think Springsteen was really "boring old news" and artistically and in many other ways a conservative force. One critic even suggested that what Springsteen presented was just another form of "cock rock."[4] How does one account for the variations in response?

FUNCTIONS OF ROCK MUSIC

Analysis of the political implications of the Springsteen sensation of the 1980s first requires reconsideration of how rock music functions in this culture. From the first recognitions among social science intellectuals in the mid–1960s that something was indeed happening here, the literature on the functions of rock has been increasingly voluminous and conflicted.[5] To return to a question raised earlier, how are popular songs indicators of social behavior or attitudes? How does the audience interpret the meaning of rock texts, if by *texts* one means both lyrics and total musical package as it is included in recordings for sale, on video, and in personal appearances—that is, arrangement, rhythm, accompaniment, stage performance, and the band members' public images and personalities as well as their interactions with each other? Reading and hearing the lyrics of Springsteen's songs repeatedly, hearing them as "social facts" in themselves,[6] I find a significant portion of them have thematic interest and intrinsic merit, more than most of hundreds of other popular song lyrics studied over the 25 years since this observer first heard Bob Dylan and developed more than a passing interest in social and political functions of popular song.

This reading, by a political scientist who came to consciousness in the 1960s, focuses on social and political themes. Striking in the body of Springsteen's work is the recurrent use of the "dream" (also a significant theme in the blues and in the songs of David Byrne of the Talking Heads) and the linking of the image to a "promise of America" theme with a related subtheme of its failure and how that "tears one apart." Clearly, through most of his career Springsteen has found the traditional promises and vision of America to be unfulfilled for large sectors of the population. He has said as much in several interviews. This suggests rethinking the dominant vision of America or recognizing that the promise not only is simply unfulfilled, but that for many it can *never* be fulfilled, given the way things are organized. Whether that "message" reaches the audience is doubtful, given what is known and what has been demonstrated in the empirical literature on perception of the meaning of lyrics in popular song.[7] What is the impact on those who hear the message?

Springsteen is widely quoted on the misinterpretation of his songs, particularly "Born in the USA." As he put it: "I opened the paper one day and saw where they had quizzed kids on what different songs meant to them and they asked them what "Born in the U.S.A." meant. 'Well, it's about my country,' they answered. Well, this *is* what it's about—that's certainly one of the things it's about—but if that's as far in as you go, you're going to miss it, you know?"[8]

Robert Hilburn has argued that "listeners have been so conditioned to expect banality that a large percentage of the pop audience no longer even understands a good song when it hears one."[9] This, he suggests, is the result of MTV and bland radio formats. This observation is quite consistent with the results of a number of empirical studies done as early as the mid–1960s.

Springsteen has said, "I don't think people are being taught to think hard enough about things in general, whether it's about their own lives, politics, the situation in Nicaragua, or whatever."[10] The consequence of this fact (not exactly a revelation to those social scientists who have studied public opinion, nor even the smaller number who have studied popular music), he argues, is that "if you do not develop the skills to interpret that information—you're going to be easily manipulated, or you're going to walk around simply confused and ineffectual and powerless."[11]

Curiously, Hilburn has suggested that "rock 'n' roll is *no longer* [if it ever was!] looked to by the mass pop audience as information or art, but as simply entertainment."[12] Here one reaches a basic and complex problem of analysis, much more complex than Hilburn suggests. Clearly, rock is part of the dialogic social process that is popular culture.[13] The popularity of any rock recording derives from many sources, only in a minority of cases "directly extracted and/or deduced from its apparent substantive content."[14] The audience responds to popular musical figures for a variety of reasons: One woman fan said in an article on Springsteen's popularity, "Bruce has nice buns!"[15]

Recognizing the freedom of the audience to use popular culture for its own purposes, one must carefully approach thematic analysis of lyrics. They cannot be the sole source of data on singers or audiences.[16] This doesn't preclude the analysis of lyrical content, especially where a popular artist such as Springsteen unequivocally indicates the general message being communicated through introductions. To what degree and to what effect such messages "get through" are more problematical questions. Record companies who undertake expensive market analysis are not interested in such questions and do not publish their results. Their primary aim is increasing the sales of the product. But enough empirical literature of a general sort exists to provide some good indications of the effects of Springsteen's efforts. Record sales and concert grosses are indicative of appeal, though not necessarily of understanding and acceptance of intended messages. However, one *can* analyze the political significance of identified themes, the relation of that thematic content to political-economic context, the self-conception of the artist, and the historical limitations within which politically relevant popular song has operated.

MUSICAL COMMODITIES AND SOCIAL FUNCTIONS

Standing with 70,000 in the audience at the Silverdome immersed in the spectacle of the Springsteen concert, I was struck by the realization that unlike music in any society in history, in the United States a popular music has been created and marketed as a commodity that serves as a form of collective, self-critical dialogue. It provides individuals materials around which to construct social relationships and self-images. Virtually every person in contemporary society establishes self-identity, at least in part, in relation to elements of popular culture.[17]

Popular music with the apparent mass market appeal of a Springsteen or a Michael Jackson or the enduring influence of Bob Dylan, or especially Elvis Presley, functions as substitute imagery. It serves the historical function of art, that "of helping individuals find themselves, know who they are."[18] As substitute imagery, rock songs relate "a feeling toward the whole" while speaking to people as individuals.[19]*

Beyond such functions, rock is what Alan Gowans terms an "art of conviction" and an "art of persuasion." Arts of conviction set forth the fundamental beliefs and realized ideals of society.[20] Arts of persuasion create images to move people to form different beliefs. One interpreter argued that "rock music in the middle and late 1960s *primarily* functioned as an art of persuasion. Consciously and unconsciously it propagated an alternative way of viewing our society and induced its audience to consider, if not accept, new values and beliefs about how life should be lived." At this period, it is asserted, rock functioned as the "crown of creation, . . . the premier art form of the counter-culture."[21] The interpreter goes on to argue that in the 1960s "rock's mass communications network broadcast a lifestyle which obviously differed from the accepted standards of American society. The dissemination and absorption of its subterranean values reinforced behavioral changes, and as these changes became widespread basic lifestyles were affected."[22]

As a self-fulfilling empirical demonstration of the impact of the music, by the

---

*Listening to Springsteen's "Factory" on the album *Darkness on the Edge of Town* reminded me of the years my father spent in exhausting 12-hour days as the foreman on the paint line in a small truck plant. He was "used up" by the job and fired just before his eligibility for retirement. "Bobby Jean," from the *Born in the USA* album, a song seemingly directed at a woman who had been a friend but who was no longer part of his life, brought back memories of women friends from the past each time I heard it.

same interpretation, "rock's role as a reflector and reinforcer of these changes becomes readily apparent via an examination of the major lyrical themes of the period."[23] Although in accord with much conventional wisdom and personal recollections and perceptions, this view becomes mired in circularity when its own lyrical themes are suggested as empirical indications of its effects on society. The general direction of the argument is, of course, supported in critical and descriptive literature.[24] Yet it is contradicted by a number of empirical studies.[25] Achieving an adequate understanding of the issues requires a review of some of the highlights of existing theoretical and empirical literature.

There is a revelatory irony in the fact that Springsteen, one of the best-selling, most-admired figures in American popular music (speech writers for Ronald Reagan repeatedly quoted him in 1984, and in 1988 Democratic vice-presidential candidate Lloyd Bentsen adopted Springsteen's "No retreat, baby; no surrender" line in the closing weeks of the campaign) has portrayed in his songs an often devastating vision of an America of broken promises and "dreams that tear you apart," of a runaway society grinding up human hopes and aspirations. How many people related to his music because of these themes? Or did they appreciate his songs as examples of his sincere and authentically personal expression—in the way one might listen to a friend?

To review, the most simplistic analogy behind much empirical inquiry sees the committed artist "injecting" the audience with ideas. Whether dealing with the effects of mass media generally or more specifically with the question of whether the audience for a song "gets the message," this "hypodermic" hypothesis [26] suggests that the very fact of exposure alters the audience's values and behavior. Others imply that the very fact of a song's existence, regardless of its circulation, sales, understanding, or acceptance, is indication of its effects. A voluminous body of theoretical and empirical literature on mass communication, popular music, studies of persuasion and propaganda effects from World War II to the present, and literature on attitude change, to the contrary, show opinion and attitude change to be extremely complex processes, dependent on conditions, situations, and historical context.

Irving Janis and Carl Hovland, in a classic review of factors relevant to studying any effort at persuasion, distinguished four broad categories of multiple factors: (1) observable communication stimuli (content characteristics in content, communicators, media, and sociohistorical and environmental situation characteristics); (2) predispositional factors in the individual and audience (general and specific predispositions to particular types of appeals); (3) internal mediating processes in the individual (attention, comprehension, and acceptance); (4) observable communication effects (changes of opinion, perception, affect, and action or behavior). Within each category could be an infinite number of possible subdivisions.[27] Given these complexities, to arrive at any "scientifically" definitive determination of rock music's effects on the audience is probably impossible, considering the diversity of contexts into which works are projected and the variant needs and uses of the audience.

From debates that began in the late 1960s, the literature shows both conventional wisdom and professional opinion is divided, holding that contemporary music is either apolitical or extremely political. Journalistic commentators such as Hilburn have suggested that the political *content* of contemporary popular music (not simply the blue-collar protest rock of Bruce Springsteen, John Cougar Mellencamp, Bob Seger, and others, but most of the various schools in pop and rock) is more developed and more theoretically sophisticated than in earlier periods. Other observers, such as John Street in *Rebel Rock,* see complexity and contradiction.[28]

Social science writing about the functions of rock music has been directed largely at understanding either what the music does *to* the audience—are they "radicalized," for example—or to what degree they "get" the specific message conveyed in the lyrics, that is, to what degree they are aware of, comprehend, or accept the message. Other writing seeks to understand the demographics of consumption: Who buys what? Who listens to what? These leave out perhaps the most important dimensions—those dealing with what the audience *does* with the music, how they use it, and the larger implications of the patterns of their use. To understand such questions requires a review of some fundamental relationships.

COMMODITIES AND CORPORATIONS

The popular artist is involved in the creation of a commodity for sale through the network provided by a major corporation. While the recording is a type of commodity specific to late capitalism, the song itself "retains links with an earlier stage of social development. Captured on record, the song becomes a commodity to be transformed into profit for the industry."[29] This is but one of the functions served. Companies in their relentless search for profit will comb through the grass roots of popular song to find whatever is new, whatever people will buy, whatever people want and will create themselves if they cannot buy; they thus provide a crucial area of free space for composer and artist.

All record companies operate according to marketing decisions, and it is one of the specific features of the music business that there are different kinds of products worth marketing. Although they may be different products in terms of sound, however, in one sense all records are the same: They are the results of the same process of material production. This offers a productive contradiction: Because they are the same, to a large extent it does not matter what is in the grooves—as long as it sells.[30]

An effect of such a system is the ever-present possibility of some kind of alternative voices being heard. Thus CBS could assert in the mass advertising campaigns of the 1968–70 period, "The Man Can't Bust Our Music" and "The Revolutionaries Are on Columbia Records!" and it was *not* sheer hype. Despite the profit-making functions of the system, this situation creates a two-way relationship in the production of songs and records. In one view of the relationship companies virtually expropriate songs and artists and transform them for their ends to compete in the market. In another view, "the companies' products can themselves be transformed by the culture which receives them." In other words, the meaning of a record is not simply determined by the social relations of its production. It is affected also by the social relations of its consumption, that is, by its use: "Because records are interpreted, because they stimulate song, their consumption is not merely passive."[31]

Any recording or concert is a social fact in itself, intrinsically interesting from the perspective of critic or historian; but the fullest interpretation of meaning comes from the meanings brought to such creations by both artist and audience.[32]

Given sales of over 15 million copies of such an album as Springsteen's *Born in the USA* and exposure to tens of millions via television, what does such consumption and exposure mean? Knowledgeable observers have been cited as saying that most buyers of the album probably *mis*interpreted the meaning of it, identifying it with the superpatriotism and xenophobia of Ronald Reagan or of Sylvester Stallone in the film *Rambo*. Given the similarities of Springsteen and the Stallone of the *Rambo* films, in terms of muscles, bandanas, and tattered shirts, that view may not be so far off the mark.

Yet as Greil Marcus searingly explicated "Born in the U.S.A.," for the elite audience of *Artforum,* it seemed there could be little doubt of the composer's intentions:

The song is about the refusal of the country to treat Vietnam veterans as something more than nonunion workers in an enterprise conducted off the books. It is about the debt the country owes to those who suffered the violation of the principles on which the country was founded, and by which it has justified itself ever since.[33]

How many listeners heard it that way? Was there perhaps intentional ambiguity in the lyrics, and that made the record a big hit among all listeners, since one could get *any* reading out of it one wanted? Marcus saw it very differently:

The song links Vietnam veterans to the Vietnamese—or rather (because when he is on, Springsteen personalizes everything he touches), one veteran tries to make that link. . . . Springsteen's veteran shouts at an unseen judge [that he was sent to a foreign land . . . to kill Yellow men]. He was, he knows, sent off to kill a cipher, and he knows that he was sent as a cipher. The furious irony in his voice, ten years building, turns the racist phrase inside out and makes both ciphers real.[34]

For at least *some* of the millions who attended the live Springsteen concerts in 1984–85, and subsequent performances with the Amnesty International Human Rights Now! tour in 1988, the message and meaning the composer had in mind were evident. Interviews with Springsteen left no doubt of his critical vision of an America that had let the best of itself slip away. But what was the potential political effect of these performances and recordings? And of the minority who *correctly* "heard" the music?

EMPIRICAL SOCIAL SCIENCE AND POPULAR MUSIC

How does one test the frequent proposition that rock can "catalyze the hopes of a generation"? Principal sources of quantitative evidence are surveys of high school and college students. Based on a survey of Michigan high school students, John Robinson and Paul Hirsch reported that "only" a minority of from 10 to 30 percent of the sample correctly identified the "intended messages" in songs they selected as representative protest music.[35] Evidence consistent with this was presented in a widely cited series of reports by R. Serge Denisoff and Mark Levine based on analysis of survey data from college students in San Francisco. In their view "only" minorities of the sample correctly interpreted the meanings of two songs, "Eve of Destruction" and "Universal Soldier," taken as antiwar protest songs.[36] The interpretive "only" is emphasized because it seems a product of conventional wisdom rather than existing theory regarding political information and consciousness. What passes for knowledge of human behavior in ordinary discourse is often simply empirically not true.

A 1983 student survey by Emily Edwards and Michael Singletary seeking information on images of the media among students and their perception of mass media images in four popular songs found that among samples reporting familiarity with songs, comprehension of lyrics ranged from 18.1 to 58.7 percent.[37] The latter figure is considerably higher than the earlier Robinson and Hirsch or Denisoff and Levine studies. In the Robinson and Hirsch research about 70 percent of respondents reported being attracted to popular music by the overall "sound" rather than lyrics.[38] Edwards and Singletary found that, consistent with that view, the majority of listeners do not pay close attention to lyrics: Only 25 percent of their sample said lyrics were the aspect of a song most likely to determine their liking it; 31 percent said tempo; 14 percent were attracted by instrumentation; 13 percent, the vocalist; 10 percent, the musicians.[39]

Support for an alternative interpretation comes in a study by William Fox and James Williams based on a survey of 730 undergraduate sociology students at the University of Iowa seeking data on political preference and type of music consumed.[40] These investigators viewed their data as "generally incompatible with the argument that contemporary music is largely apolitical. Rather, evidence indicates that music has a differential appeal to young persons of varying political orientations."[41] A problem here is that all "rock" music is lumped together, obscuring possible differences among artists attractive to politically attentive and leftist students. Considering music consumption, one interesting finding showed that "liberal students tend to attend rock and popular music concerts more frequently, buy more record albums and tapes, and spend more time listening to records and tapes than do their conservative peers."[42] Conservative students in the sample tended to spend more time in radio listening and show a greater preference for current popular hits than did liberal or leftist students, who tended to like folk music, the blues, and protest music substantially more than did the conservatives.

John Orman's *The Politics of Rock Music* reports differences in the orientation of supporters of Jackson Browne, Bruce Springsteen, and punk/new wave in the period fall 1980–spring 1981.[43] It was carried out among self-designated supporters of the three preference groups at Fairfield University, a Jesuit school in Connecticut. One must be careful here in drawing too many conclusions. The student body of a Catholic school is not an adequate reflection of that generation of college students. Using attitudes toward certain symbols and historical figures (the United States, Jesus, Karl Marx, and Ronald Reagan are some examples) the Fairfield groups were differentiated according to their variant responses.

Results of the Fairfield study showed 33 percent of the Jackson Browne fans (n = 69), 34 percent of the Springsteen fans (n = 47), and 47 percent of the punk/new wave group (n = 61) to be self-designated liberal or radical. For the Browne fans former president Gerald Ford, incredibly, ranked the highest among living politicians in the United States; for Springsteen fans it was Jimmy Carter; for the punk/new wave group it was 1980 third-party presidential candidate John Anderson. The Springsteen supporters were characterized as slightly to the left of the Browne supporters. This is surprising, in Orman's view, because of Browne's identification with progressive causes. (The attitudes of the Springsteen fans reflect the image of the singer at the time of the tour for *The River* album, which was then underway. Springsteen's working-class identification was evident then, but the singer's significant politicization and deepening radicalism of the period of the "Born in the USA" tour of 1984–85—to the extent it was even evident—would, of course, not be reflected.) Based on his interpretation of the sample, in Orman's judgment "most rock music of the 1980s is clearly apolitical, and this seems to be an accurate reflection of the apolitical state of the 1980s rock fan."[44] But obvious alternative interpretations can be made. The absence of much support for Ronald Reagan in the year of his election to the presidency suggests some significant oppositional opinions might be at work.

REINTERPRETING THE RESULTS

Much more is evident here than most of the authors suggest. First, that the attraction of rock music appears to be in the generalized "sound" for the majority of listeners does *not* mean the music is not political nor politically relevant. Rock music is based heavily on the blues; as Ben Sidran so effectively put it, the blue notes convey nonverbal information—they represent a "galvanization of meaning and pitch."[45] Previous studies miss the basic attraction of the music, its liberating "feel," which, of course, lies in the "sound" rather than the lyrics. Some see this aspect as purely pleasureful. Lawrence Grossman, for example, has drawn an analogy between the vibrator used as a sexual aid and the vibrations of live music.[46] Yet as Sidran makes clear, the sound and the feel fulfill important functions that are significantly political: It was not always the lyrics which "blew the minds" of white youths attracted to rock 'n' roll in the 1950s. The lyrics of Chuck Berry, Little Richard, or Elvis were only a small part of the total musical package that drove audiences to a frenzy, though they did, in Richard's case, often encode some wild information![47] Berry's lyrics, as pointed out by Keith Richards in the 1988 film *Chuck Berry: Hail, Hail, Rock and Roll*, contained subtly-stated social commentary. But a major point of black music is its *non-literary*, oral expressive quality. (Of course, as pointed out in Chapter 4, this is not to say that the blues does not contain significant lyrical elements, nor that these lyrical elements are not an important contribution to the appeal of the music.)

Second, if one takes as a rough estimate with some empirical foundation the figure of "only" 10 to 30 percent of listeners who are attentive to lyrics, there remains a massive population—indeed millions, in the case of some of the biggest-selling albums—who *are* reached by song lyrics or who may consciously seek out singers and songs expressive of their views. Given findings of Converse and of other students of the belief systems of mass publics,[48] these figures are remarkable, considering the general lack of constraint in the belief systems of mass publics and the minority of the population who might by any standard be considered ideological. This fact, combined with the very explicit, politically relevant introductory raps and commentary by a Bruce Springsteen, suggests that exposure to explicitly political rock might play a much more significant role in reinforcing orientations of those in the audience who are disposed toward progressive action.

Indeed, based on the Fox and Williams findings, there is much to suggest that the audience exercises a good deal of initiative in selection of music in accord with its values.[49] Their study confirms that, amazingly, liberals and leftists find the blues recordings (and they have to do it on difficult-to-obtain specialty labels) in spite of the abominable treatment of the music by the conglomerates of the music industry! One may postulate that the audience probably make some very clear differentiations among popular rock artists, using or even, as Jacques Attali suggests in his revelatory *Noise: The Political Economy of Music,* "*re*-composing" the music in accord with their developing belief systems.[50]

If existing empirical literature tells very little about how the audiences use the music, artists like Springsteen have seen it and felt it; they know how songs like "Born to Run" become invested with meaning far beyond what originally existed in the mind of the composer. Thus, as Springsteen pointed out in an interview: "The song 'Born to Run' means a lot more to me now than it did then [1974]. I can sing it tonight and feel like it breathes in all those extra years. . . . It's one of the most emotional moments of the night. I can see all of those people and that song to them is like—that's *their song*, man. *It's almost as much the audience's as it is mine.*"[51]

From the outset many of these studies fail to ask the right questions, nor do they sensitively follow up responses or use many open-ended questions. There is a tendency to underinterpret the meaning of the results, relying too heavily on conventional wisdom, failing to consider the relation of findings to existing literature or theory. Often more interesting details from which to develop future hypotheses are obscured in efforts to draw inferences from categories that simply fail to make good sense.

To understand the individual relationship between a person and the music he or she selects, alternative approaches must be taken. The existing body of empirical studies based on surveys, at least those published in available social science journals, have not come close to doing that. Perhaps company marketing studies present other data, but such studies are generally neither known nor available to the public. Ideally, unstructured depth interviews could explore the uniqueness of personal use and preferences. In fact, a good deal can be learned simply by asking people their reasons for liking a particular artist or kind of music.

Rock music is a complex form of popular culture that is more than meets the ear. It starts with the creative expression of the artist. That is transformed into a marketable commodity, the recording. How that recording is used determines what it is. As Gowans points out, "Popular/commercial arts are far more than the cultural expression of an individual. . . . Whatever artistic expression they manifest is subordinated . . . to *social* function."[52] Popular music as an interactional or dialogic form of expressive activity in the context of reciprocity between artist and corporation, and corporation and consumer, and within the limits of what will generate a profit for the corporation, allows the listener to *create* a world of meaning by manipulating the imagery in the songs. To gain access to that world of meaning much greater degrees of creativity will be required from empirically oriented investigators.

The best and most enduring popular music shows a symbiotic relation between the creativity of the artist and the needs of the audience. Recalling Stuart Hall's notion of "contested terrain," the meaning of any popular artifact is the product of a variety of determining forces and demands, which inevitably involves a struggle over meaning.[53] Just as the artist's creativity is mediated through the corporations that market recordings and through radio and television disc and video playlists, audience needs are also mediated; but the reciprocity exists, nonetheless.

The problem of how meaning is determined is one of *signification*. What inflections in meaning are introduced by the nature of the corporate commodity process and which are contributed by the initial creators? What is the role of the publics who consume mass popular culture? Some of the basic issues were set out long ago by Simon Frith in *Sound Effects*.[54] There are the "realist" approaches that assume media operate with a degree of "transparency," communicating the meaning of artists but suggesting that "who controls" is perhaps the most significant factor in affecting what the audience receives. All media attempt to do this or to some degree create a sense or illusion of realism. It is a central aim of Hollywood films and most news media. To such views can be counterposed those of theorists who stress the way media "construct" reality for the audience. Radical music critics usually analyze rock, not in terms of form and content, but in terms of production and consumption, suggesting "the ideological meaning of music lies in the *way* it is commercially produced in its commodity form."[55] This goes back to T. W. Adorno's analyses in the 1940s stressing a unidirectional process in which mass culture was injected by elites into a passive mass, producing an ideological effect—a formerly creative people becoming passive as a result of forced feeding of standardized commercial musical products.[56]

Walter Benjamin represented a contrasting view, stressing that the mechanical reproduction of art broke the "aura" of the authority of "the original," permitting the democratization of consumption. The ideological meaning of art or music was thus decided in the process of consumption.[57] Meaning becomes what people make of popular culture. The emergence of the long-submerged approach of M. M. Bakhtin to the consciousness of culture analysis in the 1980s signaled the increasing appeal of conceiving of the audience as creative subjects. The appeal of both notions, of course, may say significant things about the analysts using them, serving as projective tests of unconscious political impulses in culture critics.[58] Both the elitist and creative subject perspectives can sensitize the observer to significant tendencies in the struggle for meaning in popular music, today in part deriving from the explosive energy of rock music. This is connected to its fundamentally contradictory character as creative expression and commodity, to its potential both for liberation and for domination. Popular music is more than a product—either of commercial manipulation or of the "pure aspirations of youth." As with any art form in a commercial society, only more so, it is "squeezed out between two conflicting pressures. On the one hand the publishers and manufacturers, geared to the obsolescence principle, constantly promote new crazes. On the other, working class youth seek a medium to express their experience in modern society."[59]

In popular music this contradiction exists in a particularly intensified form. Musicians must take account of it, some adopting tried commercial formulas of the past, others by insisting on being pure artists and cultural revolutionaries whose productions are not marketed or bought.

Springsteen is one of those who recognize the limitations of the above positions, seeing *each* as "a form of false consciousness, an inability to recognize both the potentialities and limitations of the situation."[60] Certainly the culture industry is powerful, but that fact does not definitively exclude progressive messages from committed artists, nor progressive uses by the receiving public. From the beginning of the "Born in the USA" tour, Springsteen was "at once the most important artist and the most hyped commodity in mass culture."[61] Yet he tried to wring from the situation new opportunities and, in spite of the mass spectacles his concerts became, seemed to be struggling to fashion a new role for the mass popular artist and to create new and ever-larger arenas for his message to be heard. In the process, he rejected or perhaps never considered how in the form of his presentation, in the context in which it was heard, the content of his message might be diminished. Even if he was heard, where could he go and where could he take his audience?

The limited success of Springsteen's highly politicized associate "Little Steven" is instructive. Little Steven, (formerly "Miami" Steve Van Zandt, a member of the Springsteen E Street Band for many years, tried a hard-line, explicitly political direction in 1984 with *Voice of America*, an ambitious effort to enter the rock mainstream with some powerful political messages. Acclaimed by some critics, it got little airplay, though Black Uhuru recorded "Solidarity" from the album. He followed it in 1987 with *Freedom, No Compromise,* including tailored-for-MTV tunes and videos with highly political messages such as "Bitter Fruit" and "Trail of Broken Treaties." It, too, got little U.S. exposure. In fact, Little Steven found each of his albums sold only about 100,000 copies, none achieving significant airplay. By the end of the 1980s he was speculating on how long his career could stand his chosen direction. If some critics applauded his work, others questioned whether he had the ability to communicate to larger numbers.[62] For example, Robert Christgau, commenting on *Freedom, No Compromise*, appraised his performances as of "just a guy who longs to let all the love and pain and ambition inside him out, and who isn't even any good at imitating those who know how. . . . Only as a writer of protest songs does he show any knack."[63] Little Steven's only great success, measured in market impact, was in bringing together a large number of politically conscious artists for the 1985 *Sun City* album, designed to support the antiapartheid policies of the white South African regime and discourage artists from performing at the Sun City resort in Bophuthatswana, a sun, sex, and gambling colony in one of the bantustans the Afrikaner government has tried to present as some kind of free state. Here, with an amazing aggregation of artists including Springsteen, Dylan, Miles Davis, and Bono Hewson of U2, was a strong political statement, technically brilliantly produced by mix-master Arthur Baker and performed with great conviction by all concerned. Perhaps because MTV gave one video some heavy exposure, the album sold very well and became "agitprop from the streets—an uncompromised political statement that managed a miraculous intrusion on the music industry's business as usual."[64] The lessons are clear: To be successful as "popular" music, highly political music in the contemporary United States must be great music *and* break into heavy MTV rotation. It cannot sell on the basis of the worthiness of the cause or by riding the coattails of past association with a pop icon like Springsteen. That seems to be the hard reality of the structure of media bias.

SPRINGSTEEN'S SIGNIFICANCE

Springsteen's music for two decades has, at least in live performances, certainly embodied the visceral abandon, the losing of one's self, that terrified parents in the 1950s and started riots—joyous explosions of good feelings—in theaters. At the beginning of the 1970s Peter Guralnick in his *Feel Like Goin' Home* (1971), widely praised as one of the best books on American music, would say: "Rock 'n' roll today, . . . is a middle-class phenomenon almost exclusively.

What for us was a liberating act . . . has become . . . something a great deal more serious and infinitely less important.''[65] He argued, ''That's why all attempts at revival are bound to fail. To bring it back you'd have to bring back the Eisenhower Era and the McCarthy Hearings.'' Rock 'n' roll was, as the Coasters said, ''a secret message delivered with a sneer and taken with a grain of salt. . . . [A] source of endless energy and bound-less amusement.''[66]

Maybe the Reagan era of the 1980s was a rerun of the 1950s. During that time Springsteen seemed to have revived the rocking joy of 1950s rock 'n' roll. Perhaps, one can surmise from his biography *Born to Run*,[67] he was so ''out of it'' and into himself and the guitar that all the counterculture illusion and dis-illusionment of the 1969–72 period passed him by. As John Fogerty and Creed-ence Clearwater Revival maintained a studied distance from Bay area ''flower-power'' with their working-class pessimism symbolized by Fogerty's ''Wrote a Song for Everyone'' with its line that suggested (in response to counter-culture/ flower power proclamations of change) things were *still* the same and *not* dif-ferent.[68] Springsteen, clearly an admirer of Fogerty's work, seemed separate from everything significant about the late 1960s except some of the best of its singles, which he can play almost endlessly as encores. It was not until the 1980s that his work bears evidence of his having thought about the impact of Vietnam.

There may have been a lot *less* happening in mainstream America from 1967 to 1972 than self-important middle-class kids who had done too many acid trips thought.[69] If Springsteen embodies or personifies a ''promise'' of rock 'n' roll that began in the 1950s, with significant additions in the 1960s, it is in the best senses of *both* eras by asserting its possibilities for everybody. His audience included not just drugged-out, alienated, but financially well-off middle-class suburban kids who suffered through the boredom of homogenized consumer culture but also the working-class kids who watched their fathers and mothers physically or emotionally die, bit by bit, in the drudgery of daily work in the factory or office or the repressive social relations of traditional family and home. Springsteen's identification with the situation of ordinary working people, and his efforts to help them see what they—indeed the whole society—have lost, remains a remarkable quality of his art.

What is especially unique about Springsteen is that in the 1970s and the 1980s he continued the alienation and critical distance from U.S. society expressed by Bob Dylan for the generation of the 1960s and, a bit later, for example, by John Fogerty writing for Creedence Clearwater Revival in the 1968–72 period. But Springsteen did so by *inverting* some of the overt countercultural critiques of the 1960s: Operating *within* the assumptions of the dominant, male-defined culture—hard work, patriotism, cars, girls, marriage, and the promise of the American dream—his criticism comes back in a more profound and basic way. He proposes no war, no drugs to alter consciousness—just life in the USA for ordinary people. From a different and broader class perspective, yet proceeding from *within* the central assumptions of the culture, he finds it *doesn't work; it is lethal*. It grinds you down; it engenders dreams that tear one apart; it delivers a promise that is not just a lie, but something worse. And that something gnaws at one, for it is a promise—a happiness based on consumption and idealized myths of the possibilities of love relationships so arresting and seductive that one gets trapped, sometimes to explode into flight or violence. Thus his anthem "Born to Run," first a song of flight, of the "empty freedom of escape," but over the years transformed into something more, transformed by the artist's acceptance of the "burden of responsibility" to his fans and the larger culture.[70] He has described it as something he sees, now, as about "searching" rather than flight. It is a song he continued to sing through his 1988 tour and will have to sing throughout his career.[71]

Springsteen's music in the course of his first decade evolved from the substitute imagery of breaking out and fleeing as in "Thunder Road" and "Born to Run"— the latter itself evolving as the audience has invested it with meaning so that it is, as we have seen, perhaps more the audience's song now than the composer's— to an identification with those who could not flee ("Reason to Believe," "Down-bound Train"); those who tried to flee ("Seeds") but found nowhere to run; or those who couldn't take it anymore and ran amok, robbing and killing ("Johnny 99").

From *Darkness on the Edge of Town* (1978), containing "Badlands," "Prom-ised Land," "Factory," "Racing in the Street," and "Streets of Fire," to the present, one can discern a starkly realistic portrayal of the cultural contradictions of life in the backwash of postindustrial capitalism. There is an almost despairing lyrical critique of the lies and dreams that in "The Promised Land" tear one apart. About Springsteen's voice in this song and its line that suggests one could use a knife to cut the pain out of one's heart, Marcus suggested, it "takes you out of yourself: it connects you to the singer and to everyone else. Hell is not other people. The world is suddenly remade into a utopia of what it would mean to speak so plainly and be understood so violently, a utopia in which one immediately loses one's way. Driving, you could run into a tree. Shaving, you could cut your throat."[72]

Yet the lyrical despair one senses in so much of Springsteen's work is often literally blown away in the wall of sound that raises the lyrics to the level of exultation, suffusing some of the most grim lyrical judgments on American culture and society with the sheer joy of making music. This may be an intentional expression of the singer's sense of the contested and ambiguous reality of the "promise" of American life.

Since the album *Darkness on the Edge of Town* (1978), as Steve Perry put it, "much of his music has embodied a struggle between the recognition of grim circumstances and the will to make life count in those circumstances."[73] Some-times the critique has been so despairing, as in *Nebraska* (1982), the stark guitar and vocal album recorded at home, that critics have fallen all over themselves to assure the listeners that he really did find some "Reason to Believe." But they were wrong. If at the end of every day people do find some reason to believe, it is *not* because, in Springsteen's view, there has been much reason to do so. In spite of everything? Possibly. But only, as Marcus argued, if one does not see what one is looking at, or listen to what one hears.

Since then, it oftens seems that Springsteen has sought musically to wring every element of hope from essentially insoluble contradictions between circumstance and human will. His live shows, often lasting over four hours, are extended feats of endurance and conviction, as anyone who has seen one will testify. It is almost as if he were reaching for, searching for, hope beyond hope—something no music, or perhaps *only* music, can achieve or sustain.

Certainly the massive response to his world tour in 1984–85 demonstrates an audience who apparently seek something. But what is it? Is it a reason to believe in the face of an existence that for many is a marking of time during the boring passage from birth to death? At least Springsteen seems to affirm life. In contrast to Bob Dylan's consistent principled refusal to assume responsibility for what he saw as demands of the audience to give direction to their lives, Springsteen's image seems to convey to many that he somehow cares, that he is sincere. He seems, in John Street's phrase, to have come to accept ''the inescapable burden of belonging.''

More recently, his album *Tunnel of Love* turns in another, personally introspective, even confessional direction, exploring inner worlds, the private, personal terror of interpersonal relationships. Christgau has suggested that ''by depicting the fear of commitment as sheer terror, he does the impossible: renews L-O-V-E as pop subject.''[74] These are universal themes, for all people feel the real pain of interpersonal agonies much more than can focus on the complexities of the dissolution of the promise of America. Because the record was not exactly a rock 'n' roll record in its sparse instrumentation, its appeal to the rock audience was limited: It sold ''only'' something over three million units. But its themes touch the lives of many, and as Springsteen's own marriage broke up in 1988, the confessional quality of his songs gained new resonance.

These issues might be described as part of the personal politics of pain. During the 1980s, teaching on a state university campus one often saw audiences of only 25 or so turn out for meetings on peace in Central America while several hundred would show up for lecture/discussions of ''smart women, foolish choices'' or ''women who love too much'' based on self-help, popular psychology bestsellers. Many hundreds more attended Alcoholics and Narcotics Anonymous meetings in the same city. By this standard *Tunnel of Love* may hold more relevance for interpersonal politics than anything Springsteen did previously.

Yet his commitment to broader themes of human rights and social change remained undiminished. Responding to the appeal of Peter Gabriel he joined the Amnesty International Human Rights Now! tour in 1988 seeking to contribute his celebrity status and perceived personal integrity to a cause in which he seemed to believe deeply.

Throughout Springsteen's career, there seems to be, so far as one can judge from all the interviews, biographical profiles, and gossip, a continuing process of personal transformation and self-conscious exploration of ideas, alternatives, and explicit efforts not to get separated from fans or what is really happening in the country. Perhaps to a larger degree than other rockers, Springsteen has strategically donated large amounts to charities ranging from local food banks to British coal miners and union locals in Los Angeles, Pittsburgh, and elsewhere; and he has bankrolled the Vietnam Veterans of America with a benefit show and continued financial support. Because he is one of the richest entertainers, he can, of course, afford to do this. Perhaps he has to in order to legitimate his huge income.* Nonetheless, he has sought out union people all over the country and continues to read and be transformed by books such as Joe Klein's *Woody Guthrie: A Life*, which he repeatedly mentioned at concerts and in the introduction to "This Land Is Your Land" on the five-record "live" collection; novels and stories by Flannery O'Connor and William Price Fox; and histories by Henry Steele Commager. His interview with Chet Flippo revealed a man who had thought a lot about what has been happening to America, who didn't like the direction in which things were going, and who tried to say a lot about it in his music *and* do something about it as well:

[D]uring the Seventies . . . the hustle became legitimized. First through Watergate. That was a real hurting thing, in that the cheater, the hustler, the dope pusher on the street— that was legitimization for him. It was: you can do it, just don't get caught. Someone will ask, what did you do wrong? And you'll say, I got caught . . . *Born to Run* was a spiritual record in dealing with values. . . . *Nebraska* was about the breakdown of all those values . . . about a spiritual crisis, in which man is left lost. . . . [H]e has nothing left to tie him into society anymore. He's isolated from the government. Isolated from his job. Isolated from his family. . . . [I]solated from his friends. . . . That happens in this country, don't you see, all the time.[75]

And in an interview with Kurt Loder in *Rolling Stone:*

[P]eople want to forget. There was Vietnam, there was Watergate, there was Iran—we were beaten, we were hustled, and then we were humiliated. . . . [P]eople got a need to feel good about the country they live in. But what's happening, I think, is that that need— which is a good thing—is gettin' manipulated and exploited. And you see the Reagan reelection ads on TV—you know: "It's morning in America." And you say, well, it's not morning in Pittsburgh. It's not morning above 125th Street in New York. It's midnight, and, like, there's a bad moon risin'.[76]

He has clearly appreciated the contradictions of American life. And he seemed for a time to have stepped into the middle of these contradictions and to have sought to wring from them significant opportunities to work out new ideas concerning the role of the artist and to demonstrate new commitments. Given

---

*According to *Forbes,* October 3, 1988, Springsteen was the seventh highest paid entertainer in the country in 1987 and 1988, earning $61 million for those two years.

the organizational underdevelopment of American politics, however, where *could* he go? Perhaps the emergence of Jesse Jackson as a populist people's tribune in 1988 temporarily obviated the need for Springsteen's role, or at least diminished the pressure on him as a popular cultural tribune of the people; but his involvement in the 1988 Amnesty International tour demonstrated the continued depth of his commitment to using his music for political ends.

The real importance of the Springsteen phenomenon of the mid–1980s lies less in itself and more in the continued moral bankruptcy of a political system against which a rock star had to serve the function of tribune of the poor and dispossessed, the strung out, beaten down, losers in an American dream gone out of control. In doing so, Springsteen tried to take on the role sought earlier by Guthrie and Seeger, and later served, though not sought, by Dylan.

Springsteen has been widely perceived as a nice guy who works hard to make people happy at his shows. For two decades he has done it as well as (some say better than) any mass culture figure ever has, and for more people, though Michael Jackson has certainly surpassed him in units sold. But even Springsteen appreciates the limits of what he can do through music, though he believes it *is* political and "it makes a difference." As he said in an interview: "I don't know that much about politics. I guess my politics are in my songs, whatever they may be. My basic attitude is people-oriented, you know. . . . [H]uman politics. I feel that I can do my best by making songs. Make some difference that way."[77] That would be a sensible solution for anyone who had thought a good deal about the possibilities of transforming American society in an unrevolutionary time. He seems to have tried to make another kind of affectively empowering difference.

To make that difference he seems to believe strongly in the need for personal contact:

You gotta bring it to people. Up real close, as close as you can get. . . . 'Cause *if you want it for yourself, you gotta want it for everybody*, 'cause it's all connected. In the end it's all part of the same thing. Which is why Elvis' message was so profound. It reaches everybody, everywhere. Doesn't matter where or what the problems are or what the government is like. It bypasses those things. It's a heart to heart, it's a human thing. . . . [S]omebody comes out, they shout and yell, they have a great night, it's a rock 'n' roll show. It makes a difference, makes them think about something different.[78]

All this is significantly political depending on how one conceives it. If affective empowerment is as significant as Jesse Jackson has argued, it is. If caring about what is happening to people, and basic humanity means anything, it is. If providing the substitute imagery that might help people make sense of their life struggles in a society that promises more than it delivers means something, it also is. And there is a good deal more: The Springsteen phenomenon is only one part of a developing story of an evolving popular consciousness seeking to find a role for itself through a collective discourse made up of elements of national popular culture. In Springsteen's case, there has been an acute sensitivity to the lives of ordinary people, together with populism and class identification, and a critique of the promise of a political economy that spins out lies and engenders dreams that can never be fulfilled. Asked by Flippo whether doing the Stones' "Street Fighting Man" as an encore during the 1984–85 tour was a political statement, Springsteen replied, "I don't know. I like that one line in the song [about how a poor boy has no options but to play for a rock 'n' roll band]. It's one of the greatest rock 'n' roll lines of all time. It just seemed right for me to do it."[79]

Neither Springsteen nor the Stones have been exactly "poor boys," but it is not unrealistic to think that any moderately perceptive observer, and especially such an insightful one as Bruce Springsteen, has read as well as invested some meaning in the line that suggests the political game as played is presently without any solution. That might explain Springsteen's rather nondirective responses to efforts of the Reagan campaign to coopt his themes during the 1984 presidential race. In 1988 Jesse Jackson seemed to awaken and stir some of the same themes Springsteen and other blue-collar rockers have used. But the fact they have sold considerably more recordings than Jackson has garnered votes in two runs for the presidency suggests their voices will serve to articulate human needs, dreams, and desires far into the future.

NOTES

1. Lawrence Goodwyn, *Democratic Promise: The Populist Moment in America* (New York: Oxford University Press, 1976), p. ix.

2. Amiri Baraka, et al., "The Meaning of Bruce," *Spin*, vol. 1, no. 7 (November 1985): 51.

3. My reactions were similar to those I read in reviews not long after by Jack Newfield, "A Spark Starting a Fire," *Village Voice*, September 24, 1985; David Corn, *In These Times*, September 25–October 1, 1985; Steve Perry, "Reason to Believe," *In These Times*, February 12–18, 1986, pp. 23–24.

4. John Street in *Rebel Rock: The Politics of Popular Music* (New York: Basil Blackwell, 1986), notes the "creative conservatism" of Springsteen, who, he finds, represents "all that is most conservative and all that is best" in rock. James Lull, "Listeners' Communicative Uses of Popular Music," in *Popular Music and Communication*, ed. James Lull (Newbury Park, Calif.: Sage, 1987), p. 145, finds that "some modern music fans find Springsteen as boring old news." Considering the sensistivity to women I often found in the body of Springsteen's work, it amazed me to find him placed in the category of "cock rocker" by John Shepard in "Music and Male Hegemony," in *Music and Society*, ed. R. Leppert and S. McClary (New York: Cambridge University Press, 1987).

5. Among the works surveying and interpreting the rock phenomenon I found most interesting and theoretically sophisticated Simon Frith, *Sound Effects: Youth, Leisure, and the Politics of Rock 'n' Roll* (New York: Panteon, 1982). The best writing by far is Greil Marcus, *Mystery Train: Images of America in Rock 'n' Roll Music*, new ed. rev. and expanded (New York: E. P. Dutton, 1982). The most resolutely tough-minded is

Dave Harker, *One for the Money: Politics and Popular Song* (London: Hutchinson, 1980). His neo-Trotskyist theoretical position illuminates the political limits of rock quite unlike any other work. Uneven, but useful, are John Orman, *The Politics of Rock Music* (Chicago: Nelson-Hall, 1984), and Don J. Hibbard, *The Role of Rock* (Englewood Cliffs, N.J.: Prentice-Hall, 1983). Orman's work summarizes the literature on audience response and reports on some useful previously unpublished empirical work. The Hibbard work is useful for its extensive notes and citations of contemporary critical material from obscure sources.

6. Regarding the fallacies involved in the interpretation of lyrical content and inferences drawn therefrom, see the incisive commentary and debate between Norman K. Denzin and James T. Carey, "Problems in Analyzing Elements of Mass Culture: Notes on the Popular Song and Other Artistic Productions," *American Journal of Sociology* 75 (1970): 1035–1041.

7. For a review of the empirical literature see R. Serge Denisoff and John Bridges, "The Sociology of Popular Music: A Review," *Popular Music and Society,* vol. 9, no. 1 (1983): 51–62.

8. Quoted by Robert Hilburn in syndicated column in the Bozeman, Mont., *Daily Chronicle*, Entertainment Supplement, December 25, 1987.

9. Ibid.

10. Ibid.

11. Ibid.

12. Ibid.

13. M. M. Bakhtin, *The Dialogic Imagination* (Austin: University of Texas, 1981); Denzin and Carey, "Elements of Mass Culture," p. 1035.

14. Ibid., p. 1036.

15. "Bruce has nice buns" was offered as one of six reasons for the Springsteen appeal in Mary-Ellen Banashek, "Bruce Springsteen: Why He Makes Us Feel So Good," *McCalls* (November 1985), pp. 12, 16, 18. The other explanations: "Bruce justs seems like a real nice guy"; "Springsteen believes in putting his money where his heart is"; "Bruce is a man who loves his work"; "Bruce is a real man"; and "Bruce is growing older, like the rest of us." These factors, presented in a mass circulation magazine for women, probably do characterize a significant proportion of the phenomenon. One other interesting effort at profiling the fans appeared in Merle Ginsberg, "The Fans: Springsteen's Followers Are Convinced He's Just like Them," *Rolling Stone,* October 15, 1985. Ten people are profiled, interviewed at random in the parking lot of Giant's Stadium, Meadowlands, New Jersey, August 21, 1985. Only one of the ten (a 36-year-old Vietnam veteran) might be characterized as having a politically progressive response; two others like Springsteen's "patriotism," while the rest stressed his being "regular" and "normal." The Vietnam veteran said, "I admire the man—he's a humanitarian. He focuses on vets 'cause he's an American—he cares what we've done. He doesn't shun us. He's got spirit; he motivates us. I hear he's been givin' to charities. He doesn't have to do that. About politics, to tell you the truth, I think he's right and wrong. But he does show a lot of emotion. . . . Bruce, he gives you the spirit of living. You want to take on the world and challenge it."

16. See especially the comments by Denzin and Carey in "Elements of Mass Culture," p. 1039.

17. Ibid., pp. 1037–1038.

18. Alan Gowans, *Learning to See: Historical Perspectives on Modern Popular/Com-*

mercial Arts (Bowling Green, Ohio: Popular Press, 1983), p. 20. This is one of the most significant theoretical works on popular culture.

19. Hibbard, *The Role of Rock,* p. 2.

20. Ibid., p. 3.

21. Ibid., pp. 3–4.

22. Ibid.

23. Ibid., p. 52.

24. For at least partial confirmation of such a view see R. Serge Denisoff and Mark H. Levine, "Generations and Counter-culture: A Study in the Ideology of Music," *Youth and Society* 2 (September 1970): 33–58; James E. Harmon, "The New Music and Counter-culture Values," *Youth and Society* 4 (September 1972): 61–83; and, Gary Burns, "Trends in Lyrics in the Annual Top Twenty Songs in the United States, 1963–1972," *Popular Music and Society* 9 (1983): 25–40.

25. Arguments to the essentially apolitical quality of most rock include Michael Lyndon, "Rock for Sale," in *Side-Saddle on the Golden Calf,* ed. G. H. Lewis (Pacific Palisades, Calif.: Goodyear, 1972), pp. 313–21. Also in Lewis, ed., see Sol Stern, "Altamont: Pearl Harbor to the Woodstock Nation," pp. 321–40. Perhaps the most insightfully critical comments are found in Leon Rosselson, "Pop Music: Mobiliser or Opiate?" in *Media, Politics and Culture,* ed. C. Gardner (London: Macmillan, 1979), pp. 40–50. Also see the response in Gardner, ed., Gary Herman and Ian Hoare, "The Struggle for Song: A Reply to Leon Rosselson," pp. 51–60.

26. Paul M. Hirsch, "Sociological Approaches to the Pop Music Phenomenon," *American Behavioral Scientist* 14 (January 1971): 376. For discussion of models of effects of mass communication see Sidney Kraus and Dennis Davis, *The Effects of Mass Communication on Political Behavior* (University Park, Pa.: Pennsylvania State University Press, 1976), pp. 155ff. Especially insightful is Dennis McQuail, "The Influence and Effects of Mass Media," in *Media Power in Politics,* ed. D. A. Graber (Washington, D.C.: Congressional Quarterly Press, 1984), pp. 36–53.

27. See the entry "Persuasion" by Irving Janis in *International Encyclopedia of the Social Sciences,* vol. 12, ed. Sills, and the extensive bibliography of relevant literature. Also Irving L. Janis and Carl I. Hovland, "An Overview of Persuasibility Research," in *Personality and Persuasibility,* Yale Studies in Attitude and Communication, vol. 2, ed. I. L. Janis et al. (New Haven: Yale University Press, 1959).

28. Hilburn column. One of the best-reasoned recent discussions is Street, *Rebel Rock.* Street's work relies largely on his keen powers of observation and vast knowledge of two decades of popular music. He says virtually nothing concerning relevant empirical social science findings.

29. Herman and Hoare, "The Struggle for Song," p. 52.

30. Ibid., p. 54.

31. Ibid., pp. 52–53.

32. Denzin and Carey, "Problems . . . ," p. 1035.

33. Greil Marcus, "In Your Heart You Know He's Right," *Artforum,* November 1984.

34. Ibid.

35. John P. Robinson and Paul Hirsch, "Teenage Response to Rock and Roll Protest Songs," Paper presented to American Sociological Association meeting, San Francisco, 1969; Robinson and Hirsch, "It's the Sound That Does It," *Psychology Today,* 1969; Hirsch, "Sociological Approaches."

36. R. Serge Denisoff and Mark H. Levine, "The Popular Protest Song." *Public Opinion Quarterly,* 35 (Spring 1971).

37. Emily D. Edwards and Michael Singeltary, "Mass Media Images in Popular Music," *Popular Music and Society* 9 (1984).

38. Robinson and Hirsch, "It's the Sound That Does It."

39. Edwards and Singletary, "Mass Media Images."

40. Fox and Williams, "Political Orientation and Music Preference."

41. Ibid., p. 370.

42. Ibid.

43. John Orman, *The Politics of Rock Music* (Chicago: Nelson-Hall, 1984), pp. 59–79, 175–83.

44. Ibid., pp. 179–83.

45. Ben Sidran, *Black Talk* (New York: DaCapo Press, 1981), pp. 12–13.

46. Lawrence Grossman, "Is There Rock after Punk?" *Critical Studies in Mass Communication* 3 (1986): 52.

47. Greil Marcus, "Real Life Top Ten," *Village Voice*, February 18, 1986, p. 83, and W. T. Lhamon, Jr., "Little Richard as a Folk Performer," *Studies in Popular Culture* 8 (1985). Lhamon on the Little Richard "Tutti Frutti" in 1955:

The puns on "Sue" and "Daisy" titilated uninitiated audiences simply as references to good opposite-sex partners. At another level in these days of desegregation, Daisy and Sue were knowing referents to drag queens in the clubs Little Richard had presented himself as Princess LaVonne. In seeming to sanitize "Tutti Frutti," [producer Bumps] Blackwell, [co-writer Dorothy] LaBostrie, and [Little Richard] Penniman had instead sublimated with small nodes of latent excitement. Most audiences probably did not suspect any of this . . . but the singer knew, Blackwell knew, and so did the musicians. . . . Their performance took on a licentious exuberance commensurate to their release from restraint.

In Marcus' view: "In other words, rock 'n' roll began as a code its new fans didn't know they were deciphering—a code that deciphered them."

48. Philip E. Converse, "The Nature of Belief Systems in Mass Publics," in *Ideology and Discontent*, ed. D. E. Apter (New York: The Free Press, 1964), pp. 206–261. Converse categorized, in this classic formulation, only 2 to 4 percent of the electorate as true ideologues, and another 8 to 12 percent as near ideologues. For another view, suggesting a much broader conception of ideological thinking, see Lewis Lipsitz, "On Political Belief: The Grievances of the Poor," in *Power and Community*, ed. P. Green and S. Levinson (New York: Vintage, 1970), pp. 142–72.

49. Fox and Williams, "Political Orientations and Music Preferences."

50. Jacques Attali, *Noise: The Political Economy of Music* (Minneapolis: University of Minnesota Press, 1985), pp. 133–47. This process of composition by the audience "thus appears as a negation of the division of roles and labor as constructed by the old codes. Therefore, in the final analysis, to listen to music in the network of composition is to *rewrite* it: 'to put music into operation, to draw it toward an unknown praxis,' writes Roland Barthes. . . . *The listener is the operator.*" Emphasis added.

51. Springsteen, quoted by Chet Flippo, "Interview with Bruce Springsteen," *Musician*, November 1984, p. 54.

52. Gowans, *Learning to See*, p. 24.

53. Stuart Hall presents some of the most powerful theoretical perspectives on the analysis of popular culture as mass communication. A difficult but comprehensive intro-

duction to the range of his perspectives is Lawrence Grossman, "History, Politics and Postmodernism: Stuart Hall and Cultural Studies," *Journal of Communication Inquiry* 10 (Summer 1986): 61–77.

54. Frith, *Sound Effects,* pp. 42–47.

55. Ibid.

56. See especially the celebrated analysis of "The Culture Industry" by Max Horkheimer and T. W. Adorno in *Dialectic of Enlightenment* (New York: Seabury Press, 1972): 120–176, originally published in 1944.

57. Walter Benjamin, "The Work of Art in the Age of Mechanical Reproduction," in *Illuminations: Walter Benjamin,* ed. with an introduction by Hannah Arendt (New York: Schocken Books, 1969), pp. 217–52. A contemporization of Benjamin's approach is Hans Magnus Enzenberger, "Constituents of a Theory of Media," *New Left Review* 64 (November/December 1970): 13–36.

58. One is reminded of the earlier sociological disputes over mass culture analysis in the 1950s, some of which was covered in Leon Bramson, *The Political Context of Sociology,* (Princeton: Princeton University Press, 1959).

59. Editorial cited by D. Laing, *Sound of Our Time,* (London: Sneed and Ward, 1969), p. 190.

60. Ibid.

61. Steve Perry, "Reason to Believe," *In These Times,* February 12–18, 1986, p. 24.

62. See the interview with Little Steven by Sandy Carter in *Zeta Magazine* (Z) 1 (January 1988): 45–51.

63. Robert Christgau, "Christgau's Consumer Guide," *Village Voice,* December 1, 1987.

64. Carter, *Zeta Magazine,* p. 45.

65. Peter Guralnick, *Feel Like Goin' Home* (New York: E. P. Dutton, 1971), pp. 18–19.

66. Ibid.

67. Dave Marsh, *Born to Run: The Bruce Springsteen Story* (New York: Dell, 1981).

68. Ellen Willis, "Creedence Clearwater Revival," in *The Rolling Stone Illustrated History of Rock & Roll* (New York: Random House, 1980), pp. 324–26. Willis writes perceptively of John Fogerty's "reservations about the counterculture" and "sensitivities to the realities of class."

69. See particularly Sol Stern's piece (originally in *Scanlon's),* "Altamont: Pearl Harbor to the Woodstock Nation," reprinted in *Side-saddle on the Golden Calf,* ed. Lewis, pp. 313–21.

70. The phrase "burden of responsibility" comes from John Street's analysis in *Rebel Rock* (New York: Basil Blackwell, 1986).

71. Flippo, *Musician,* p. 58.

72. Greil Marcus, "In Your Heart You Know He's Right," *Artforum,* November, 1984.

73. Steve Perry, "Reason to Believe," *In These Times,* February 12–18, 1986, p. 24.

74. Christgau, "Christgau's Consumer Guide," Dec. 1, 1987.

75. Flippo, *Musician,* p. 58.

76. Springsteen as interviewed by Kurt Loder, *Rolling Stone,* December 6, 1984.

77. Ibid.

78. Ibid. Emphasis added.

79. Flippo, *Musician,* p. 58.

9

Political Possibilities of Popular Music

During the 1960s and after, Bob Dylan, the Rolling Stones, the Beatles, and others created music reflecting political conflicts of the day and through which individuals found personal identities. As such it became political-cultural raw material. Songs such as the Rolling Stones' "Street Fighting Man," "You Can't Always Get What You Want," and "Gimme Shelter" or the Beatles' "Revolution" came to political significance through the uses of millions of individuals. They were songs incorporated into personal ideological perspectives, becoming inseparable from the oppositional politics of the era. But some comparative perspective is needed: John Lennon, among the Stones and Beatles, made perhaps the most serious (some might say naive but well-intentioned), mass-oriented efforts toward fusing music and politics in his era. He had to pay the price of fighting a four-year battle with U.S. government agencies over a deportation order issued in 1972 until winning a green card in 1976.[1] Such sanctions were mild compared, for example, with those suffered by Lennon's contemporary, Chilean political activist and singer-composer-guitarist Victor Jara. In the September 1973 coup against Chile's president Salvador Allende, Jara was arrested and tortured (his hands were smashed—some reports say cut off), and his mutilated body later found. Lennon's 1980 assassination by a demented "fan" was a development of a wholly different kind in an emerging "televisual" community.

In the United States, cultural struggles have often only indirectly expressed the more explicit dimensions of ongoing organized sociopolitical struggles, though that does not make them less significant, nor less political. Bob Dylan, the most significant figure in the emergence of 1960s rock in the United States, never expressed politically transformative impulses to anyone close to him.[2] Yet although persistently refusing in any *formal* way to accept the burden of responsibility for the lives of a generation that many seemed to want to place upon him, the role he played in the popular culture of the time was central.

Dylan's apparently emotionally limited, self-absorbed personal existence reveals dynamics by which music expresses political themes. Individuals in their songs may express meanings of which they may be less than consciously aware. Does this imply an "unconsciousness" of expression, reflecting and reinforcing the spirit of an era? If so, the music and lyrics of Dylan might be an example of a personal expression that seemed to reflect the causes and issues of an era, touching the lives of millions. Likewise, in a different style and time, Mozart reflected the spirit of an era despite his apolitical stance. He expressed for an elite audience the conflicts "in the air" in the years preceding the great French Revolution through his opera *The Marriage of Figaro.* * Whether Mozart was as overtly disdainful of politics as he is portrayed as being in the film *Amadeus*, may be secondary to the power with which his music expressed emerging social conflicts in 1786 in *Figaro* and, perhaps, in 1787 in *Don Giovanni* forecasting the doom of a predatory aristocracy.

Whatever the inner workings of the minds of Mozart or Dylan, there is enough to be found in their music for the audience to integrate into oppositional political perspectives. In eras of great change or movements for change, music functions to catalyze personal perspectives while "managing" and providing substitute imagery for people seeking to express their dreams and fantasies. In revolutionary eras, of course, music serves some of the same purposes it does in nonrevolutionary periods. It does not *make* movements, nor does it alone change consciousness. R. Serge Denisoff noted eight political functions for music in relation to political movements, which apply as well to the situation of individuals seeking some gratification of personal political longings. In Denisoff's formulation music can do the following:

1. Solicit or arouse support for a movement.

2. Reinforce the value structure of individuals.

3. Create cohesion, solidarity, and morale.

4. Recruit individuals into a specific movement.

5. Evoke solutions to a social problem via action.

6. Describe a social problem in emotional terms.

7. Divide supporters from the world around them.

8. Counteract despair in social reformers, when hoped-for change does not materialize.[3]

---

*Conductor Bruno Walter once suggestsed that in Mozart's musical setting for the libretto of Beaumarchais, and especially the *aria* "Se vuol ballare" in the opera *The Marriage of Figaro* (1786), one could "hear" the approaching French Revolution. Similarly, the philosopher Herbert Marcuse (in response to a question I directed to him, concerning a definition of "revolutionary" art) suggested Mozart's opera served a revolutionary function through expressing with such beauty and power the class conflicts of that day.

In the late 1960s questions of the relation of pop music to politics were posed openly; many sought an explicitly political popular music but saw their hopes diminish during the 1970s. By the late 1980s a virtual explosion of efforts to fuse music and causes such as USA for Africa, Live Aid, Farm Aid, Amnesty International's Human Rights Now! tour, though not usually seen as revolutionary efforts, carry implications of far-reaching change in the orientations of popular artists and have helped to alter the consciousness of millions toward a greater concern for the disadvantaged in an age obsessed with having and getting and money management.

THE PROMISE OF ROCK: IS THE DREAM A LIE, OR SOMETHING WORSE?[4]

In a comment on the Bruce Springsteen of the mid–1980s, Jefferson Morley suggested Springsteen's songs were united not by "the genius of some godlike superstar nor some progressive political sensibility, but a very out-of-fashion, much derided article of faith from the Sixties; *the promise and the power* of rock music."[5] Its promise is the "authentic" 1960s spirit, which "has something to do with liberation and something to do with self-respect. It is the spirit that says you can't start a fire sitting around crying of a broken heart."[6] Though it seems an archaic reflection of the 1969 Woodstock era, this is an important common perception of the rather more complex political "promise" of rock.

Far from being "easy riders," many highly paid entertainers in the 1980s show evidence of a new acceptance of the burden of belonging to society. Popular musicians have elaborated new cultural organizational forms in seeking to raise public awareness of important issues. That each event has carried elements (statements, raps, songs) that can be read as reflective of a perceived need for more radical social change does not mean that a genuinely oppositional musical discourse exists, nor does it signal the emergence of oppositional movements. It might more accurately reflect the "televisual apparatus" into which the whole society has become integrated. In Ann Kaplan's view, for example, "Television seems able to integrate and use any kind of potentially subversive counter-culture before it has even had time to identify itself as such." While suggesting a humanizing of dominant ideology and discourse, she suggests it means that "oppositional discourses are never given an opportunity to structure a community."[7] Although hardly a new insight—it bears significant similarities to Herbert Marcuse's position in *One Dimensional Man* over a quarter century ago[8]—it is important to consider.

A defining aspect of the condition of postmodernism itself has been, Kaplan suggests, "the loss of any position from which to speak—of mechanisms for critical evaluation of social structures and ideologies."[9] Youth culture as an oppositional counterculture is in this view a naive dream:

What we have predominantly is a uni-dimensional, commercialized and massified youth culture, not really organized by youth itself but by commercial agents, that has absorbed into itself, and trivialized, all the potentially subversive positions of earlier rock move-ments. There are small sub groups that are important but, just because marginalized and lacking access to the media, they are powerless. Any attempts at oppositional discourses struggle against their reduction to glamorous "media events," to the surfaces/textures/images of opposition rather than to its actuality as something that challenges the status quo.[10]

Kaplan and Morley represent radically contrasting views. Morley in the 1980s articulates the power of the 1960s myth. Kaplan characterizes what would appear to be an overwhelming reality of a media-based, postmodern society. What real possibilities exist?

Historian E. J. Hobsbawm suggested, in writing of the French May Revolt of 1968 in which cultural protest played such a significant role, "In France . . . the new movement produced a genuine revolutionary crisis, though one unlikely to achieve revolution . . . because the social struggle, politics and a 'cultural revolution' against all forms of manipulative integration of individual behavior were combined."[11] The situation in the United States, by contrast, was char-acterized by the visibility of "the phenomena of cultural revolt, which are *symptomatic* rather than *operational*."[12] Similarly, French sociologist Alain Touraine would write in *The May Movement* that "while in France the social struggle was at the center of the movement and the cultural revolt was, one might almost say, a byproduct of a crisis of social change, *in the United States cultural revolt is central*."[13] An implication of both views is that when such cultural factors as rock or folk music loom as large as they do in the United States, it is a symptom of the *weakness* of "genuine" forms of opposition (i.e., not much "real" politics is going on). The attention directed at Bruce Springsteen throughout the late 1980s might be seen as a similar symptom, although in response, one might cite Springsteen's own line, "You can't start a fire without a spark." Does popular music provide that spark?

What is implied in the "promise" of rock? Liberation as an end, or as part of a process? Measurable and fundamental institutional change, or for some brief time the creation of a feeling, a "mood" or "sense" of freedom, joy, and release *prefiguring* the envisioned future liberation? One could go on at length formu-lating such questions, given the record of the spontaneous and contradictory politics evident in the counterculture centered in the San Francisco Bay area in the late 1960s. There, as English folk-protest singer Leon Rosselson characterized it,

rock music was the natural expression of the student-hippie community. . . . It was the alternative culture, it was peace and love, it was doing your own thing. It was community control and the battle for the People's Park in Berkeley. It was hostility towards the war in Vietnam and the commercial values of straight America. It was rejection of the institution of marriage and the work ethic. It was sex and drugs as a voyage of self-discovery. All very subversive. The music, fusing rock, folk and the Beatles [and the blues], was, at the outset, created from within the community and controlled by the musicians themselves.[14]

Although some of the music was overtly political, in its totality it reflected obliquely emancipatory impulses. Music here was the primary form of expressive communication.

Unique historical conditions facilitated the creation of the counterculture and its music; when those changed, it changed. Just as New Orleans as the cradle of jazz suffered a decline at the end of World War I when the Storyville area was declared off limits to soldiers or as Kansas City, a cauldron of swing and small-group improvisation that produced both the bop of Charlie Parker and the rhythm and blues that was the foundation of rock 'n' roll, became less prominent, the Bay area experienced changes that overtook "flower power" and counter-cultural rock and virtually all the sociocultural movements that preceded it. Massive media attention brought legions of tourists, the invasion of hard drugs, crime, police repression, commercialism, and cooptation that, in addition to existing endemic naivete and lack of coherent community organization, consumed the counterculture.

Part of the decline resulted from the larger society's partial acceptance of the cultural revolt of the late 1960s: greater sexual permissiveness (until the herpes and AIDS scares of the 1980s); widening uses of drugs (cocaine became a recreational drug for upscale consumers); greater acceptance of psychotherapy as an adjunct to self-discovery and a wide range of related humanistic psycho-therapeutic activities; greater body consciousness and resort to body work and massage therapy; organic foods and vegetarian diets; new forms of religious-spiritual inquiry that became a whole New Age movement; greater reliance on nonhierarchical styles of management and decision making. All attained their status on the national agenda in the late 1960s.

Nonetheless, at the time contradictions built into the society and music industry permitted cooptation and perversion, such that the counterculture soon became a big business. To some, "the guerillas had simply, without their even realizing it, been incorporated into the regular army of the enemy."[15] But subsequent studies show an *oppositional* outcome: A permanent and very coherent oppositional consciousness and activist orientation remain with people of that generation, especially those who were in any way culturally and politically activist. Two decades later they still conceive of themselves as acting "in struggle" and resistance to dominant values and institutions.[16]

Despite the efforts of this earlier generation, the signals of confusion and short-run political impotence were clear: isolation from the world, political naivete, an apparent inability to understand the structure of power in U.S. society, and an incapacity of such successful "political" musicians as John Lennon to distinguish between media illusion and reality, as, for instance, in his efforts to achieve peace through simply declaring it (indeed, protest-folk singer Phil Ochs tried a similar course[17]).

Contradictions between professed emancipatory beliefs and functional roles of media stars remain. It now seems evident that Bob Dylan saw or felt this contradiction, thus his refusal to assume the burden of "leadership" responsibility others have subsequently felt.

Critics have pointed to a lack of genuine, substantive radical organizational alternatives in the United States of the 1950s, leaving "negotiated" or essentially symbolic forms of revolt to take place while many others could still enjoy the benefits of consumer capitalism.[18] Rock 'n' roll, in one view, allowed young people, psychologically and to a limited degree in terms of lifestyle, a temporary "inversion" of their "real material status, identifying with the less well-off, without making any more overt political commitment."[19]

For European leftist observers coming, for example, from the left wing of the British Labour party—or any other political culture of somewhat more "disciplined" and "permanently organized" leftist organization—"political action" involves other than the apparent symbolism of gathering around the Washington Monument to sing "We Shall Overcome" in 1963 or "Give Peace a Chance" in 1969. But neither American workers nor students in the post–World War II period engaged in the kinds of mass strikes familiar in, say, the British coal industry. Such actions are simply not realistic alternatives for most people until there are relevant models to emulate. The conception of political action held by nearly 90 percent of the U.S. population in most studies consists of very individualistic acts, for example, voting in presidential elections for the candidates of one of the two pro-capitalist parties. Only minorities of around 30 percent would report even seeking to persuade someone to vote a certain way and only about 10 percent said they had given money to a campaign, though other studies, in 1981, showed as many as 61 percent claiming they had at some time signed a petition and an incredible (and probably wildly inaccurate) 12 percent claiming they had participated in a lawful demonstration. That by 1988 only half the potential electorate would opt even for voting in the presidential election raises questions either of significant overestimation of activism in such self-reporting, or alienation on a massive scale.[20]

Given historical realities in the United States, it is truly remarkable that an allegedly apolitical American public generated, first, a major and broadly based movement against racism through the 1960s and, second, a successful challenge to a foreign imperialist war that over an eight-year period completely turned the general population from majority support to overwhelming opposition; and, third, it started a cultural revolution that profoundly shook up culture and politics around the world in the late 1960s.[21] Compared with such efforts by supposedly underorganized Americans, what can British and European socialists, for example, list as achievements? If the French can point to the May Revolt of 1968, the trial of strength it represented was, for all the mass mobilization, significantly symbolic, resulting in a reaffirmation of the de Gaulle regime within a few weeks in elections (though de Gaulle himself would resign a year later).[22] If the British Labourites could call themselves socialists and briefly held state power, have they done anything in the last quarter century approaching such achievements in the United States?

In the United States, for whites to identify with any aspect of black culture was to call into question racism as one of the main tools for ideological legitimation of the hierarchy and exploitation endemic to the U.S. system. In the 1960s the struggle against racism became *the* second American Revolution. It has, perhaps, taken over two decades for that to become evident, as critical commentaries on the 1988 film *Mississippi Burning* suggested.[23] The identification with black music that lay at the foundation of rock, for example, was also a revolutionary cultural act in calling into question some other core falsehoods in U.S. society, especially the persisting denial of the power of black cultural achievements in the face of three centuries of oppression. Moreover, in making such identification, the alleged equalities before the law and of economic opportunity central to ruling liberal ideology began to be unmasked as the lies they had been for all but a privileged minority of middle-class and upper-class white males. Growing recognition that economic opportunity was *not* a possibility for every person and that every person was *not* equal before the law shredded previously ruling liberal ideology and brought a longing for a new kind of American community by the end of the 1960s.

Organizationally, the mass symbolic gatherings mounted by the civil rights movement were the product of long months of patient and disciplined work by complex national coalitions of many organizations involving coordination between blacks and whites in the face of generations of racism. Planning for the great March on Washington for Jobs and Freedom of 1963 began over a year before and was modeled on an earlier march organized by black labor leader A. Phillip Randolph in the 1940s.[24] This supposedly symbolic yet exceptionally well organized assembly also provided in "I Have a Dream" a rallying cry not simply in the quest for civil rights for over a quarter of a century after, but for any possibility of change beyond the present reality. Moreover, such dreams are an important part of the reality of living. A life without them would be unbearable. Without such an expression of a dream as King's, and the multitude of organizations that came together to express it, a more radical politics beyond it could not be conceived.[25]

Although it is correct to perceive the United States in contrast to most industrialized nations, as characterized by an underdevelopment of long-term leftist organizational forms that encompass and mobilize large proportions of the population, that does not mean mass organizations and mobilizations have not existed. Some earlier major efforts were violently suppressed.[26] Real organized alternatives to the two major capitalist parties have not existed since the suppression of the small but growing Socialist party during World War I. The United States has thus never had a major labor party, as in the United Kingdom, nor a mass-based socialist or communist party, as exist in most other major Western industrial nations. In the 1960s the most significant oppositional organizational form, Students for a Democratic Society (SDS) never had more than about

100,000 loose affiliates, even according to the most extravagant estimates.[27] These were not mass-based leftist alternatives.[28] Ordinary people cannot identify with alternatives that simply do not exist for them.

To recognize symbolic and cultural dimensions of revolt is to perceive the historical reality of politics and culture in the United States since 1920. But to assert that "genuinely *oppositional* forms of consciousness and of action were simply not available," as does British critic Dave Harker, [29] is to misunderstand and undervalue the way this central quality of U.S. politics operates. People fight where they can, using the only materials and weapons they have, in ways consistent with their continued survival. For whites in opposition and resistance, musical "negotiated" forms, on the one hand, of folk-protest (associated with Woody Guthrie and Pete Seeger) and, on the other, of rock 'n' roll (associated with Elvis Presley and Little Richard) and related lifestyle forms have not simply been "tolerated" and "possible"; they have provided forms that also served as ways to call into question fundamental aspects of U.S. society. In a context characterized by a history of repression and the consequent effective absence of more organized leftist political movements, such cultural forms of opposition have been not only realistic reflections of the realities of power but also the most *effective* uses of available channels for expression of opposition. Such cultural resistance is the distinctive form revolutionary action takes in the United States.

Given these realities, of course, one could not go far in terms of European conceptions of organizational affiliation to be considered "radical" in the late 1950s and early 1960s. Formal and openly expressed organizational connections in a political culture that did not encourage them could brand an individual as sectarian, narrow, and suspect. In the early 1960s Bob Dylan initially abandoned his attraction to Buddy Holly and rock 'n' roll and moved to the folk-protest music he found so appealing in Woody Guthrie. The Greenwich Village folk scene then provided him with a receptive audience for a folk-music politics that made him a kind of culture hero. In achieving this status he stayed clear of any formal organizational commitment, even though, Todd Gitlin points out in his perceptive study of the era, Dylan did explore the organizational possibilities and realities of movement politics at the time, attending an SDS National Council meeting in December 1963 and traveling to Mississippi, singing for black workers in the cotton fields and civil rights organizers and also visiting organizers in the mining areas of eastern Kentucky.[30]

But where could Dylan have gone in American politics had he decided to make a major organizational commitment other than SDS? There was no coherently organized party, coalition, or movement (although later there were references to "the movement," which was nowhere precisely located). There were many tendencies and very real divisions among and within the organizations that did exist. None was in anything approaching a hegemonic position on the fragmented left, in spite of tendencies by many former SDS members to romanticize the centrality of that organization.[31] For all the power and appeal of the moving original declarations by the first generation of SDS leadership such as Todd Gitlin, Tom Hayden, and Carl Oglesby and their and other contemporary recollections of that era,[32] by the later 1960s SDS chapters were often controlled by intransigent extremists utterly out of touch with majority values and sentiments who identified with idealized visions of Ho Chi Minh and Che Guevara, with little knowledge of the contemporary relevance of orientations of such earlier authentic native American radicals as Eugene V. Debs, Mary "Mother" Jones, Elizabeth Gurley Flynn, or Big Bill Haywood, or even the potentially more salable native, progressive "good government" socialism of Norman Thomas and Victor Berger, which at one point early in the century elected hundreds of local officials across the country.[33]

Considered in historical retrospect, Dylan, for a few years at least, fulfilled a significantly more important political-cultural role than any dozen such "movement leaders" of the 1960s through his more detached posture as generational voice. In his songs producing a series of lines and phrases that became part of the personal vocabularies of millions, his music was incorporated into the perspectives of those who sought to define new identities in a time of conflict and change. Ultimately, even if Dylan and other musical artists of his generation had consciously and openly sought to define themselves as organizationally based revolutionaries, they would have had to *create* organizations that united a weak and incredibly diverse array of groups and movements. That would ask of them to create something more than even the sophisticated kinds of organizational vehicles attempting to link music and cause that emerged in the 1980s, which so far have themselves engaged in a largely symbolic politics. It would be highly unrealistic to expect people of an earlier era, whose main concerns in those days were in individual self-expression, social commentary, and criticism through making music, to embark in political-organizational directions for which they had little preparation or experience and certainly no interest.

If in the early 1960s, as Harker put it, "there was *nowhere to go*; . . . there was no 'it' to get involved with, at a practical level, outside the music, and outside the protest movements,"[34] in the 1980s a different situation confronted those in opposition. Although numerous efforts to fuse music and politics have arisen, their relation to any more fundamental movements for change remains problematic, given the weakness of such movements as perceived realistic alternatives to existing institutional politics. That 50 percent of the potential U.S. electorate did not vote in the presidential election of 1988 does not necessarily indicate, proclamations of Jesse Jackson's Rainbow Coalition to the contrary, that a more radical movement would have attracted more voters, given surveys showing nonvoters' preference for Bush in 1988 or Reagan in 1984.[35]

It still perplexes analysts of popular culture that while many of Bob Dylan's songs became anthems for civil rights and later antiwar activists, and other songs seemed to express the feelings of those seeking to define their identities, the singer himself persistently, almost obsessively, asserted he was not in any overt way involved in, nor a spokesperson for, anything. Beyond that, as Joan Baez notes, he vehemently asserted that even *he* didn't know what his songs meant.[36]

The answer is, of course, that Dylan intuitively knew that he could find no better way to speak than through his songs.

Dylan's music consistently told a very different story than his enigmatic personal life and obsessive abhorrence of "guru" or "spokesman-for-a-generation" status. The personal political uses of his music for activists of his generation were staggering in their range and diversity, but all carried important political implications on personal or social levels. The sheer number of cover versions of his major early songs such as "Blowin' in the Wind" and "The Times They Are a Changin' " and the tremendous popularity and influence of groups such as the Byrds, whose recorded output was based heavily on Dylan songs performed in a kind of "Beatle-ized" instrumental style, made them unavoidable background to the lives of the whole society.

Whatever one's political persuasion, Dylan's music became part of everyday life. But if the songs "spoke" to a generation, what, precisely was the message? Where the traditional folk left sought an explicit, broadside style of topical ballad dealing with recognizable issues around which people could organize or be organized, Dylan saw things differently. Criticizing formal protest songs and identification with a concrete organization or struggle, Dylan reportedly put it thus: "It's vulgar, the idea that somebody has to say what they want to say in a message type song. . . . They always say folk music should be simple so people can understand. . . . What's happened is the union movement people, *they're* talking about keeping it simple. All these labor people, rich suburban cats telling their kids not to buy Bob Dylan records. 'Which side are you on?' That's such a waste. I mean, which side can you *be* on?''[37]

It appears that well before the Rolling Stones wrote the line in "Street Fighting Man,'' it was evident to Bob Dylan that "the game as played" was then "without solution,'' at least one with which he wished to be associated.

He said to a friend in 1964: "All I can say is politics is not my thing at all. I can't see myself on a platform talking about how to help people. Because I would get myself killed if I *really* tried to help anybody. I mean, if somebody *really* had something to say to help somebody out, just bluntly say the truth, well obviously they're gonna be done away with. They're gonna be *killed*.''[38]

Dylan's movement away from explicit protest themes coincided with the deepening radical critique then emerging in the country. In the view of Carl Oglesby, an early leading figure in SDS, "Even after abandoning the anthem writing period, when he turned to a new kind of literary epic, Dylan became more political in mood than before.''[39] This change for Dylan and for the new generation of radicals emerging in the mid–1960s grew, in Oglesby's view, out of a new recognition, a changed perspective: "The change involves understanding that laws are not written out of scruples of human instincts; that's not how they're made. If anything they are dim reflections of the realities of power. By the Sixties, Dylan and the Movement and everybody just knew the world is run by these criminals in power, knew how powerful these criminals are. The lamentable deaths, the betrayals, the losing of hope—it comes as no surprise. That's where

Dylan moved to, where the Movement moved to at precisely the same time.''[40] Against this world, again perhaps unconsciously, grew a widespread movement toward apocalyptic cultural-musical expressions in which one feels expressed the need for psychological shelter and related senses of inner freedom provided by the free space of new cultural forms. If no organizational side exists to be on, what *can* be the role of the music and its practitioners if not to provide the symbolism and substitute imagery for those involved in cultural struggles for survival ("Like a Rolling Stone," "Subterranean Homesick Blues," "Stuck inside of Mobile with the Memphis Blues Again") and more personal conflicts ("It Ain't Me, Babe")?

Given the absence of large-scale disciplined political organizations beyond the two major parties, and aside from such obvious radical minority adaptations as the Weatherman faction of SDS (based on a line of Dylan's "Subterranean Homesick Blues"), it remained for individuals to use the existing popular culture as a source of resources to fashion their own personal oppositional political perspectives as a means of resistance. Popular songs could still be made to serve such a function. Even if never having been intended to do so by their creators, "Gimme Shelter," "Purple Haze," and "All along the Watchtower" seemed to embody the despair and terrors of a time when the nation was convulsed by the agonies of a war involving millions, while Richard Nixon presided over its government.

In addition to the long-recognized instrumental functions of recruiting membership and support for an organization or movement (i.e., "Talkin' Union," "Which Side Are You On?" or "We Shall Not Be Moved" and "We Shall Overcome," though never strictly popular songs in some definitions, but *functionally* "people's" music), perhaps the most important function of music has always been in expressing and reinforcing elements of existing, broadly oppositional political culture and attitudes, thus facilitating ongoing struggles and resistance, whether organized or personal. In this way songs of Dylan and many others provided substitute imagery for a generation of the alienated, who felt separate from or opposed to mainstream America, or even harbored a sense of approaching doom.[41]

If even the best past protest rock and political folk music in the United States was merely a "negotiated" form of consciousness, what would a genuinely oppositional form look or sound like, and how might music be linked to it? Could initially negotiated forms prefigure broader, more socially inclusive transformative movements? To what degree might *music itself* be such an oppositional form?

In Stuart Hall's approach to analysis of responses to mass media discourses discussed earlier, three hypothetical positions from which content of any media discourse may be interpreted or "decoded" were identified: the dominant-hegemonic position, when the message is decoded "in terms of the reference code in which it has been encoded"; the negotiated code, which "contains a mixture of adaptive and oppositional elements"; finally, the oppositional approach, in which the receiver may "detotalize" the message in the preferred or intended code but then "retotalize the message within some alternative framework of reference."[42] This latter approach leads the receiver to read the message sent in a very different way from the intended meaning. In Hall's view, "One of the most significant political moments . . . is the point when events which are normally signified and decoded in a negotiated way begin to be given an oppositional reading. Here the 'politics of signification'—the struggle in discourse—is joined."[43]

Whether a form is genuinely oppositional or serves as an effective means of resistance depends upon the context. In the contemporary United States sound itself is oppositional. It creates a new space, reinforcing within each person the possibility of an assertively oppositional posture before existing social reality, but also—and rap is the best contemporary example—imposing a new order in sound on a context once oppressively closed. Observing videos of leading rap performers, one sees them taking over public spaces for their performances, literally seizing them with such powerful recurrent images as performers first being enclosed in jail cells and then literally exploding through walls to land, microphone in hand, directly in the middle of ongoing concerts. A sense of declaration of freedom and liberation of space pervades rap, which, as veteran jazz drummer Max Roach has put it, "lives in the world of sound—not the world of music—and that's why it's so revolutionary. What we as black people have always done is show that the world of sound is bigger than white people think."[44]

Rap arises from the experience of a culture fragmented and disintegrating, yet providing infinite opportunities for appropriation and rearrangement, *rescuing* "noise, transforming fugitive shards into sharp, pleasurable, highly self-conscious artifacts that can ride the lilt of impromptu signifying or rise to the sonic density of Ornette Coleman."[45] It constitutes the latest example of that "flash of the spirit"—the centuries-old black cultural practice of making marginality a productive space through sound. Rap represents the latest development from a culture based on oral expression that goes back centuries through African war chants, playing the dozens, field hollers, call-and-response patterns in worksong and the "lining-out" of hymns in the black church, tale telling, and more.[46]

Rap at its best mocks the narrowness of such elitist lamentations on high culture's "decline" as Allan Bloom's *Closing of the American Mind*.[47] The rappers know more about the range of linguistic convention than Bloom has ever thought. Their work reveals a sheer linguistic exuberance and verbal sophistication far beyond any conception of today's allegedly ignorant youth one finds in Bloom's diatribe against popular culture. Eric B. proclaims in "Follow the Leader" that he could take a phrase and flip it and make it a daily word.[48]

Rap embodies the tensions of acute social realities of urban life from Malcolm X through crack: "live lyrics from da bank of reality." Rap seems hard because the life it comes out of is hard, yet it demonstrates again that what is done to people is less significant than what they do with what is done to them. The harsh social reality of urban black existence charges the best rap (such as Public Enemy and Eric B. & Rakim), critic John Powers suggests, "with an enormous cultural voltage, a political message that's far more ferocious than it is precise. For all Public Enemy's ultra-militant stance, their real political force lies in their semiological assault on the listener. Car sounds, whistling kettles, random scratches. . . . [t]he band deliberately uses noise to throw a wrench in the normal channels of communication created by white society."[49] Thus rap overtly rejects validation by white society (though it sells to whites hungry for cultural opposition). Through sheer noise and disorientation rap asserts the possibilities of an empowering open-endedness in a culture whose dominant institutional politics proclaim there are no possibilities beyond "read-my-lips, no-new-taxes."

The oppositional possibilities and renewed sense of potentiality that mark the emergence of rap still does not solve the problem of linkage to wider political and social movements to transform "da bank of reality." If, theoretically, music and other forms of popular culture reflect and reinforce broad tendencies to read or interpret popular culture and media messages from oppositional perspectives, such oppositional consciousness does not imply transformative movements embodying affirmative challenge and change; however, these forms at least establish the groundwork that makes such movements possible.[50] Lacking "structured" links to preexisting communications networks of organized movements, no unified fusing of opposition tendencies occurs, though it may be prefigured in cultural linkages through new forms of community established by mass communication. Challenges to the structure of social power here fall within the category of politics Antonio Gramsci categorized as a "war of position" (as opposed to the more organized "war of movement").[51] Such positional challenges to the existing structure of social power take place at the level of ideas and public consciousness—the broad social agenda. In the supposedly open and democratic systems of Western liberal capitalism, such a politics of position is necessary and prior to fundamental shifts in the scope of public programs. In this sense music may function as a material force with significant political potential. What people will make of that potential remains an open question.

NEW FORMS LINKING MUSIC AND POLITICS

In the United Kingdom the Rock Against Racism movement, which began in 1976, prefigured most organizational efforts over the next decade. Created not long after reported apparent racist comments by Eric Clapton, it involved such groups as Steel Pulse, the Specials AKA, UB40, and the Beat (known in the United States as "The English Beat"), and brought together over 80,000 to a concert in Victoria Park, London, in 1977.[52] Its success and significance lay in its explicit merging of music and politics, providing a model for new forms of involvement for musicians in political causes that would emerge repeatedly in a variety of ways over the next dozen years, from the MUSE "No Nukes" concerts of 1978 through Live Aid and Band Aid, the Artists United against

Apartheid "We Are the World" video and record, the Farm Aid concerts, the "Sun City" record and educational project, and various other efforts to support South African resistance to apartheid and to free imprisoned black leader Nelson Mandela, through the Amnesty International Human Rights Now! tour of Bruce Springsteen, Sting, Tracy Chapman, Peter Gabriel, and others in 1988.

These efforts opened opportunities for musicians and creative/technical personnel to be engaged, using music in ways "instrumental" to what they saw to be significant causes. But what have been the effects?[53] Obviously, vast media spectacles were created, which too often tended to focus on the allegedly heroic sacrifices of performers (Phil Collins performing in Philadelphia and then flying to London to appear *again* the same day on the same show!). Although hundreds of millions of dollars, perhaps even billions, were raised, the total amounts provide only small portions of the vast sums needed to make a transforming impact on any of the problems addressed. This does *not* mean the events were without important impacts on the consciousness of audiences or participants, of course. This is so even though proponents boasted of raising more money than the foreign aid budgets of some countries, a statement itself indicative of the naivete of participants in failing to recognize the historically complementary role of most national foreign aid programs in facilitating profoundly unequal and exploitative trade relations between developed and underdeveloped worlds.[54]

The main positive effects have probably been to raise public consciousness, though too often about *which* rock and pop superstars appeared, while providing opportunities for such "name" musicians to participate.[55] Even though such focus on who was to appear in media coverage seemed to take precedence over why they were there, the appearances by all the stars provided models of public-regarding moral behavior in an era generally exalting privatization, "incentives," and sheer greed. Also, such organizations as Amnesty International have reported increased memberships after appeals on their behalf.

Some have argued, to the contrary, that the net effects did not "particularly publicize the problems of poverty and starvation, or give us better understanding of the political issues involved."[56] If the events became narcissistic star showcases in which both performers and audiences reveled, gauging whether form overcame substance and content is much more difficult. There are many reasons to postulate an opposite effect, depending on the context and the perspectives of the audience. To suggest that the authentic concerns of committed individual artists and the desires of millions of people to help the disadvantaged or speak out for human rights plays into the overall commercial strategy of MTV and the large corporations represented by many of the performers is to postulate an inert and manipulated public. Moreover, it is to suggest that in popular music there is no effective presence of, nor the possibility of creating, potentially oppositional, utopian, and revolutionary themes. Neither situation is an accurate perception. Popular culture is a complex and contested reality in the United States, but it remains the primary means of resistance and the most widely used channel for expression of emancipatory political perspectives.

The pessimistic conception of influence argued by T. W. Adorno and Max Horkheimer in their celebrated 1944 essay "The Culture Industry," a view of cultural artifacts as *acting on* people who are objects of the intentions of others, the controlling of the "culture industry," remains a significant interpretive impulse.[57] One cannot lightly dismiss the prescience of an analysis that sees how "efforts at emancipation result in the opposite—in fortifying the context of delusion in which they are caught."[58] Yet as Marcuse argued for over a quarter of a century, the accumulation of "surplus repression"[59] in the life of Western industrial systems makes future outbreaks of revolutionary impulses, so common at the end of the 1960s, a virtual certainty in the future. An explicit connection exists between music and other forms of popular culture in the process of activation and mobilization of public consciousness of such surplus repression.[60]

From efforts to create popular music with radical social effects in Germany in the 1920s, through perspectives of Walter Benjamin in the 1930s, through Guthrie and Seeger and many folk and rock artists in recent decades, an emancipatory impulse has consistently fought for a popular music that facilitates the empowering of people as creative subjects.[61] Even more significant are the numerous cases illustrated in this book that are testimony to the spirit and creativity of the oppressed and socially marginal.

As a collective dialog over popular identity and community purpose, the historically diverse forms of people's and popular music for well over a century in the United States have been some of the most important ways in which this discussion is undertaken, especially when existing political forms and institutions fail to provide either adequate forums for undertaking such discussions or channels for action. As a form of mass communication that reflects and shapes the hopes and desires of millions of individuals, contemporary popular music, embodying as it does elements of all these earlier forms, indeed serves as mass political communication.[62] It reveals unexpressed longings and provides cultural raw materials that enable each listener to use it in the service of the most basic human impulses to survive, to grow, and to create personal and collective senses of identity often in conflict with the tyranny of the present.

NOTES

1. See the discussion in John Weiner, *Come Together: John Lennon in His Time* (New York: Random House, 1984), pp. 225–78.

2. Anthony Scaduto, *Bob Dylan: An Intimate Biography* (New York: Signet Books, 1973); Robert Shelton, *No Direction Home: The Life and Music of Bob Dylan* (New York: Ballantine Books, 1987). Joan Baez, *And a Voice to Sing With* (New York: New American Library, Plume Editions, 1988).

3. In addition to the works of Denisoff, see David King Dunaway, "Music as Political Communication in the United States," in *Popular Music and Communication*, ed. J. Lull (Newbury Park, Calif.: Sage Publications, 1987), pp. 36–51. The functions are drawn from R. Serge Denisoff, *Sing a Song of Social Significance* (Bowling Green, Ohio: Popular Press, 1983).

4. The heading comes from a line of Springsteen's "The River," which asks whether a dream is a lie if it doesn't come true, or something even worse.

5. Jefferson Morley, *Rolling Stone,* October 10, 1985, p. 24.

6. Ibid.

7. E. Ann Kaplan, *Rocking around the Clock: Music Television, Post-Modernism, & Consumer Culture* (New York: Methuen, 1987), p. 152.

8. Herbert Marcuse, *One Dimensional Man* (Boston: Beacon Press, 1964).

9. Ibid.

10. Ibid.

11. E. J. Hobsbawm, *Revolutionaries* (New York: New American Library, 1973), pp. 234–44.

12. Ibid.

13. Alain Touraine, *The May Movement* (New York: Alfred A Knopf, 1971), as cited by Hobsbawm, *Revolutionaries*, p. 244. Emphasis added.

14. Leon Rosselson, "Pop Music: Mobiliser or Opiate?" in *Media, Politics and Culture,* ed. Carl Gardner, (London: Macmillan, 1979), p. 46.

15. Ibid.

16. For example, see Richard Flacks and Jack Whalen, *After the Barricades: The Sixties Generation Grows Up* (Philadelphia: Temple University Press, 1989), and Doug McAdam, *Freedom Summer* (New York: Oxford University Press, 1988). An earlier study suggesting a similar continuity is Joseph R. DeMartini, "Social Movement Participation, Political Socialization, Generational Consciousness, and Lasting Effects," *Youth & Society*, vol. 15, no. 2 (December 1983): 195–223.

17. See the accounts of Ochs' "War Is Over" rallies in Marc Eliot, *Death of a Rebel* (New York: Anchor Books, 1979), pp. 129–33, 143–44, 244–45.

18. "Negotiated" and "opposition" consciousness, together with "dominant/hegemonic" as modes of interpreting the message of popular culture texts were terms developed by Stuart Hall and associates at the University of Birmingham Centre for Cultural Studies during the 1970s. See Stuart Hall, "Encoding/Decoding," in *Media, Culture, Society* (London: Hutchinson, 1980), pp. 128–138.

19. Dave Harker, *One for the Money*, p. 116.

20. On the kinds of political activities engaged in by citizens in the United States compared with those in Great Britain, West Germany, and France, see Russell J. Dalton, *Citizen Politics in Western Democracy* (Chatham, N.J.: Chatham House Publishers, 1988). This is a comprehensive overview of several decades of voting and participation studies and contains an extensive bibliography.

21. I am indebted to George Lipsitz for reminding me of these developments.

22. Hobsbawm, *Revolutionaries*.

23. See letters to *The Nation*, February 13, 1989, by Dorothy Zellner and Abbie Hoffman and also in the same issue Nicolaus Mills' review of Seth Cagin and Philip Dray, *We Are Not Afraid* (New York: Macmillan, 1988) and Doug McAdam, *Freedom Summer* (New York: Oxford University Press, 1988).

24. See Herbert Garfinkel, *When Negroes March* (Glencoe, Ill.: The Free Press, 1959). David J. Garrow, *Bearing the Cross* (New York: Vintage Books, 1988), pp. 265–86. My own work as research assistant to Herbert Garfinkel during 1963–64 involved reading all back issues of several major Negro newspapers issued during the year prior to the 1963 March on Washington and clipping every reference to planning the march and

activities of each of the major figures. The march did not simply materialize. It was the product of a long process of organization.

25. One notes a similarity of views with Rudolf Rocker, a preeminent figure in the international anarchist movement in the first half of the twentieth century. See the second volume of his autobiography, *The London Years* (London: Robert Anscombe, 1956), p. 174, on the function of dreams and dreamers.

26. Wolfe, *The Seamy Side of Democracy: Repression in America,* second edition, revised (New York: Longman, 1978).

27. Estimates of SDS strength may be found in Kirkpatrick Sale, *SDS* (New York: Random House, 1973).

28. On the changing universe of popular movements see Carl Boggs, *Social Movements and Political Power* (Philadelphia: Temple University Press, 1987), pp. 39ff. On SDS see Sale, *SDS*. A good historical overview is Irwin Unger, *The Movement: A History of the American New Left, 1959–1972,* (New York: Dodd, Mead, 1974).

29. Harker, *One for the Money.*

30. Gitlin, *The Sixties,* p. 198.

31. See, for example, Sale, *SDS*, for expression of the view that the New Left collapsed because of SDS disintegration.

32. Tom Hayden, *Reunion: A Memoir* (New York: Random House, 1988); James Miller, *Democracy Is in the Streets* (New York: Simon & Schuster, 1987); David Caute, *The Year of the Barricades: A Journey through 1968* (New York: Harper & Row, 1988); Richard Goodwin, *Remembering America: A Voice from the Sixties* (Boston: Little, Brown, 1988).

33. See, for example, Jerry W. Calvert, *The Gibraltar: Socialism and Labor in Butte, Montana, 1895–1920* (Helena, Mont.: Montana Historical Society, 1988), and the extensive bibliography on socialism of that era therein. Especially relevant is James Weinstein, *The Decline of Socialism in America, 1912–1925* (New York: Vintage Books, 1967).

34. Harker, *One for the Money,* p. 118.

35. See *New York Times* voter/nonvoter profiles published immediately after the 1984 and 1988 elections.

36. See the revealing exchange between Dylan and Joan Baez in Baez's *And a Voice to Sing With* (New York: New American Library, Plume Editions, 1988), p. 86.

37. Quoted by Harker, *One for the Money,* p. 118.

38. Quoted by Scaduto, *Dylan,* p. 205–206.

39. Ibid.

40. Ibid.

41. See Betsy Bowden's excellent analysis of this and other Dylan songs in *Performed Literature: Words and Music by Bob Dylan* (Bloomington: Indiana University Press, 1982).

42. Stuart Hall, "Encoding/Decoding," in *Culture, Media, Language* (London: Hutchinson, 1980), pp. 128–38.

43. Ibid., p. 138.

44. Quoted by John Powers in his "One Plus One" column, "Play This Column Loud," *LA Weekly,* January 13, 1989, p. 10.

45. Ibid., p. 10.

46. Ibid.

47. Allan Bloom, *The Closing of the American Mind* (New York: Simon and Schuster,

1987). Bloom may be a distinguished scholar in the area of classical political thought—his translation of Plato's *Republic*, for example, is excellent—but his ignorance of the richness, intelligence, and complexity of the varieties of rock and popular music, together with the shallowness and simplistic cultural elitism evident in what amounts to a silly, ill-informed diatribe against popular music in one section of his book, raise the gravest doubts concerning the value of his larger critical project.

48. "Play This Column," Powers, p. 12.

49. Ibid.

50. Insightful on the conditions under which social movements arise is Jo Freeman, "On the Origins of Social Movements," in *Social Movements of the Sixties and Seventies,* ed. J. Freeman (New York: Longman, 1983), pp. 23–30.

51. See Antonio Gramsci, *Prison Notebooks* (New York: International Publishers, 1971), pp. 229–46.

52. See the account in John Street, *Rebel Rock: The Politics of Rock Music* (New York: Basil Blackwell, 1986), pp. 76–78.

53. One insightful survey is Andre J. M. Prevos, "Singing against Hunger: French and American Efforts and Their Results," *Popular Music and Society* 11 (1987): 57–74.

54. There are numerous critical studies the link between of foreign aid programs and imperialist and neocolonial trade policies. Some of the initially significant have included Teresa Hayter, *Aid as Imperialism* (Baltimore: Penguin, 1971), and Harry Magdoff, *The Age of Imperialism* (New York: Monthly Review Press, 1969).

55. E. Ann Kaplan, *Rocking around the Clock* (New York: Methuen, 1987), p. 85.

56. Ibid., p. 85.

57. T. W. Adorno and Max Horkheimer, "The Culture Industry: Enlightenment as Mass Deception," *Dialectic of Enlightenment* (New York: Herder and Herder, 1972; orig. pub. 1944), pp. 120–76.

58. Albrecht Wellmer, cited by Jurgen Habermas, *Legitimation Crisis* (Boston: Beacon Press, 1975), p. 125.

59. "Surplus repression" is a central concept in Marcuse's *Eros and Civilization* (Boston: Beacon Press, 1955; New York: Vintage Books, 1962), pp. 32–35. It refers to the restraint necessary to social domination, in contrast to the normal repressions of instinct required for civilization to exist. A year before his death, in March 1978, Marcuse reaffirmed his belief in the future power of the concept in an impassioned address at the San Francisco meetings of the American Philosophical Association.

60. Marcuse notes that centrally crucial role in *Counter-revolution and Revolt* (Boston: Beacon Press, 1972). He seemed to back away from it somewhat in *The Aesthetic Dimension: Toward a Critique of Marxist Aesthetics* (Boston: Beacon Press, 1978).

61. Here the efforts of Paul Hindemith, Bertolt Brecht, Hans Eisler, and others deserve to be recalled. See, for example, John Willett, "Brecht: The Music" in John Willett, *The Theater of Bertolt Brecht: A Study from Eight Aspects* (New York: New Directions/London: Methuen, 1959).

62. On the variety of interpretations of music as mass communication, see James Lull, ed., *Popular Music and Communication* (Newbury Park, Calif.: Sage Publications, 1987).

Bibliography

Works listed contributed informing theoretical perspectives or proved especially helpful in clarification of concepts. Readers should consult the notes for each chapter for much additional source material, especially books on specific musical genres, as well as most journal and magazine articles, record album notes, and recommended recordings.

Adams, Frank. *Unearthing Seeds of Fire: The Idea of Highlander*. Winston-Salem, N.C.: John F. Blair, 1975.

Adorno, T. W., and Max Horkheimer, "The Culture Industry: Enlightenment as Mass Deception." In *Dialectic of Enlightenment*, edited by T. W. Adorno and Max Horkheimer, pp. 120–176. New York: Herder and Herder, 1972.

Allen, Robert C., ed. *Channels of Discourse: Television and Contemporary Criticism*. Chapel Hill: University of North Carolina Press, 1987.

Ames, Russell. *The Story of American Folk Song*. New York: Grossett and Dunlap, 1955.

Arendt, Hannah. *On Revolution*. New York: Viking Press, 1965.

Atali, Jacques. *Noise: The Political Economy of Music*. Minneapolis: University of Minnesota Press, 1987.

Avineri, Shlomo. *Social and Political Thought of Karl Marx*. New York: Cambridge University Press, 1967.

Baez, Joan. *And a Voice to Sing With*. New York: New American Library, Plume Editions, 1988.

Bakhtin, M M. *The Dialogic Imagination: Four Essays*. Austin: University of Texas Press, 1981.

Bastin, Bruce, *Red River Blues: The Blues Tradition in the Southeast*. Urbana: University of Illinois Press, 1986.

Bay, Christian. *The Structure of Freedom*. New York: Atheneum, 1965.

Becker, Howard. *Outsiders*. New York: The Free Press, 1963.

Belenky, Mary Field, et al. *Women's Ways of Knowing: The Development of Self, Voice, and Mind*. New York: Basic Books, 1988.

Bellah, Robert, et al. *Habits of the Heart*. Berkeley: University of California Press, 1986.

Bender, Thomas. *Community and Social Change in America*. New Brunswick, N.J.: Rutgers University Press, 1978.

Benjamin, Walter. "The Work of Art in the Age of Mechanical Reproduction." In *Illuminations: Walter Benjamin*, edited with an introduction by Hannah Arendt, pp. 217–252. New York: Schocken Books, 1969.

Berlin, Edward. *Ragtime: A Musical and Cultural History*. Berkeley: University of California Press, 1980.

Berman, Marshall. *The Politics of Authenticity*. New York: Atheneum, 1970.

Berman, Marshall. *All That Is Solid Melts into Air*. New York: Simon & Schuster, 1982.

Berryman, Phillip. *Religious Roots of Rebellion*. Maryknoll, N.Y.: Orbis Books, 1985.

Billington, James H. *Fire in the Minds of Men*. New York: Basic Books, 1980.

Black, Earl, and Merle Black. *Politics and Society in the South*. Cambridge, Mass.: Harvard University Press, 1987.

Blesh, Rudi, and Harriet Janis. *They All Played Ragtime*. Fourth Edition. New York: Oak Publications, 1971.

Boggs, Carl. "Revolutionary Process, Political Strategy, and the Dilemma of Power." *Theory and Society* 4 (1977): 359–393.

Boggs, Carl. *Social Movements and Political Power*. Philadelphia: Temple University Press, 1986.

Boggs, Carl, and Ray Pratt. "The Blues Tradition: Poetic Revolt or Cultural Impasse?" In *American Media and Mass Culture*, edited by Donald Lazare, pp. 279–292. Berkeley: University of California Press, 1987.

Borneman, Ernest. "The Roots of Jazz." In *Jazz*, edited by Nat Hentoff and Albert McCarthy, pp. 1–20. New York: DaCapo Press, 1978.

Botkin, B. A. "The Folksong Revival: Cult or Culture?" In *The American Folk Scene: Dimensions of the Folksong Revival*, edited by David A. DeTurk and A. Poulin, Jr., pp. 95–100. New York: Dell, 1967.

Boughton, Viv. *Black Gospel*. London: Blandford Press, 1985.

Bowden, Betsy. *Performed Literature: Works and Music by Bob Dylan*. Bloomington: University of Indiana Press, 1982.

Breines, Wini. *Community and Organization in the New Left, 1962–1968*. New York: Praeger, 1982.

Buhle, Mari Jo, and Paul Buhle. "The New Labor History at the Cultural Crossroads." *Journal of American History* 75 (June 1988): 151–157.

Buttimer, Anne. "Social Space in Interdisciplinary Perspective." In *Surviving the City*, edited by John Gabree, pp. 15–29. New York: Ballantine Books, 1973.

Byars, Jackie. "Reading Feminine Discourse: Prime Time Television in the U.S." *Communication* 9 (1987): 289–303.

Cagin, Seth, and Philip Dray. *We Are Not Afraid*. New York: Macmillan, 1988.

Calvert, Jerry W. *The Gibraltar: Socialism and Labor in Butte, Montana, 1895–1920*. Helena, Mont.: Montana Historical Society/Seattle: University of Washington Press, 1988.

Carpenter, Edmund and Marshall McLuhan. "Acoustic Space." In *Explorations In Communications*, edited by E. Carpenter and M. McLuhan, pp. 65–70. London: Jonathan Cape, 1970.

Chambers, Iain. "A Strategy for Living: Black Music and White Subcultures." In *Resistance through Rituals*, edited by Stuart Hall and Tony Jefferson, pp. 157–166. London: Hutchinson, 1976.

Chambers, Iain. *Urban Rhythms*. New York: St. Martin's Press, 1985.

Chapple, Steven, and Reebee Garofalo. *Rock and Roll Is Here to Pay*. Chicago: Nelson-Hall, 1977.

Charters, Samuel. *The Bluesmen*. New York: Oak Publications, 1967.

Charters, Samuel. *The Poetry of the Blues*. New York: Avon Books, 1970.

Charters, Samuel. *The Country Blues*. New York: DaCapo Press, 1975.

Clarke, John, Stuart Hall, Tony Jefferson, and Brian Roberts. "Subcultures, Cultures, and Class." In *Culture, Ideology and Social Process: A Reader*, edited by Tony Bennett et al., pp. 53–82. London: The Open University Press, 1981.

Cohen, Norm. *Long Steel Rail: The Railroad in American Folksong*. Chicago: University of Illinois, 1981.

Collier, James Lincoln. *The Making of Jazz: A Comprehensive History*. New York: Delta Books, 1978.

Cone, James H. *The Spirituals and the Blues*. New York: Seabury Press, 1972.

Czitrom, Daniel. *Media and the American Mind*. Chapel Hill: University of North Carolina Press, 1982.

Davis, Fred. *Yearning for Yesterday: A Sociology of Nostalgia*. New York: The Free Press, 1979.

DeMartini, Joseph R. "Social Movement Participation, Political Socialization, Generational Consciousness, and Lasting Effects." *Youth & Society* 15 (December 1983): 195–223.

Denisoff, R. Serge. "Protest Movements: Class Consciousness and the Propaganda Song." *Sociological Quarterly* 9 (Spring 1968): 228–244.

Denisoff, R. Serge, and Mark H. Levine. "Generations and Counter-culture: A Study in the Ideology of Music." *Youth & Society* 2 (September 1970): 33–58.

Denisoff, R. Serge. "The Popular Protest Song: The Case of 'The Eve of Destruction,' " *Public Opinion Quarterly* 35 (Spring 1971): 117–122.

Denisoff, R. Serge, and Richard A. Peterson, eds., *The Sounds of Social Change*. Chicago: Rand McNally, 1972.

Denisoff, R. Serge, and John Bridges. "The Sociology of Popular Music: A Review." *Popular Music and Society* 9 (1983): 51–62.

Denisoff, R. Serge. *Sing a Song of Social Significance*. Bowling Green, Ohio: Popular Press, 1983.

Denisoff, R. Serge. *Tarnished Gold*. New Brunswick, N.J.: Transaction Books, 1986.

Denzin, Norman K., and James T. Carey. "Problems in Analyzing Elements of Mass Culture: Notes on the Popular Song and Other Artistic Productions." *American Journal of Sociology* 75 (1970): 1035–1041.

DeTurk, David, and A. Poulin, Jr., eds. *The American Folk Scene: Dimensions of the Folksong Revival*. New York: Dell, 1967.

Dickstein, Morris. *Gates of Eden: American Culture in the 60's*. New York: Basic Books, 1977.

Dixon, Robert M. W., and John Godrich. *Recording the Blues*. London: Studio Vista, 1969.

Dubois, W. E. B. *The Souls of Black Folk*. New York: Fawcett World Library, 1961.

Dubovsky, Melvyn. *We Shall Be All: A History of the Industrial Workers of the World.* Chicago: Quadrangle Books, 1969.

Dunaway, David King. *How Can I Keep from Singing?: Pete Seeger.* New York: McGraw-Hill, 1981.

Eliot, John. *Models of Psychological Space.* New York: Springer-Verlag, 1987.

Eliot, Marc. *Death of a Rebel: Starring Phil Ochs and a Small Circle of Friends—A Biography.* New York: Anchor Books, 1979.

Ellison, Ralph. *Shadow and Act.* New York: Signet Books, 1966.

Epstein, Dena J. "A White Origin for the Black Spiritual? An Invalid Theory and How It Grew." *American Music* (Summer 1983): 53–59.

Evans, David. *Big Road Blues: Tradition and Creativity in the Folk Blues.* Berkeley: University of California Press, 1982.

Evans, Sara. *Personal Politics: The Roots of Women's Liberation in the Civil Rights Movement & The New Left.* New York: Vintage Books, 1982.

Evans, Sara, and Harry Boyte. *Free Spaces.* New York: Harper & Row, 1986.

Fahey, John. *Charley Patton.* London: Studio Vista, 1970.

Feagin, Joe. "Slavery Unwilling to Die: The Background of Black Oppression in the 1980's." *Journal of Black Studies* 17 (December 1986): 173–200.

Ferguson, Marilyn. *The Aquarian Conspiracy: Personal and Social Transformation in the 1980s.* New York: Granada Publications, 1983.

Ferreira, Christine. " 'Like a Virgin': The Men Don't Know, But the Little Girls Understand." *Popular Music and Society* 11 (1987): 5–16.

Fisher, Miles Mark. *Negro Slave Songs in the United States.* Secaucus, N.J.: Citadel Press, 1978. Originally published in 1953.

Fiske, John. "*Cagney and Lacey*: Reading Character Structurally and Politically." *Communication* 9 (1987): 399–426.

Flacks, Richard, and Jack Whalen. *After the Barricades: The Sixties Generation Grows Up.* Philadelphia: Temple University Press, 1989.

Foner, Philip S. *The Case of Joe Hill.* New York: International Publishers, 1965.

Fox, William S., and James D. Williams. "Political Orientation and Music Preferences among College Students." *Public Opinion Quarterly* 38 (1974): 353–371.

Franklin, John Hope. *From Slavery to Freedom: A History of Negro Americans.* New York: Vintage Books, 1969.

Frazier, E. Franklin. *The Negro Church in America.* New York: Schocken Books, 1963.

Freeman, Jo, ed. *Social Movements of the Sixties and Seventies.* New York: Longman, 1983.

Freidan, Betty. *The Feminine Mystique.* New York: Dell, 1963.

Freire, Paulo. *A Pedagogy of the Oppressed.* New York: Seabury Press, 1974.

Frith, Simon, and Angela McRobbie. "Rock and Sexuality." *Screen Education* 29 (Winter 1978–79): 3–19.

Frith, Simon. *Sound Effects: Youth, Leisure, and the Politics of Rock & Roll.* New York: Pantheon, 1981.

Frith, Simon. "Towards an Aesthetic of Popular Music." In *Music and Society*, edited by Richard Leppert and Susan McClary, pp. 133–149. New York: Cambridge University Press, 1987.

Frith, Simon. "Confessions of a Rock Critic." *New Statesman,* 23 (August 1985). Reprinted in Simon Frith. *Music for Pleasure*, pp. 163–68. New York: Routledge, 1988.

Frith, Simon. *Music for Pleasure: Essays in the Sociology of Pop*. New York: Routledge, 1988.

Garfinkel, Herbert. *When Negroes March*. New York: The Free Press, 1959.

Garon, Paul. *Blues and the Poetic Spirit*. London: Eddison Bluebooks, 1975.

Garrow, David J. *Bearing the Cross: Martin Luther King Jr. and the Southern Christian Leadership Conference*. New York: Vintage Books, 1988.

Genovese, Eugene. *Roll, Jordan, Roll: The World the Slaves Made*. New York: Pantheon, 1974.

Gentile, Mary. *Film Feminisms*. Westport, Conn.: Greenwood Press, 1985.

Gillette, Charlie. *The Sound of the City*. Revised and Expanded Edition. New York: Pantheon, 1983.

Gilligan, Carol. *In a Different Voice: Psychological Theory and Women's Development*. Cambridge, Mass.: Harvard University Press, 1982.

Gitlin, Todd. *The Whole World Is Watching: The Media in the Making and Unmaking of the New Left*. Berkeley: University of California Press, 1980.

Gitlin, Todd. *The Sixties: Years of Hope, Days of Rage*. New York: Bantam, 1987.

Glen, John M. *Highlander: No Ordinary School*. Lexington: University Press of Kentucky, 1988.

Goldstein, Richard. *Goldstein's Greatest Hits*. New York: Tower, 1970.

Gombin, Richard. *Origins of Modern Leftism*. Baltimore: Penguin, 1975.

Goodwyn, Lawrence. "Populist Dreams and Negro Rights: East Texas as a Case Study." *American Historical Review,* 76 (1971): 1435–1456.

Goodwyn, Lawrence. *Democratic Promise: The Populist Moment in America*. New York: Oxford University Press, 1976.

Gowans, Alan. *Learning to See*. Bowling Green, Ohio: Popular Press, 1983.

Gramsci, Antonio. *The Prison Notebooks*. New York: International Publishers, 1970.

Green, Archie. *Only a Miner: Studies in Recorded Coal-Mining Songs*. Urbana: University of Illinois, 1972.

Grossman, Lawrence. "History, Politics and Postmodernism: Stuart Hall and Cultural Studies." *Journal of Communication Inquiry* 10 (Summer 1986): 61–77.

Guralnick, Peter. *Feel like Goin' Home*. New York: E. P. Dutton, 1971.

Guralnick, Peter. "Searching for Robert Johnson." *Living Blues* 53 (Summer-Autumn, 1982): 27–41.

Guralnick, Peter. *Lost Highway: Journeys and Arrivals of American Musicians*. New York: Vintage Books, 1982.

Guralnick, Peter. *Sweet Soul Music: Rhythm and Blues and the Southern Dream of Freedom*. New York: Harper & Row, 1986.

Gusfield, Joseph. *Community: A Critical Response*. New York: Harper & Row, 1975.

Habermas, Jurgen. *Legitimation Crisis*. Boston: Beacon Press, 1975.

Hall, Edward T. *The Hidden Dimension*. New York: Anchor Books, 1969.

Hall, Stuart, and Tony Jefferson, eds. *Resistance through Rituals: Youth Subcultures in Post–War Britain*. London: Hutchinson, 1976.

Hall, Stuart. "Encoding/Decoding." In *Culture, Media, Language,* edited by Stuart Hall et al., pp. 128–138. London: Hutchinson, 1980.

Hall, Stuart. "Notes on Deconstructing 'The Popular.' " In *People's History and Socialist Theory*, pp. 227–240. Boston: Routledge & Kegan Paul, 1981.

Hamm, Charles. *Yesterdays: Popular Song in America*. New York: W. W. Norton, 1983.

Hammond, John, with Irving Townsend. *John Hammond on Record*. New York: Ridge Press/Summit Books, 1977.

Hampton, Wayne. *Guerilla Minstrels*. Knoxville: University of Tennessee Press, 1986.

Harding, Vincent. "Religion and Resistance among Antebellum Negroes, 1800–1860." In *The Making of Black America*, I, edited by August Meier and Elliott Radwick, pp. 179–200. New York: Atheneum, 1969.

Harding, Vincent. *There Is a River: The Black Struggle for Freedom in America*. New York: Vintage Books, 1983.

Harker, Dave. *One for the Money: Politics and Popular Song*. London: Hutchinson, 1980.

Harmon, James E. "The New Music and Counter-Culture Values." *Youth and Society* 4 (September 1972): 61–83.

Harris, William H. *The Harder We Run: Black Workers since the Civil War*. New York: Oxford University Press, 1982.

Hasse, John Edward, ed. *Ragtime: Its History, Composers and Music*. New York: Schirmer Books, 1985.

Hayden, Delores. "Capitalism, Socialism, and the Built Environment." In *Socialist Visions*, edited by Steven R. Shalom. pp. 59–81. Boston: South End Press, 1983.

Hebdige, Dick. *Subculture: The Basis of Style*. New York: Methuen, 1979.

Hebdige, Dick. *Cut 'n' Mix*. London: Methuen, 1987.

Heilbut, Anthony. *The Gospel Sound: Good News and Bad Times*. Revised and Updated. New York: DaCapo Press, 1985.

Hein, Hilde. "Aesthetic Consciousness: The Ground of Political Experience." *Journal of Aesthetics and Art Criticism* 35 (Winter 1976).

Herman, Gary, and Ian Hoare. "The Struggle for Song: A Reply to Leon Rosselson." In *Media, Politics, and Culture*, edited by Carl Gardner, pp. 51–60. London: Macmillan, 1979.

Hibbard, Don. *The Role of Rock*. Englewood Cliffs, N.J.: Prentice-Hall, 1983.

Hirsch, Paul M. "Sociological Approaches to the Pop Music Phenomenon." *American Behavioral Scientist* 14 (January 1971): 371–388.

Hobsbawm, E. J. *Primitive Rebels: Studies in Archaic Forms of Social Movement in the 19th and 20th Century*. New York: W. W. Norton, 1959.

Hobsbawm, E. J. *Revolutionaries*. New York: Meridian, 1973.

Holland, Norman. *The Dynamics of Literary Response*. New York: Oxford University Press, 1968.

Hughes, C. Alvin. "A New Agenda for the South: The Role and Influence of the Highlander Folk School, 1953–1961." *Phylon* 46 (September 1985): 242–250.

Jameson, Fredric. "Reification and Utopia in Mass Culture." *Social Text* 1 (1979): 130–148.

Jameson, Fredric. *The Political Unconscious*. Ithaca, N.Y.: Cornell University Press, 1981.

Janis, Irving L., and Carl I. Hovland. "An Overview of Persuasibility Research." In *Personality and Persuasibility*, edited by I. L. Janis et al. Yale Studies in Attitude and Communication. Vol. 2. New Haven, Conn.: Yale University Press, 1959.

Jay, Martin. *The Dialectical Imagination: A History of the Frankfurt School and the Institute of Social Research, 1923–1950*. Boston: Little, Brown, 1973.

Jones, LeRoi (Baraka, Amiri). *Blues People*. New York: Morrow, 1963, 1971.

Kaplan, E. Ann. *Women and Film: Both Sides of the Camera*. New York: Methuen, 1983.

Kaplan, E. Ann. *Rocking around the Clock: Music Television, Postmodernism & Consumer Culture*. New York: Methuen, 1987.

Keil, Charles. *Urban Blues*. Chicago: University of Chicago Press, 1966.

Kellner, Douglas. "TV Ideology and Emancipatory Popular Culture." In *Television: The Critical View*, Fourth Edition, edited by Horace Newcomb, pp. 470–503. New York: Oxford University Press, 1987.

Kerber, Linda K. "Separate Spheres, Female Worlds, Woman's Place: The Rhetoric of Women's History." *Journal of American History* 75 (June 1988): 9–39.

Klein, Joe. *Woody Guthrie: A Life*. New York: Ballantine Books, 1982.

Kousser, J. Morgan. *The Shaping of Southern Politics: Suffrage Restriction and Establishment of the One Party South, 1880–1910*. New Haven, Conn.: Yale University Press, 1974.

Kraus, Sidney, and Dennis Davis. *The Effects of Mass Communication on Political Behavior*. University Park, Pa.: Pennsylvania State University Press, 1976.

Kuhn, Annette. *Women's Pictures: Feminism and Cinema*. London: Routledge & Kegan Paul, 1982.

Laing, Dave. *The Sound of Our Time*. London: Sheed & Ward, 1969.

Lanternari, Vittorio. *The Religions of the Oppressed*. New York: Alfred A. Knopf, 1963.

Lasch, Christopher. *Haven in a Heartless World: The Family Beseiged*. New York: Basic Books, 1977.

Lawrence-McIntrye, Charshee. "The Double Meanings of the Spirituals." *Journal of Black Studies* 17 (June 1987): 379–401.

Lazere, Donald, ed. *America Media and Mass Culture*. Berkeley: University of California Press, 1987.

Lefebvre, Henri. "The Marxian Concept of Praxis." In *The Sociology of Marx*, Henri Lefebvre, pp. 25–58. New York: Vintage Books, 1969.

Levine, Lawrence. *Black Culture and Black Consciousness*. New York: Oxford University Press, 1977.

Lewis, Lisa. "Form and Female Authorship in Music Video." *Communication* 9 (1987): 355–377.

Limon, Jose E. "Western Marxism and Folklore: A Critical Introduction." *Journal of American Folklore* 96 (January-March 1983): 34–52.

Lipsitz, George. *Class and Culture in Cold War America: "A Rainbow at Midnight."* New York: Praeger, 1981.

Lipsitz, George. " 'This Ain't No Side Show': Historians and Media Studies," *Critical Studies in Mass Communication*, 5 (1988): 147–161.

Lipsitz, George. "The Struggle for Hegemony." *Journal of American History* 75 (June 1988): 146–150.

Lipsitz, George. "Mardi Gras Indians: Carnival and Counter-narrative in Black New Orleans." Paper Presented at Annual Meeting, American Studies Association, Miami, October 27–30, 1988.

Lipsitz, Lewis. "On Political Belief: The Grievances of the Poor." In *Power and Community*, edited by Philip Green and Sanford Levinson, pp. 142–172. New York: Vintage Books, 1970.

Lomax, Alan. Notes. *Roots of the Blues*. New World Records NW252. New York: New World Records, 1977.

Lombardi-Satriani, Luigi. "Folklore as Culture of Contestation." *Journal of the Folklore Institute* 2 (June-August 1974): 99–122.

Long, Elizabeth. *The American Dream and the Popular Novel*. Boston: Routledge & Kegan Paul, 1985.

Lovell, James. *Black Song: The Forge and the Flame*. New York: Paragon Books, 1986.

Lull, James. "Listeners' Communicative Uses of Popular Music." In *Popular Music and Communication*, edited by James Lull, pp. 140–74. Newbury Park, Calif.: Sage, 1987.

Lupsha, Peter. "Explanation of Political Violence: Some Psychological Theories versus Indignation." *Politics and Society* 2 (Fall 1971): 89–104.

McAdam, Doug. *Freedom Summer*. New York: Oxford, 1988.

McQuail, Dennis. "The Influence and Effects of Mass Media." In *Media Power in Politics*, edited by Doris A. Graber, pp. 36–53. Washington, D.C.: Congressional Quarterly, 1984.

Malone, Bill C. *Southern Music—American Music*. Lexington: University Press of Kentucky, 1979.

Malone, Bill C. *Country Music, U.S.A.* Austin: University of Texas Press, 1985.

Mander, Jerry. *Four Arguments for the Elimination of Television*. New York: Morrow, 1978.

Marcus, Greil. "Lies about Elvis, Lies about Us." *Village Voice,* November 18, 1981 (*Village Voice Literary Supplement,* December 1981).

Marcus, Greil. *Mystery Train*. Revised Edition. New York: E. P. Dutton, 1982.

Marcus, Greil. "In Your Heart You Know He's Right." "Speaker to Speaker" (column). *Artforum*, November 1984.

Marcus, Greil. "Speaker to Speaker" (column). *Artforum*, December 1985.

Marcus, Greil. "Critical Response." *Critical Studies in Mass Communication* 3 (1986): 77–81.

Marcus, Greil. "When You Walk into the Room—Robert Johnson: The Sound and the Fury." *Village Voice,* December 9, 1986.

Marcuse, Herbert. *Eros and Civilization: A Philosophical Inquiry into Freud*. New York: Vintage Books, 1961. Originally published in 1955.

Marcuse, Herbert. *One Dimensional Man*. Boston: Beacon Press, 1964.

Marcuse, Herbert. *Counter-revolution and Revolt*. Boston: Beacon Press, 1972.

Marcuse, Herbert. *The Aesthetic Dimension*. Boston: Beacon Press, 1978.

Marre, Jeremy, and Hannah Charlton. *Beats of the Heart: Popular Music of the World*. New York: Pantheon, 1985.

Maslow, Abraham H. "A Theory of Human Motivation." *Psychological Review* 50 (1943): 370–396.

Meier, August, and Elliott Rudwick. *From Plantation to Ghetto*. Revised Edition. New York: Hill and Wang, 1970.

Meier, August, and Elliott Rudwick. *Black History and the Historical Profession, 1915–1980*. Urbana: University of Illinois, 1986.

Meyrowitz, Joshua. *No Sense of Place: The Impact of Electronic Media on Social Behavior*. New York: Oxford University Press, 1985.

Mills, C. Wright. *White Collar*. New York: Oxford University Press, 1951.

Mills, C. Wright. *The Sociological Imagination*. New York: Oxford University Press, 1959.

Mills, C. Wright. "On Knowledge and Power" (1955). In *Power, Politics, and People:*

The Collected Essays of C. Wright Mills, edited by Irving Louis Horowitz, pp. 599–613. New York: Ballantine Books, 1963.

Miller, Jim, ed. *The Rolling Stone Illustrated History of Rock & Roll.* New York: Random House, 1980.

Monaco, Paul. *Ribbons in Time: Movies and Society since 1945.* Bloomington: University of Indiana Press, 1987.

Morris, Aldon. *The Origins of the Civil Rights Movement.* New York: The Free Press, 1984.

Murray, Albert. *Stomping the Blues.* New York: Vintage Books, 1982.

Neff, Robert, and Anthony Conner. *Blues.* Boston: David Godine, 1975.

Newcomb, Horace. "On the Dialogic Aspects of Mass Communication." *Critical Studies in Mass Communication* 1 (March 1984): 34–50.

Nisbet, Robert. *The Quest for Community.* New York: Oxford University Press, 1953. Reprinted as *Community and Power.* New York: Galaxy Books, 1962.

Oates, Stephen B. *Let the Trumpet Sound: The Life of Martin Luther King, Jr.* New York: Harper & Row, 1982.

Okihiro, Gary, ed. *In Resistance.* Amherst: University of Massachusetts Press, 1986.

Oliver, Paul. *The Meaning of the Blues.* New York: Collier Books, 1963. Originally published in 1960 as *The Blues Fell This Morning.*

Oliver, Paul. *Conversation with the Blues.* New York: Horizon Press, 1965.

Oliver, Paul. *The Story of the Blues.* New York: Chilton Books, 1969.

Olsen, Tillie. *Silences.* New York: Delta Books, 1982.

Orman, John. *The Politics of Rock Music.* Chicago: Nelson-Hall, 1984.

Palmer, Bruce. *"Man over Money": The Southern Populist Critique of American Capitalism.* Chapel Hill: University of North Carolina Press, 1980.

Palmer, Robert. *Deep Blues.* New York: Penguin Books, 1982.

Parenti, Michael. *Inventing Reality: The Politics of the Mass Media.* New York: St. Martin's Press, 1986.

Pateman, Carole. *Participation and Democratic Theory.* New York: Cambridge University Press, 1970.

Pateman, Carole. "Feminist Critiques of the Public/Private Dichotomy." In *Public and Private in Social Life,* edited by S. Benn and G. Gaus, pp. 281–303. New York: St. Martin's Press, 1983.

Pateman, Carole. "The Theoretical Subversiveness of Feminism." In *Feminist Challenges: Social and Political Theory,* edited by Carole Pateman and Elizabeth Gross, pp. 1–10. Boston: Northeastern University Press, 1986.

Pateman, Carole, and Elizabeth Gross, eds. *Feminist Challenges: Social and Political Theory.* Boston: Northeastern University Press, 1986.

Pells, Richard. *Radical Visions and American Dreams: Culture and Social Thought in the Depression Years.* New York: Harper Torch Books, 1974.

Postman, Neil. *Amusing Ourselves to Death: Public Discourse in the Age of Television.* New York: Penguin, 1986.

Pratt, Linda Ray. "Elvis, Or the Ironies of a Southern Identity." In *Elvis: Images and Fantasies,* edited by Jac L. Tharpe, pp. 40–51. Jackson: University Press of Mississippi, 1979.

Pratt, Raymond B. "Toward a Critical Theory of Revolution." *Polity* 11 (Winter 1978–79): 172–199.

Pratt, Ray. "Ways of Hearing." Paper Presented at Annual Meeting, Popular Culture Association, Louisville, Ky., March 1985.

Pratt, Ray. "The Politics of Authenticity in Popular Music: The Case of the Blues." *Popular Music and Society* 10 (1986): 55–78.

Pratt, Ray. " 'Is a Dream a Lie if It Don't Come True, Or Is It Something Worse?': A Commentary on Political Implications of the Springsteen Phenomenon." *Popular Music and Society* 11 (1987): 51–74.

Prevos, Andre J. M. "Singing against Hunger: French and American Efforts and Their Results." *Popular Music and Society* 11 (1987): 57–74.

Raboteau, Albert. *Slave Religion*. New York: Oxford University Press, 1978.

Radway, Janice. *Reading the Romance: Women, Patriarchy, and Popular Literature*. Chapel Hill: University of North Carolina Press, 1984.

Rawick, George, ed. *The American Slave: A Composite Autobiography*. Multiple Vols. Westport, Conn.: Greenwood Press, 1972.

Rawick, George. *From Sundown to Sunup: The Making of the Black Community*. Westport, Conn.: Greenwood Press, 1972.

Reuss, Richard A. "The Roots of American Left Wing Interest in Folksong." *Labor History* 17 (1971): 259–279.

Rieger, Eva. " 'Dolce Semplice?'—On the Changing Role of Women in Music." In *Feminist Aesthetics*, edited by Gisela Ecker, pp. 135–149. Boston: Beacon Press, 1986.

Rinzler, Ralph. "Roots of the Folk Revival." In *The Folk Music Source Book*, edited by Larry Sandberg and Dick Weissman, pp. 96–100. New York: Alfred A. Knopf, 1976.

Rodnitzky, Jerome. *Minstrels of the Dawn*. Chicago: Nelson-Hall, 1976.

Rosen, Marjorie. *Popcorn Venus: Women, Movies, and the American Dream*. New York: Coward, McCann & Geoghegan, 1973.

Rosselson, Leon. "Pop Music: Mobiliser or Opiate?" In *Media, Politics and Culture* edited by Carl Gardner, pp. 40–70. London: Macmillan, 1970.

Rowbotham, Sheila. *Woman's Consciousness, Man's World*. New York: Penguin, 1973.

Rowe, Mike. *Chicago Blues*. New York: DaCapo, 1981. Originally published as *Chicago Breakdown*. New York: Drake, 1975.

Russell, Ross. *Jazz Style in Kansas City and the Southwest*. Berkeley: University of California Press, 1973.

Russell, Ross. *Bird Lives!: The High Life and Hard Times of Charlie "Yardbird" Parker*. London: Quartet Books, 1980. Originally published in 1972.

Russell, Tony. *Blacks, Whites and Blues*. London: Studio Vista, 1970.

Ryan, Michael, and Douglas Kellner. *Camera Politica*. Bloomington: University of Indiana Press, 1988.

Sale, Kirkpatrick. *SDS*. New York: Random House, 1973.

Samuels, Stuart. "The Age of Conspiracy and Conformity: *Invasion of the Body Snatchers (1956)*". In *American History/American Film: Interpreting the Hollywood Image*, edited by John O'Connor and Martin A. Jackson, pp. 203–218. New York: Frederick Ungar, 1980.

Sandberg, Larry, and Dick Weissman. *The Folk Music Source Book*. New York: Alfred A. Knopf, 1976.

Scaduto, Anthony. *Bob Dylan: An Intimate Biography*. New York: Signet Books, 1973.

Schafer, John. *New Sounds*. New York: Harper & Row, 1987.

Schuller, Gunther. *Early Jazz*. New York: Oxford University Press, 1968.

Scovill, Ruth. "Women's Music." In *Women's Culture: The Women's Renaissance of the Seventies,* edited by Gayle Kimball, pp. 148–162. Metuchen, N.J.: The Scarecrow Press, 1981.

Shaw, Arnold. *Honkers and Shouters: The Golden Years of Rhythm and Blues*. New York: Collier Books, 1978.

Shaw, Arnold. *Black Popular Music in America*. New York: Schirmer, 1985.

Shelton, Robert. *No Direction Home: The Life and Music of Bob Dylan*. New York: Ballantine Books, 1987.

Shepard, John. "Music and Male Hegemony." In *Music and Society*, edited by Richard Leppert and Susan McClary, pp. 151–172. New York: Cambridge University Press, 1987.

Sidran, Ben. *Black Talk*. New York: DaCapo Press, 1981.

Slater, Philip. *The Pursuit of Loneliness: American Culture at the Breaking Point*. Boston: Beacon Press, 1970.

Smith, Dorothy E. "A Sociology for Women." In *The Prism of Sex: Essays in the Sociology of Knowledge,* edited by Julia A. Sherman and Evelyn Torton Beck, pp. 135–188. Madison: University of Wisconsin Press, 1979.

Smith, Dorothy E. *The Everyday World as Problematic*. Boston: Beacon Press, 1987.

Southern, Eileen. *The Music of Black Americans: A History*. New York: W. W. Norton, 1971.

Stallard, Karin, Barbara Ehrenreich, and Holly Sklar. *Poverty in the American Dream: Women and Children First*. Boston: South End Press, 1983.

Starobin, Joseph. *American Communism in Crisis, 1943–1957*. Cambridge, Mass.: Harvard University Press, 1972.

Stearns, Marshall. *The Story of Jazz*. New York: Mentor Books, 1958.

Stephens, Ronald J. "What the Rap is About: A History and Criticism of Contemporary Rap Music and Culture." Department of African-American Studies, Temple University, Philadelphia. Paper originally presented at the Speech Communication Association annual convention, New Orleans, November 5, 1988.

Steward, Sue, and Cheryl Garratt. *Signed, Sealed, and Delivered: True Life Stories of Women in Pop*. Boston: South End Press, 1984.

Stott, William. *Documentary Expression and Thirties America*. New York: Oxford University Press, 1973.

Street, John. *Rebel Rock: The Politics of Popular Music*. New York: Basil Blackwell, 1986.

Szwed, John F. "Afro-American Musical Adaptation." In *Afro-American Anthropology: Contemporary Perspectives,* edited by Norman W. Whitten and John F. Szwed, pp. 219–230. New York: The Free Press, 1970.

Thomas, Alexander, and Samuel Sillen. *Racism and Psychiatry*. New York: Brunner/Mazel Publishers, 1972.

Thompson, E. P. *The Making of the English Working Class*. New York: Vintage Books, 1963.

Thompson, Robert Farris. *The Flash of the Spirit: African and Afro-American Art and Philosophy*. New York: Random House, Vintage Books, 1984.

Titon, Jeff. *Early Downhome Blues: A Musical and Cultural Analysis*. Urbana: University of Illinois Press, 1977.

Toshes, Nick. *Country*. New York: Scribners, 1985.

Unger, Irwin. *The Movement: A History of the American New Left, 1959–1972.* New York: Dodd, Mead, 1974.

Wallace, A. F. C. "Revitalization Movements." *American Anthropologist* 58 (April 1956): 264–281.

Wallace, A. F. C. *Religion: An Anthropological View.* New York: Random House, 1966.

Walsh, Andrea S. *Women's Film and Female Experience.* New York: Praeger, 1984.

Washington, Joseph R. *Black Sects and Cults.* New York: Doubleday, 1972.

Waterman, Guy. "Ragtime." in *The Art of Jazz*, edited by Martin Williams, pp. 11–31. New York: Grove Press, 1960.

Weinberg, Loren S. "Political Socialization of Community Activists." Ph.D. Dissertation, Department of Political Science, University of Colorado, Boulder, 1982.

Weiner, Jon. *Come Together: John Lennon in His Time.* New York: Random House, 1984.

Weinstein, James. *The Decline of Socialism in America, 1912–1925.* New York: Vintage, 1967.

Whitburn, Joel. *The Billboard Book of Top 40 Hits.* Revised and Enlarged Third Edition. New York: Billboard Publications, 1987.

Wilhelm, Sidney. "The Economic Demise of Blacks in America: A Prelude To Genocide?" *Journal of Black Studies* 17 (December 1986): 201–254.

Williams, Martin, ed. *The Art of Jazz.* New York: Grove Press, 1960.

Williams, Martin, ed. *Jazz Panorama.* New York: Collier Books, 1964.

Williams, Raymond. *Marxism and Literature.* New York: Oxford University Press, 1977.

Willis, Ellen. "Creedence Clearwater Revival." In *The Rolling Stone Illustrated History of Rock & Roll*, edited by Jim Miller. New York: Random House, 1980.

Willis, Ellen. "Janis Joplin." In *The Rolling Stone Illustrated History of Rock & Roll*, edited by Jim Miller. New York: Random House, 1980.

Willis, Ellen. "Sins of the Fathers." *Village Voice*, December 15, 1987.

Wolfe, Alan. *The Seamy Side of Democracy: Repression in America.* Second Edition, Revised. New York: Longman, 1978.

Wolin, Sheldon. *Politics and Vision.* Boston: Little, Brown, 1960.

Woodward, C. Vann. *The Strange Career of Jim Crow: A Brief Account of Segregation.* New York: Oxford University Press, 1957.

Yankelovich, Daniel. *New Rules.* New York: Random House, 1981.

Yinger, J. Milton. "Religious Movements among American Negroes." In *The Scientific Study of Religion*, pp. 254–260. New York: Macmillan, 1970.

Index

ABOUT THE AUTHOR

RAY PRATT has taught political science at Montana State University in Bozeman, Montana, since 1971. He was born in Detroit, Michigan, and attended public schools in Lansing, Michigan. Graduating from Michigan State University with majors in history and sociology, he completed a Master's in political science at Michigan State and a Ph.D. in political science at the University of Oregon. He has done post-doctoral work at the University of Michigan, Ann Arbor, and University of California, Santa Barbara. He has taught at Michigan State, Oregon, Washington University at St. Louis, and Montana State University.